The 7 Vital Parenting Skills and Confident Kids

A 7 Full-Length Positive Parenting Book Compilation for Raising Well-Adjusted Children

Frank Dixon

Book Description:

"Parents can only give good advice or put them on the right paths, but the final forming of a person's character lies in their own hands." –Anne Frank

In The 7 Vital Parenting Skills and Confident Kids book, best-selling parenting advice expert Frank Dixon offers loving parents powerful positive parenting skills and effective family communication techniques that any Mom or Dad can use to help your child to overcome adversity and be confident children with compassion for others. This valuable parenting skills book offers a unique benefit to families with children of different ages, as it provides game-changing tips for parenting teens, as well as several books for teaching toddlers positive behaviors and also dealing with ADHD kids of all ages and an entire book on preventing child anxiety during the Covid-19 pandemic and quarantine.

In this exhaustive positive parenting book compilation, you will receive 7 full-length best-selling books, covering the most important topics for providing a happy home and a loving family in today's challenging environment for raising children:

• 7 Effective Methods for Calming Kids Anxiety During the Covid-19 Pandemic: Easy Parenting Tips for Providing Your Kids Anxiety Relief and

Preventing Teen Depression Caused by Coronavirus Isolation

• 7 Vital Parenting Skills for Understanding Teenagers and Communicating with Teens: Proven Parenting Tips for Developing Healthy Relationships for Teens and Reducing Teen Anxiety

• 7 Vital Skills for Parenting Teen Girls and Communicating with Your Teenage Daughter: Proven Parenting Tips for Raising Teenage Girls with Self-Confidence and Coping Skills

• 7 Vital Skills for Parenting Teen Boys and Communicating with Your Teenage Son: Proven Positive Parenting Tips for Raising Teenage Boys and Preparing Your Teenager for Manhood

• 7 Vital Parenting Skills for Improving Child Behavior and Positive Discipline: Proven Positive Parenting Tips for Family Communication without Yelling or Negativity

• 7 Vital Parenting Skills for Teaching Kids With ADHD: Proven ADHD Tips for Dealing with Attention Deficit Disorder and Hyperactive Kids

• 7 Proven Strategies for Parenting Toddlers that Excel, from Potty Training to Preschool: Positive Parenting Tips for Raising Toddlers with Exceptional Social Skills and Accelerated Learning Ability

Whether you have rambunctious or hyperactive preschool kids, or you are dealing with an unmotivated teen or stressed out teenage girl, each best-selling book contains the 7 most important parenting skills and communication skills that you must master to help your child to feel loved and become a successful an well-adjusted young adult.

Before we begin, I have something special waiting for you. An action-packed 1 page printout with a few quick & easy tips taken from this book that you can start using today to become a better parent right now!

It's my gift to you, free of cost. Think of it as my way of saying thank you to you for purchasing this book.

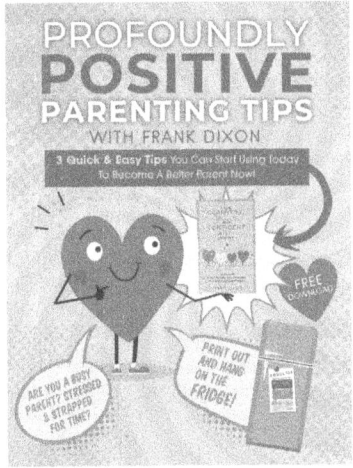

Claim your download of Profoundly Positive Parenting with Frank Dixon by scanning the QR code below and join my mailing list.

Sign up below to grab your free copy, print it out and hang it on the fridge!

Sign Up By Scanning The QR Code With Your Phone's Camera To Be Redirected To A Page To Enter Your Email And Receive INSTANT Access To Your Download

Before we jump in, I'd like to express my gratitude. I know this mustn't be the first book you came across and yet you still decided to give it a read. There are numerous courses and guides you could have picked instead that promise to make you an ideal and well-rounded parent while raising your children to be the best they can be.

But for some reason, mine stood out from the rest and this makes me the happiest person on the planet right now. If you stick with it, I promise this will be a worthwhile read.

In the pages that follow, you're going to learn the best parenting skills so that your child can grow to become the best version of themselves and in doing so experience a meaningful understanding of what it means to be an effective parent.

Notable Quotes About Parenting

"Children Must Be Taught How To Think, Not What To Think."

— Margaret Mead

"It's easier to build strong children than to fix broken men [or women]."

- Frederick Douglass

"Truly great friends are hard to find, difficult to leave, and impossible to forget."

— George Randolf

"Nothing in life is to be feared, it is only to be understood. Now is the time to understand more, so that we may fear less."

— Scientist Marie Curie

Table of Contents

**7 VITAL PARENTING
SKILLS FOR IMPROVING CHILD
BEHAVIOR AND POSITIVE DISCIPLINE 233**

7 Vital Parenting Skills for Understanding Teenagers and Communicating With Teens

Proven Parenting Tips for Developing Healthy Relationships for Teens and Reducing Teen Anxiety

Frank Dixon

Book Description

Is your teen being rebellious? Do they talk back and not obey rules? Are they always hiding stuff from you or lying to your face? Are they being difficult on purpose and seeking complete independence?

Teenagers, with the numerous changes going on, can be challenging to handle. Their sudden need for privacy and independence can drive you nuts. Your once obedient and compassionate child seems to have grown into this monstrous hulk, ready to charge whenever something doesn't go according to their plans.

So how do you handle the temper tantrums, prevent arguments and disagreements, establish some ground rules, and ensure that they follow them? This parenting book has the answer.

Written in a simple and undeviating manner, it equips parents with 7 vital, strategic, effective, and well-researched skills, which, if implemented, will send all their concerns and worries out the door. To give you a quick overview of what to expect, take a look at the many important topics it covers:

- Importance of setting a positive example
- The need for positive attention and spending quality time with them

- Handling teenage anxiety and helping teens overcome it
- Picking up the right battles to fight for
- The best strategies to set realistic expectations for teens
- Purpose of allowing teenagers some room and space to breathe
- The important role effective communication plays

All these topics and many more are discussed in detail to help parents seeking advice and recommendations on what to do and what not to. The 7 vital parenting skills we discussed will definitely help you raise them to become responsible, independent, emotionally-intellectual, and happy adults.

been derived from various sources. Please consult a licensed professional before attempting any techniques outlined in this book.

By reading this document, the reader agrees that under no circumstances is the author responsible for any losses, direct or indirect, that are incurred as a result of the use of the information contained within this document, including, but not limited to, errors, omissions, or inaccuracies.

Introduction

Remember the night your baby kept you awake all night, crying and needing to be fed, and all you could think to yourself was that this will soon pass? Well, now you have the same child, grown up into a teenager and that night of sleeplessness feels like a beautiful dream. You had thought that having lived through the middle-of-the-night feedings, temper tantrums and hectic school routines, you will finally have some years of quiet and calm. Alas, those golden years don't seem to catch up to you any time soon because you now have a rebellious, raging with hormones, disobedient, rude, and ill-mannered child in the house and have no clue how to deal with them.

For many parents, teen years are a rather confusing period. Their kids are showing intense growth, fluctuations in their moods, and emotional instability. But they aren't just difficult, they also have upbeat energy that is hard to compete with, a growing and idealistic mindset, a deep interest in what's right and wrong, and thoughtfulness. They are finding themselves and learning to associate themselves and nurture their talents, skills, and passions.

It is scary yet beautiful.

There is no given timeline as to when adolescence begins. For most girls, it starts around the age of 13 and for boys, much later when they are 14 to 16 years of age. In different parts of the world, the average varies, which means everyone's normal is slightly different. Many of us, for most of our lives, have believed that reaching puberty means the development of sexual characteristics, such as an increase in breast size, onset of pubic hair, and menstrual periods in girls. In boys, the earliest signs of puberty are the growth of their testicles and scrotum. But these are just physical changes. Many emotional and behavioral changes take place too, but since they aren't visible changes, they often get neglected, which is where problems begin to sprout from. The most common behavioral changes happen around their parents. As they seek more independence, they start to separate from their parents. They become more concerned than ever about what others think of them, especially their peers. They try different looks, pursue multiple interests and passions, and try to fit in the world. When they struggle with these, episodes of distress happen. Conflicts with parents also increase. A classic example of this could be a teenage daughter arguing with her mother because she wants to wear something more provocative and edgy than what her mother had selected for her. After all, all her friends are dressing in the same manner. The argument can lead to serious accusations such as, "You want me to make a fool out of myself wearing that", or, "You don't care about what my friends will think of me if I go wearing what you chose for me."

This time of emotional ups and downs has been of great interest to psychologists and scientists for many years. For many years, they have been trying to break through the stereotypical image of what being a teen feels like and want to learn more about what goes on in their heads.

The more knowledge we have, the better parenting skills we can bring into practice to minimize the number of conflicts and disagreements.

Therefore, in this book, we look at how teenagers behave, the many changes they go through, why they seem so stressed and anxious and how, as parents, we can help them navigate through this complicated chapter of their lives with grace. To begin with, we look at various parenting skills, which if applied, can help parents understand their growing children better and help them cope with the challenges they face by offering emotional support. There are many questions we shall look at such as, "Am I giving my child enough room and explore themselves or being a control-freak", or "If I need to allow them more independence to engage in age-appropriate activities or not", or, "If I am being the right role model for them or not."

So let's begin!

Chapter 1: Brain Vs. Hormones

S ince most of the changes that take place reflect or have an impact on the way teenagers behave, we must discuss these early on so that we start off on the right foot and ease into the normality of living with a teenager in the latter part of the chapter.

Two prominent changes suggest the onset of maturity in teenagers. The first is bodily changes and the second, emotional. Both are regulated by the hormonal fluctuations in their bodies. They help with the development of the brain as well as the inception of puberty which triggers many bodily changes, suggesting sexual maturity.

Hormonal changes guide the body through puberty and this, for the most part, includes the increase in the levels of testosterone in boys and estrogen in girls. They are responsible for the majority of behavioral changes such as mood swings, aggression, depression, anxiety, and more.

Secondly, the changes in the level of maturity of the brain. New and promising research studies propose that the brain continues to mature well after teenagers turn 18. We now also know that hormonal changes don't trigger the changes in the brain but the brain triggers the hormonal changes. Yet, there is still no certainty of what triggers what, as it is observed that late bloomers or children who don't undergo puberty due to hormonal issues also have a perfectly mature brain working normally. There have been no visible differences in the way they question things, assess risks, or get along with their peers.

Some of the most common changes in the brain during the teenage years include neural messages and neural connections.

Neural messages speed up thanks to the addition of myelin to the neurons. This makes everything get through faster.

Secondly, a large number of neural connections in the prefrontal cortex are pruned which makes things like planning, organization, and implementation of tasks more efficient. This happens during adolescence when the brain takes a time-out, which means, during this specific period, the functioning of the brain is less effective – thus the poor decision-making skills and risk assessment.

These two, when together, the result is some noteworthy behavioral changes most commonly linked with teenagers. For instance:

Limited Functioning of the Brain: The changes in the prefrontal cortex – the region of the brain responsible for regulating logical thinking and its aspects – causes lapses in good judgment and risk assessment. This is what makes them high on energy at all times which results in an enhanced need for risk-taking and life-threatening behavior. Since they aren't thinking straight, they subject themselves to exploration which doesn't always end well for them. Drunk driving and drug overdose, to name a few.

Increased Need for Excitement: Since messages are traveling faster than ever, teenagers experience an increased need for sensory input. It usually manifests itself as adrenaline-seeking. Ever wondered why places like theme parks and clubs target teenagers specifically? It is because they are more likely to respond well to activities that involve some form of risk or excitement.

Heightened Emotional Responses: Teenagers, during adolescence, also feel things more strongly. You may spot them causing a scene out of the blue, crying their eyes out over something trivial, and walk back to their room after slamming the door into your face. There are days when they will be over the moon with joy and happiness and also days when they won't come out of their room for the entire day unless to eat. In girls, such mood swings are more prevalent as they tend to feel things more deeply.

Focus on Self: Let's get one thing straight: teenagers aren't deliberately trying to be rude or selfish. They genuinely have a troubled time deciphering emotions in others, again, due to the rewiring of the prefrontal cortex. This makes them rather self-centered. They don't care about the impact their actions and words have on others.

Goals When Living With a Teenager

Keep in mind, all teenagers are different and unique. Give them some space and time to open up to you and while they do, encourage and appreciate any form of communication they try to have with you. Other than that, there are some ground rules as per an article in Psychology Today that all parents must abide by when they have a teenager in the house.

Learn to Ignore Disobedience

We are all aware of the eye rolls when told to do something uninteresting. It can make your blood boil but you have to control your emotions. If they notice that it irritates you, they will do it more often. Shake it off and don't feel disrespected. Although since it isn't an acceptable way to handle orders, sit them down when they are in a good mood and try to bring it up by telling them how disrespected you feel when they do it.

Change Their Definition for the Word 'Sexy'

If you have a teenage daughter, tell her that sexy doesn't always mean knee-high skirts or crop tops that barely cover anything. Tell her the kind of message she is sending by wearing such revealing clothes. Let her know that if she truly wishes to look sexy, then she should go with what feels comfortable and not with what everyone's wearing. Sexy can also mean intelligence, straightforwardness, and confidence. Their goal shouldn't just be to invite male attention but to make the right statement. It has nothing to do with revealing clothes.

If you are raising a teenage boy, he must know not to give in to peer pressure and get involved in things beyond his age such as alcohol, smoking pot, taking ecstasy pills, or sniffing chalk without proper knowledge of what it can do to their systems. No, it isn't sexy – just self-threatening.

Have the "Talk"

For many parents, it is one of the most dreadful days when they have to sit down with their teenager and go through the details of sex, sexual orientation, and protection. Peggy Orenstein, in her book Girls and Sex, tells her readers that although many girls act tough when demanding equality on the field and in the classroom, they succumb to the pressures of sexual activity due to their partner's wishes. As they are more informed than ever about these things, we need to have a clear and detailed dialogue with them about why they should never settle for anything demeaning to please someone. The same is the case with most teenage boys. Influenced by what their friends are doing or into, they indulge themselves in self-harming or reckless behavior in the name of fun.

Apologize for Bad Behavior

It can be called miraculous if you never fought about anything with your teenager. You must have yelled, shouted, or shamed them for their choices in a weak moment when you felt that things were slipping out of your hand. However, now is the time to teach them a valuable lesson i.e. the power of forgiveness! If you have thrown your power around, misused it around them or shamed them in one way or the other, own up to it and apologize. An apology requires commitment and sincerity and it is an essential thing to teach your teenager. It requires that the guilty submits to their mistakes without any shame and expects being treated fairly in return. If they model it and begin to admit to their mistakes, they will be more willing to rectify them instead of just giving up or hiding in fear.

Show Patience Towards Their Lack of Empathy

They can be egomaniacs and stubborn. They may not understand your need to have some space to yourself because you are feeling down. They may also seem too involved in their problems and issues. This lack of empathy is normal for a teenager to demonstrate. Don't be too surprised or hurt by how selfish they can be. It is just a phase.

Be Cautious When Discussing Their Friends

They may not like the way you talk about their friends or understand why you don't like them. As their focus changes from family to their friends, they may become sensitive about them. Therefore, whenever approaching the topic of discussing their friends, take caution. If you have a bad feeling about a friend of theirs, don't just say it out loud. Use other strategic ways to make them understand why you think they are a bad influence. For instance, you can concoct a story about how you also had a friend like theirs and how you ended by being hurt because of them.

Act Like a Grown-Up

Remember who the adult is in the house. Make them know it too. This doesn't mean making decisions for them or laying down strict rules and regulations in the house. It means that they know who is in charge of having the last say in the house and why they must do what they are told. Teenagers need us as their role models and moral compasses. You have to be compassionate and considerate but also authoritative. They must know that they can never exploit the privileges they enjoy.

Chapter 2: The 7 Vital Parenting Skills to Understanding Teenagers

M ost parents think it is they who deal with the most challenges, but it is only one side of the story. Teenagers are equally clueless about the changes happening inside them. They feel unprepared to cope with them in healthy ways and thus, become more anxious than ever. Teenage anxiety is a real thing and also one of the most worrying types of anxiety. If we look at the statistics in the US alone, approximately 4.4 million children aged 3 to 17 have anxiety. That accounts for an astounding 7.1% of the teenage population. One point nine million of these teens develop symptoms of depression, and need serious help and therapy.

Something is very wrong here and everyone – the media, society and adults are to blame. Since there is not much we can do about the internet or the society that poses high standards and expectations from teenagers, what we can do is help them be prepared for it. Chances are, if they are already past their sixteenth birthday mark, you don't have much time left. They will soon be out, relying on the mercy of others, their knowledge, and academics to help them find their place in the world.

Therefore, we thought about this in detail and wanted to present parents with a collective list of strategies and methods, which if implemented correctly, can help teenagers relieve some of the stress they feel.

In a world that judges us more for our choices and not for our strong character and academics, it has become easier to just pull someone's leg and bring them down. Cyberbullying has been on the rise too. Screenshots and videos of highly-intimate messages are shared all over the internet without the consent of the other involved party and left to be blamed and shamed. Teenagers, influenced by their peers, want to do things they would never approach with a sane mind because why not – if everyone is doing it, it must be okay. Remember the tide-pod challenge? Did you know some of the teenagers stopped breathing and had to be put on a ventilator to stay alive? The point is, kids will always want to try things that entice some level of thrill and excitement. They would want to try things, just for the sake of trying.

So what can we do?

Help them make better choices. Help them take calculated risks. They shouldn't go in blindly or run after things without assessing the associated risks. They should be confident enough to call out the stupid people who put theirs and others' lives at risk just for some likes and comments under their name. They should know when to call it quits before things get out of hand. They must know how to deal with their emotions , no matter how overwhelming they are. They should never lose control over them and know to deal with them in better and healthy ways.

So how can we teach them these?

Vital Parenting Skills

Let's look briefly at each one in action and see how it can help both parents and teenagers to be on the same page, cultivate better communication, and have strong interpersonal relationships.

With our 7 vital parenting skills! What are they? Let's introduce them to you.

Vital Parenting Skill #1 - Setting a Positive Example

First and foremost, teenagers need a parent figure they can look up to. Most of the behaviors children pick up are the ones they observe others around them doing. You must have had those moments where your toddler tried to imitate the way you talk on the phone or how their father washes the car. Therefore, it is essential that whatever they are learning from us is high-quality, healthy, transparent, and rewarding. It is our job to ensure that whatever habits and behaviors they take from us help them grow up to be a better person. Think of it as choosing the best materials to lay the foundation of a building. High-quality cement, sturdy bricks, strong iron rods, etc. If you want it to stay high and tall and be praised by everyone, you need to ensure it can stand on its own.

Vital Parenting Skill #2 - Giving Positive Attention

The second thing they need from you is positive attention. When kids feel valued and looked after, they feel safe and secure. They feel supported and confident. Parents should, therefore, spend quality time with their kids from the start to impart the right values and habits. Family times can mean a lot of things. It can mean doing things of interest together, going on trips together, watching TV, eating dinners, or simply taking the time to talk. Ideally, there should be a weekly ritual where the whole family gets together and shares the top highlights of the week. In chapter four, discussing this in detail, we shall see how positive attention helps teenagers in the longer run.

Vital Parenting Skill #3 - Reducing Teen Anxiety

Another vital skill that parents must have or practice is teaching their children ways to cope with negative emotions such as anger, anxiety, depression, and other mental health conditions in a positive way. They must use means that don't add to their teenager's stress levels and engage them in things that help alleviate it.

Vital Parenting Skill #4 - Picking Battles

Not all battles are worth fighting. Some errors and mistakes are to be ignored and not argued over. There is no point in deliberately trying to create rifts over trivial things, as you don't want your teenager to look at you as a constant nagger. This will ruin the relationship you share with them and they will start to distance themselves from you. They will begin to avoid you when at home and not reply to you when questioned, because they don't want another fight. If you are trying to understand them and make communication better between you two, then you need to be smart about the things that can lead to a heated conversation. You need to understand their need for privacy and not keep losing your temper every time they leave their dirty clothes on the floor instead of putting them in the laundry basket. Instead, you have to find strategic ways to deal with the problems that bother you and in this chapter, we shall look at some in detail.

Vital Parenting Skill #5 - Setting Reasonable Expectations

The next essential skill on the list is reasonable expectations. Many parents, unknowingly, burden their children with more than their weak shoulders can handle. They push them into extra-curricular activities they are not interested in and prevent them from following their passions. There is no harm in wanting to increase the prospects of your teenager leading a successful life by asking them to become an accountant instead of a chef or a musician but science is now proving that kids who choose to follow their dreams are much happier and content with their lives than those who don't. Therefore, as a parent, you have to set the right expectations for them and help them craft a path to live, but it needs to be up to them. You can't just leave them in the dark. You have to help them figure out the things they want from their life and help them achieve them. This is both a skill and a necessity.

Vital Parenting Skill #6 - Make Communications Stronger

Another parenting skill that parents must practice is working on the communication between them and their teenagers. This is, by far, the hardest thing to do, keeping in mind that they have a mind of their own. As parents, you have to ensure that they are not doing things they shouldn't be doing behind your back or keeping secrets that can be self-harming. You have to identify the barriers to communication and work on them to improve it.

Vital Parenting Skill #7 - Giving Them Some Room to Breathe

Finally, parents don't need to act as a disciplinarian or authoritarian. They have to allow their kids some space to explore age-appropriate things. If you are too strict and unforgiving, they may go behind your back and still do the things that you don't want them to do. Instead, you have to let them come to you with their problems without probing them about them too much. You have to let them have some moments to themselves, try to figure out things their way and only intervene when they allow you to.

All these are discussed in the following chapters in much detail with the "whys" and "hows" to help the readers gain a better sense of what goes on in the mind of their teenager and how to understand them better.

Chapter 3: Essential Parenting Skill – Setting a Positive Example

C hildren are born without social skills or social knowledge. They eagerly wait to find someone they can mimic. That someone is mostly the one closest to them – their parents. You are your child's very first teacher and guide. You teach them how to eat, clean, and sleep. You teach them how to sit straight, walk, jump, or chew a bubble gum without digesting it. Did you know that our kids are more affected by what we allow them to witness than what we tell them? It is interactions and visual evidence that hold more value in their eyes. They might not want to clean their rooms but will eventually learn to do it if they see you cleaning up yours. They might not want to try different foods if they see you sticking to some basics. They will not model good behavior or pick up good habits if you don't practice them. Whatever behaviors they pick up, they pick up from us, which is why it is highly crucial to set the right example.

You have to live by the rules you want them to abide by. You have to lead a life that reflects the values and morals you want to instill in them. You have to walk the talk because if you don't, they won't either. You can't go complaining about how messy they are if you are messy too. You have to be a positive role model they grow up watching. Your goal should be to make them want to be like you, even when they become teenagers.

As parents, we often underestimate the value of healthy habits and behaviors. We don't invest the amount of time or energy needed to mold our children in the best manner possible. We leave them in the hands of the world, their peers, teachers, and even strangers to teach them things. We think if they don't do it now, someday experience will teach them. What if this is where we fail as parents? What if, not being the right role model is the biggest mistake? What if this is the reason why they feel so insecure about themselves, suffer from low self-esteem, and are always stressed?

Thus, it is about time you start thinking about what you are leaving your son or daughter with. Have you made them competent enough to follow their passions and live a successful, brave, and autonomous life?

Lack of a Role Model and Teenagers

In 2019, during one of the largest surveys by the Prince's Trust, it was revealed that 67% of adults who have grown up without a positive figure of the same gender were more likely to be unemployed than those who grew up with one ("Youth Index 2019," 2019). The survey stated that 2.170 people were interviewed between the ages of 16 and 25. The following were some other significant findings that pose the importance of a positive role model in the lives of teenagers.

- One in every 3 men had no positive figure to look up to. One in every 4 women stated the same.

- The lack of a positive role model impacted the mental wellbeing of those affected significantly.

- They had an overall negative outlook on life.

- They had trouble staying employed for longer periods as opposed to their peers.

- They were three times more likely to suffer from mental illnesses like depression and anxiety, and told the interviewers that they didn't recall the last time they felt proud of themselves.

- 50% of the women who grew up without a female positive figure in their lives told that at some point in their lives, they had felt suicidal.

- One in 4 teenagers reported that they lacked a sense of identity.

- One in 5 men said they had turned to illegal drugs and engaged in criminal activities due to the stress of being unemployed.

All these statistics are proof that a positive role model in a teenager's life is pivotal. It can be life-changing for most and save them from ending up in jail or staying unemployed.

And that is not all, in another survey conducted by Barna Group, looking at the need for positive role models for teens, found that the majority of the teenagers had listed their parents as the ideal role models in their lives (Teen Role Models: Who They Are, Why They Matter, 2011). No, it wasn't celebrities or athletes or influencers. Parents were the most highly regarded individuals because they offered moral support, encouragement, and love.

Who Are Role Models?

This is an important question to ask ourselves. Who are role models? Are they just the subject of emulation and admiration? Are they the ones who inspire others to strive for success via their attributes and achievements? Are they the ones who are always present and interact with their children giving them consistent attention?

Well, they are all that and more. Role models are the ones teenagers look up to when searching for their identities. They are the ones who lend an ear to listen, pat us on the shoulder when we do something good, cheer on for us when we feel unconfident, and shelter us from harm.

Being the Super Hero They Need in Their Lives

Being a role model requires forethought, effort, and self-control. It isn't easy to keep your cool when your child misbehaves or pushes your buttons intentionally. But since you have to set the right example, you choose composure and calmness over yelling and punishment. This is a huge responsibility you have on your shoulders and being aware of it can motivate you to do better. For instance, if you don't want your child to learn to yell, you have to stop yelling too. Other than that, you will have to:

Preach by Example

The first thing you need to do is stop being a pretender and walk the talk. With children, "do as I say" doesn't work – at least not in the longer run. They need to observe the consistency in your words and actions. It's simple really.

- If you want them to eat healthily, you eat and cook healthy.

- If you want them to limit the use of technology in the house, you do the same first.

48

- If you want them to not lie or use it as a means to get away with something, you have to stop lying about being sick and skipping work.

You have to make them appreciate you for being true to the rules you want to preach.

Examine Your Behavior and Reactions

Since they are looking up to you at all times, you must model the right behaviors via your actions and reactions. For example, you must know how to control your stress and anger, how to respond and handle unforeseen problems, how to express your anger and other negative emotions, how to deal with mistakes, responsibilities, competitions, and loss, how to take care of your body and mind, etc. If you are doing well, then you are setting the perfect example for them to follow.

Be Forgiving of Mistakes

No one is perfect. Mistakes are bound to happen. However, what's important is the way the situation is handled. Your teenager needs to see if you are forgiving or accepting when someone makes a mistake. They need to see if you deal calmly when things go wrong or berate the perpetrator. They need to see if you play the victim card and blame others or own up to your mistakes and shortcomings? They need to see you apologize when you are in the wrong, and look for strategies to not do better the next time.

Address Conflicts Sensibly

You have to make them see you deal with your problems in a calm and composed manner. They don't need to see you throwing things at your spouse or the neighbors over a small fight. Because chances are, if later, you go up to their room to preach them about the importance of conflict management, they are going to call you out. They also need to see you manage your goals such as weight loss or eating healthy foods so they learn to stay true to their commitments. Even if you fail, you have to tell them that it is alright so that they don't feel pressured constantly to aim for perfection.

Practice Modesty and Respect Towards Others

Your kids don't only see you, they hear you too. What language you speak, how you approach others, talk to them, or speak about them behind their backs are things that say a lot about your character. They listen to how you talk to your partner, your friends, relatives, neighbors, or strangers at a department store. They notice if you show respect towards them or not. They notice the tone and pitch of your voice. They notice how you practice tolerance when stuck in traffic or when someone bypasses you on the highway. They notice the way you cuss or use abusive language when in a foul mood. They notice how you speak to them and in what tone. They notice if your words are harsh and threatening or compassionate and kind. They notice if you misbehave as a response when angry or if you keep your cool. To set the right example, you have to be cautious of the way you speak around them and the language and tone you use.

Chapter 4: Essential Parenting Skill – Giving Positive Attention

I t is natural for parents to want to discipline their teenagers when they misbehave. They point out their faults, yell at them, or try to correct them with punishments. Though it makes sense, this approach to parenting can backfire.

New studies discussed later in the chapter reveal that positive disciplining or attention has proven more effective in changing behavior in the long-run. The simplest way to do so is by praising the behaviors you want them to demonstrate as opposed to calling out the behaviors that you deem to be negative.

But that certainly doesn't mean that parents have to look away every time their teenager misbehaves and only applaud them for the good things they do. Since more clarification is needed, let's begin with what positive attention is and how it can benefit teenagers by improving communication and reducing anxiety.

Positive attention requires that you praise your child for good behavior or a job well done and ignore, at least at the moment, the negative behavior. The goal is to offer parental attention – one of the things teenagers need the most. When we put positive attention into practice, it involves catching your teenager when they are doing something good.

Positive parenting can take many forms. It can include physical contact (hugs, kisses, and pats on the back) or emotional support like verbal and non-verbal praises such as high-fives and rewards. According to Lindsay Gerber, a clinical psychologist at the Child Mind Institute, parents need to be more specific and descriptive. This means that they don't only need to say, "Good job", but rather, "Good job cleaning your room. It looks so clean. I am so proud of you." She believes this increases the likelihood of replication of that behavior.

The Power of Positive Attention

Not only that, but there are also many other studies and research articles that link positive attention with improved behavior, happiness, and satisfaction in adolescents. For instance, one study suggests that positive attention from parents improves psychosocial functioning in teenagers (Joussemet et al., 2008). Another suggests reduced symptoms of depression, and better self-esteem (Duineveld et al., 2017). Another study suggests that positive attention from parents, peers, and educators build social self-efficacy in them (Coleman, 2003).

Spending quality time with children has also reported improvements to their self-esteem. They feel more validated by the emotional support offered to them and feel confident about the relationships in their lives. Another key factor here is that positive parental attention also boosts a child's academic aspirations. They are more confident to follow their passions, dedicate themselves to achieving their goals, and show greater interest in extracurricular activities. Finally, giving your teen positive attention can establish a healthy relationship between you two, which will reduce their behavioral problems and set them up for success.

5 Ways to Give Positive Attention

So what activities or interests can you two sign up for in order to spend some quality time together? How can you take time to appreciate them and celebrate their small victories and good behaviors? Take a look!

Ask Them About Their Day

Teenagers can succumb to the pressures of social media, friendships, and relationships, etc. They need some positivity in their lives and someone to talk to about the worries and stresses they experience. As a parent, you can offer them the moral and emotional support they need. All you have to do is ask them about their day every day, hoping they will open up to you. Asking our children this simple question allows them to see that you care about their wellbeing, worry about their happiness, and wish to offer comfort, in case they need it. When they will feel looked after, valued, and validated, they will be more open and compassionate.

Seek Their Opinion Over Things

They aren't little children anymore. They have had a taste of the outside world which means they are growing up to become sensible. Including them in household decisions such as deciding on a monthly grocery list, seeking their opinion on what they think about the house chores, what should be cooked for dinner, etc. This will make them feel valued and respected. When their input is taken into consideration, they will also feel more confident in expressing themselves with you.

Help Them Follow Their Passions

As a parent, another way you can provide them positive attention is by showing interest in their lives and the goals they wish to achieve. You can sit them down and have a detailed chat about where they want to be and what they want to be doing in the next 10 years.. You can help them map out a plan or map out the steps they need to take to achieve their goals.

Plan a Trip Together

It's another thing to go on one and another to plan one. Both promise equal fun so engage them in both. Spend time together to decide where you should go, what clothes and accessories you should pack along, what places you should visit, etc., etc. If a trip isn't a possibility, for now, you can go on smaller ones over the weekend together. You can go on a hiking trip, boating, to the beach, shopping, or visiting places of interest, etc.

Develop Healthy Habits

These include eating well, exercising, writing a gratitude journal, and sharing your thoughts. As they say, you have to be the role model they need. You have to set the right example if you want them to change. For instance, we all know that regular physical activity alleviates stress by releasing dopamine in our systems, which makes us feel good. They are less likely to listen and obey you when you tell them to exercise, and more likely if you get on board with them too. Besides, you can always keep checking in on them too.

Chapter 5: Essential Parenting Skill - Reducing Teen Anxiety

N ational Institutes of Health suggests that nearly every 1 in 3 teenagers aged 13 to 18 experiences an anxiety disorder (Any Anxiety Disorder, 2017). According to the Child Mind Institute, 9% of all teenagers suffer from some form of an anxiety disorder (social, GAD, panic, separation, etc.).

In recent years, the statistics are unbelievably bad. If we look at the rates of suicides and suicidal attempts, the picture gets even darker. This leaves many parents with some concerns and worries. Is their child suffering from an anxiety disorder? Are they happy with their lives? Are they happy with us as their parents? Are we doing enough to foster happiness and joy in their lives?

Although feeling anxious is a normal reaction, it becomes problematic when it happens all the time. But why is my teenager stressed? They don't have to worry about putting food on the table, paying the bills, or raising kids. What can be so heart-breaking or scary that they choose to indulge in self-harm activities or try to commit suicide?

Let's discuss some of the most common, yet overlooked reasons that add stress in the lives of our adolescents.

Factors That Contribute to Teen Anxiety in Today's World

If we go back in time and remember when we were adolescents, were we as anxious? Were we that stressed? Was there so much societal pressure to live up to? So how did we get here? Where did we go wrong in raising our kids as independent, happy, and confident adults? Several factors contribute to anxiety and impatience in teenagers today. These include:

Unrealistic Expectations and Pressures to Succeed

We have so many expectations from our children today that they are collapsing under the burdens of it. During a survey, an interviewer asked incoming college freshmen if they felt overwhelmed by the expectations their peers and parents had of them or not. Forty one percent of them said yes in 2016, compared to 28% in 2000 (Eagan et al., 2016). You can do the math. The data has doubled in the last few years. We want them to be good at school, take part in social causes, learn a new language, join karate, play an instrument, be a part of a sports team and what not, without even realizing that we are setting them up for failure.

The World Is Becoming Scarier

We have seen a rapid increase in school shootings, violence, bullying, and lockdowns. People have been exposed to all sorts of crimes on the street and in their homes. The world is no longer a safe place for them to live in. So it is acceptable to feel scared and threatened. They see it every day on their phones, on TVs and thus, feel like they have to be cautious at all times.

Social Media Is Becoming Addictive

Children and adolescents are bullied online. They also feel like they don't have enough. They notice the big things others are doing, what resources they have, how privileged they are, and then they look at their sad and boring lives and become depressed. They feel nothing remarkable will ever happen to them and this lowers their self-esteem. They compare themselves to others and feel like they aren't beautiful, intellectual, or wealthy enough to compete with them, and it further makes them feel like a loser.

Adult Responsibilities Are Making Them Anxious

We have also loaded them with adult responsibilities, knowing very well that their brain is still developing to take on them. They lack the skills they need to finish them and it causes frustrations. They want to go back to the time when things were easier and less complicated. They are fed up with the constant reminder that they need to grow up and act responsibly.

They Lack Healthy Coping Mechanisms

They know little about emotional skills or how to deal with their problems and anxiety. As parents, we emphasize more on their academics than on their emotional health. According to a national survey, the majority of teenagers feel unprepared to start college and live on their own (Morin, 2017). They suffer from separation as well as social anxiety and it is much higher in naturally shy teenagers. They don't have sufficient knowledge or skills to combat stress, take care of themselves, or manage their time.

Exposure to Drugs and Alcohol

Teens crave thrill and excitement. They want to know what it feels like to get high or drunk and thus, often expose themselves to things that are hard to pull them out of. They know they shouldn't indulge in such activities and yet they do, just because there has always been something very exciting about trying the thing that is forbidden. They become addicted, and they will become anxious every time they feel the need for it and not have it around them. They will also exhibit many behavioral problems that will ruin their relationships with others.

Peer Pressure Is Higher Than Ever

Teenagers are also under a lot of pressure from their friends. If they are surrounded by negative or unhealthy friends, they will indulge in activities they aren't supposed to indulge in, just because their friends do. They want to live up to the expectations of them and follow in their footsteps, even when they are taking them in the wrong direction. In the case that your teenager's friends are all getting good grades, excelling at extracurricular activities, and getting scholarships from excellent colleges and your teenager isn't, you can imagine the amount of stress they are in.

How Can You Help?

Management of teenage anxiety is essential. It is an important life skill that you need to teach them. If they feel anxious, panicked, or stressed out, they need to know what to do in all of these situations and prevent it from becoming worse. First of all, you need to tell them that it is a completely normal reaction to have and it will go away in time. You must also tell them that they shouldn't allow it to come in the way of things they need to do and continue without submitting to it. For example, they may have a big class presentation coming up that is causing them to sweat. Sit them down and talk to them about how they don't need to let it get into their heads and mess everything up. You can also teach them some breathing techniques to allow a good flow of oxygen to the brain to keep them calm and composed.

Managing anxiety is an important life skill. As a parent, here's what you need to do:

1. Acknowledge their fears. Don't tell them that they are being foolish and dramatic. If they seem genuinely scared, then you need to take them seriously and help them overcome it. For example, if your teenager is scared of needles and needs to get a flu shot, you need to acknowledge it and help them cope with it.

2. Encourage them to take on the things they are afraid of. However, there is no need to go overboard and force them into doing it. It will only add to their fears.

3. If they want to withdraw from something out of fear or anxiety, let them - without creating a fuss about it. Let them know that it is up to them if they want to quit but do let them know that you have confidence that they will manage it well if they choose to go after it.

4. Appreciate their efforts to overcome stress and anxiety, no matter how small they are. They need to know that they can count on you to be on their side instead of shaming them for being a loser.

5. Have conversations about the time when you were scared of something and then later overcame it. Sit them down and talk to them about the things that helped you overcome your fears. Stories that inspire and motivate can boost their self-confidence.

6. Keep them nourished with healthy food choices, especially young girls, Encourage the intake of fresh fruits and vegetables in their diet, motivate them to keep their bodies in shape, and promote good sleeping habits. All these things help lower anxiety and stimulate the release of feel-good hormones whilst building their immunity and stamina.

7. Listen to them when they come to you. Again, giving them positive attention is one of the most important things. It is very difficult for teens to open up about their problems with a parent or sibling. They only do so when they have run out of ideas or things have gotten out of control. Therefore, when they come to you to seek advice, listen actively. Help them with whatever support, ideas, or the positive dose of energy that they need so that it reduces some of their stress.

Chapter 6: Essential Parenting Skill – Picking Battles

T here are rare things that shake a parent's confidence in the way they are raising their kids. They don't question their parenting style unless their children start to exhibit bad behavior. They examine the shortcomings and challenges they still face but there is one problem – their kids are no longer kids. They are grownups who have a mind of their own. They don't just listen to you and adhere to what you say. They question. They counter your orders with their preferences. They refuse to do the things you tell them because they no longer need to be told what to do. The communication channels are also broken and no longer flow easily. It's like treading carefully into a field full of mines. The minute you take the wrong step, things blow up.

Conflicts Can Ruin Relationships

Conflicts between parents and teenagers are a common sight. With their hormones raging, teenagers often get so heated that they start to talk back, misbehave, or ignore their parents. They fight because they want to change their relationship with their parents. They have always been in the backseat of the car and now they want to be in the driver's seat. They want to live by their own rules and make decisions that concern themselves on their own. They want to be included in important discussions about the family instead of just agreeing to things mindlessly. They want to shake their parents into this new reality where they want them to see them as a new, more intellectual, and exciting person. They act over-dramatic, make mountains out of molehills, and try to push their parents into agreeing to things they are proposing.

They also want their parents to appreciate them for who they are becoming or have become even when it isn't a positive change. These quarrels, if not handled maturely, can lead to rifts between delicate relationships. For starters, it can disrupt the peace in the household and among siblings. It can also lead to blame, shame and unraveling old grievances and past failures. It can make both the parent and the teenager feel misunderstood and hurt. It can lead to anger and abuse in rare cases where one or both the parties use physical or verbal abuse to hurt one another. Some teenagers have also left their homes and moved in with their partners or friends because they feel their parents don't see them for who they are, and they are done with all the fights and violence it leads to.

Therefore, the responsibility to handle conflicts efficiently lies on the parents, as they are supposedly the more sensible ones in the relationship. This leads us to one of the most important parenting skills in today's time, picking our battles.

What Battles Are Worth Fighting and What Aren't?

Picking our battles means we critically analyze what arguments are worth stretching and what aren't. It involves thinking and deciding whether to go into action mode or not. It also means that we choose things with a profitable reward and leave the ones that pose no return on investment. As parents, we need to choose to either go into the fight or flight mood.

There will always be some issues worth fighting over and some that aren't. Your goal is to identify the ones that are and hold your ground. As for the rest, you can choose to ignore it. To make things interesting, we have created a flight and fight list to help parents understand if they are picking up the right issues to fight over or not.

The Flight List

These are the issues that can be left and ignored because fighting over them doesn't change things or bring out any positives. You will understand it more once you view the list.

Their Appearance or Clothing

It doesn't matter – at least not in the longer run – if they wish to have a certain hairstyle, get their hair dyed, or dress according to their style. They may choose to act emo and dye their hair all black or dress like a rockstar with a leather jacket on at all times. The point is, preferences change with time. They may feel in the zone right now but these choices and preferences will eventually change. They will learn to carry themselves better when they enter the professional world. So there isn't a point in starting a conflict over it every time.

A Messy Room

Some kids can't stand a dirty room. Some don't have the time to clean their rooms. A messy room isn't something you want to deal with. They can be messy eaters and careless about how their room looks, as long as they can find something clean to wear to school. Therefore, being too aggressive about it won't do you or them any good. Let it be. They will learn to behave when they move into a place of their own and spend hours looking for something.

Eating Times and Habits

Some teenagers, especially girls, give their parents a hard time with their eating habits. They will start a new diet every other week and starve themselves. They will survive on detox cleanses that taste like vomit because they have to shed a few pounds for an upcoming event. For guys, you can find them standing by the fridge, eating anything they can find in the middle of the night and then leave the kitchen a mess. Now, we do believe that healthy eating habits must be encouraged, but there are ways to go about it.

The Fight List

This list has the things you have to fight about if you see them not adhering to them. For example:

Paying Respect to Others

If they don't show others the respect that they deserve, they need to be confronted about it. It is never okay for them to be disrespectful towards their peers, parents, or teachers. They must not show prejudice toward someone or think of themselves as privileged in any way.

Curfews

They must, at all times, adhere to the rules and limitations set by you. Of course, there can be exceptions such as a class that ended late, a flat tire, or an urgent problem with a peer. They must still know to inform you about it.

Their Grades

There is no going around it. If their grades are poor, the reasons need to be discussed in a calm yet stern manner. You can scold them for not completing their homework on time or not spending time preparing for their exams.

Skills You Need to Pick Your Battles Wisely

How can you pick your battles wisely and without creating a scene every time with your teenager? Below are some great skills to use to make the right choice.

Understand the Reasons for Arguments

The first thing you need to know is why you are fighting about something. Teenagers have different personalities and styles. Some teenagers just fight for the sake of arguing. Some are shy and avoid confrontation. Some know the right things to say to change your mind and make you listen. Thus, knowing the reason for an argument combined with the personality of your child will help you pick the right battle worth fighting about.

What Are You Trying to Achieve

What is it that you wish to achieve with the conflict? What is the outcome you want? Do you just want to prove them wrong and yourself right? If so, it isn't worth the fight. Or do they want to handle waywardness and leave a positive impact on their wellbeing if they choose to change? If so, it is a worthy cause.

Getting the Timing Right

Sometimes, we are fighting the right cause but choose an inappropriate time. Kids, when in a bad mood, won't listen to you, no matter how meaningful and rewarding the outcome could be. Therefore, if you want them to listen and obey, choose the right time to have an argument or discussion.

Can a Compromise Be Made?

Is it possible that the conflict ends on a positive note where both of you settle on the same thing? Demands can be negotiated and knowing how to negotiate can reduce the pressure on you. You want them to respect you and obey you. They want the same respect in return. So try to find a middle ground where both of you leave with something, no matter how little.

Chapter 7: Essential Parenting Skill - Setting Reasonable Expectations

T hink about this for a minute. Would you go to the meat shop to buy shoes? Sounds silly, correct? But many of us do this. Not this exactly, but we set the wrong expectations for others. Remember the quote about the fish being judged on her ability to climb a tree? It's senseless. So how can we judge our teenagers over the capabilities or talents they don't have?

If your teenager had the worst experience playing volleyball with her team twice, where once, she came back with a bloody nose and told you she doesn't want to play anymore, would you still push her? If so, then maybe you do look for shoes in a meat shop.

A lot of times, parents become overexcited while setting expectations for their children. If they showed a slight interest in one skill, they want them to become a pro at it. However, setting unrealistic expectations can be damaging to their self-esteem because every time they fail or disappoint you, they lose a little part of themselves out of shame and guilt. They start to lose all confidence in their abilities and see themselves as a failure. This lack of interest can land them in dark places where they seek release from all the frustration they feel about themselves.

So in this chapter, we seek answers on how parents can set realistic expectations for their children, without burdening them with too much. We shall also see the impact of setting high, low, and reasonable expectations in the second half of the chapter.

But first, what questions should you ask yourself when setting realistic expectations for your teenager?

Questions to Ask Yourself

You must know the difference between setting and having expectations. Setting expectations is a more logical and realistic approach, where you look at your child's capabilities and then set a reasonable goal for them to achieve. Having expectations is more of a wish, where you set unrealistic expectations and pray that your child lives up to them. To clarify it further, ask yourself if you are setting the right expectations or demanding them.

The first thing you need to ask is how you can know if the expectation is realistic or not. Do you think your child possesses the expertise and strength to live up to it or assume that they will develop expertise once they start trying?

Is the expectation based on something you want and something that your child wants? Again, you have to remain focused on the things they want. True, you are a better judge of what is best for them but setting unrealistic expectations won't get you the thing you want. It will only make your child feel incompetent. Maybe what you want from them is something you had wanted when you were a little child. But is it what your child wants too?

The third question to ask yourself is about the influences that push you. Are your actions and demands directed towards the betterment of your child or are you following a tradition your family had?

The Effects of High, Low and Just Right Expectations For Teenagers

Parental expectations, if set realistically, can help foster a child's self-esteem and nurture healthy development. However, this relies on the fact that expectations are set just right – meaning they aren't too high or ridiculously low. As a parent, your goal is to find a balance between the two, and hope for an outcome that doesn't affect your child negatively.

When expectations are set too high, they become unattainable for teenagers. They feel they have to be perfect and when they fail, they feel powerless and incompetent. Repeated failures can result in a lack of interest where the child either gives up too easily without trying or prevents attempting it all together.

On the other hand, when expectations are set too low, teenagers may feel a lack of direction and purpose in life. When parents don't set goals that push them into the unknown a little, they feel unmotivated. They feel like they aren't good enough to accomplish anything and thus, the low expectations from their parents. They need to have a goal and purpose in life.

Lastly, when the expectations set are just right i.e. they aren't too high or low, it helps the teenager develop a healthy sense of self-worth and competence. Realistic expectations allow children to do well and encourages them to keep moving forward without putting a lot of pressure on themselves.

Setting Realistic Expectations – the Basics

Choosing the right expectations for your teen shouldn't feel challenging. You just need to get a few basics right and hopefully, you will have a teen that excels at everything they put their mind to. Therefore, take a look at how you can set the right expectations from an early age to minimize behavioral issues in the future.

Different Children, Different Expectations

Just because your older child was good at sports doesn't mean your other one will excel in it too. Every child is different and has their own set of talents and skills. Therefore, when setting expectations, try not to burden your children with something they don't have the skills or interest for.

This can frustrate them and they may feel that you have been unfair to them.

One Responsibility at a Time

Children want to make their parents proud, and the best way to feel that pride is when they live up to the expectations that parents have for them. However, if we put too much pressure or burdens on them at once, they might lose their confidence and not be able to give their best shot. Thus, let them take on one task at a time to learn about responsibility before handing them a list of what is expected of them. The more reasonable and few expectations there are at the start, the better. It will build their self-esteem and boost their confidence in themselves.

Begin Small and Then Grow

You can't expect your teenager to pick up on all the skills they need to achieve something set by you in a day. You need to give them time as well as the resources or directions when you expect something from them. Habits take time to develop and if something seems too hard the first time, there are fewer chances that your child will show interest in it later. Therefore, let them have a few wins and feel confident in themselves before setting up the bigger ones. Let them have the taste of independence and self-reliance a little, and then help them take on the bigger expectations driven by that motivation after winning.

Give It to Them in Writing

Finally, sometimes, the directives we give them are forgotten as the moment passes. For instance, maybe you were stuck in traffic with your teenager and decided it was the right time to instill some good expectations. The expectations may seem clear but can be misunderstood by them as a lecture. Therefore, if you are expecting them to do something or setting a goal for them, you have to make sure they know that it is one. The best way to do so is to put it in writing so it can't be forgotten or ignored.

Chapter 8: Essential Parenting Skill – Make Communication Stronger

A s children grow, the changes in the way we communicate reflect the type of relationship we have with them. They are seeking more independence and exploring new things –things that aren't always the kind you would support. Therefore, communication may take a toll and become obsolete. But it doesn't have to. Effective communication should be the goal *always*. It doesn't matter how small or big they are, you have to keep the channels of communication open and welcoming. Effective communication happens when we allow ourselves the exposure to not just verbal words but also non-verbal gestures. We don't only hear but listen. If done properly, it can help your teenager feel more relaxed around you and have a stronger and deeper bond with you, where they don't need to hide things from you anymore. You can have even the most difficult of conversations over the dinner table without feeling awkward about it.

You must keep in mind that any communication becomes effective only when:

- Both parties feel free to talk about their feelings, be heard, and understood.

- You have the opportunity to share things without being judged.

Communicating with teens is always a challenge because of the changing dynamics in the household too. Previously, they were more dependent on you for everything, had more free time on their hands to be able to sit down and watch TV with you, but not anymore. Thus, it gets harder to know what is going on in their lives and be able to help them reduce some of the anxiety they feel.

The Goal of Effective Communication

Somewhere along the line, we all believe that effective communication happens when we understand each other's words, right? Wrong. It happens when we understand the feelings and emotions underlying their words. For instance, if your teenager comes up to you and suggests something like, "Can I skip school tomorrow? I hate going on school trips, there is so much drama." What do you think would be a great answer to that?

1. Are you saying you want to skip school because of the drama?

2. Do you feel bothered by the drama on the school trip or is there something more to it that you are not telling me?

The first one misses the point completely, as you just parroted back their words to them. The second one, however, focuses more on their feelings and ideas about the school trip, where, chances are, she feels ignored or bullied, or just anxious.

When teenagers feel that they are listened to emotionally, they feel cared for. The goal of any effective communication that happens between the two of you is this. You don't have to cut to the chase, offer them the solution to a problem they are facing right away, and get done with it. You have to do more than that. You have to understand and validate their feelings.

How Effective Communication Can Cultivate Healthy Relationships With Teenagers

So how do we help our teenagers by making communication more intimate and effective? For starters, you have to deliver clear and consistent messages. You have to give them your complete attention when they come to you to talk about something. You have to let them know, both with your words and actions, that you won't judge them, mock them, or shame them. This means your messages or words should be a pure reflection of what you think about the problem. You can't say anything else and let your body tell a different story. Other than that, here are a few tips to remember:

Be an Approachable Adult

This means your teen shouldn't have to think twice before coming up to you. They should know with certainty that you wouldn't judge them. They should know that their problems will be resolved and there will be no overreaction or shaming involved.

Provide Them With Opportunities

Sometimes, the reason teenagers avoid talking to their parents is that they always find them busy with something. Communication can't happen like this. Both partners have to be clear headed, and know that something important is being discussed. Go on a short trip together or ask them to help you do something together. Maybe that will help them open up to you.

Be Supportive

If they come to you with something, don't criticize. Anyone can make a mistake. Their mistakes may seem rather naive and deliberate but don't act too worried or stressed. Instead, help them figure out ways to make amends. Criticism will only make them feel worse about themselves and hurt their self-esteem.

Prevent Power Struggles

Power struggles happen when one or both individuals want to be proven right. Your teen may hold a strong opinion and so do you. Don't belittle the whole conversation about who is right and who isn't. This will only end with hurt feelings on both ends and, may very well, become the reason for an argument. If that happens, your child won't come up to you the next time.

Focus on Interests

If you are trying hard to talk about something with them, focus on the things that interest them to spark conversations. Sometimes, when we talk about the things we love, we get so comfortable in our conversations. That should be the goal here too. You aren't trying to make a point or lecture them about something, you just talk about stuff that interests them and hope that they respond to it.

Validate Their Feelings

As parents, it is quite natural for us to want to fix and resolve the problems our children face. Your intent might be the same. However, sometimes, they just want to feel validated and heard. They want to know that you understand what they are going through. Nothing more, just that!

Don't Accuse or Assume

Let them tell you what happened. Even if you know the truth or think that you know what happened, let them have the chance to get it off their chest before you start to accuse or assume things. Don't probe leading questions in between to disrupt the flow. Let them tell you what bothers them and then ask them if they just wanted to vent or if needed any help with it.

Chapter 9: Essential Parenting Skill - Giving Them Some Room to Breathe

T he need for privacy is another developmental milestone for children. It is a natural request that teenagers make as a part of growing up. As they start to face challenges, search for their place in the world and go through many physical changes, they may act shy or wary of things concerning them.

For many parents, this is rather challenging. For years, they have been the only provider of their needs, and all of a sudden, they want them out. It can be both hurtful and difficult to adjust that they are no longer a priority in the lives of their children. But just because they want to have the door of their room closed at all times, tell you not to look in their school bag or befriend them on social media accounts doesn't mean they are hiding something from you. It can simply mean that they feel protective about their choices and the information about themselves. It can only be considered a red flag if they have started to depict some behavioral changes and acting a little weird.

The Need for Privacy in a Teenager's Life

Teens don't only need independence as they grow, they also want to be trusted to do things by themselves. They want to be seen as mature, and trustworthy adults who can take responsibility for things and handle their problems. Giving your teenagers some privacy and space can allow them to develop into inspiring adults. The level of trust you have in them makes them feel confident and capable.

Teens, when they endure physical changes become cautious about themselves. The child who once felt comfortable bathing naked in the pool on a sunny day doesn't feel that way anymore. They will lock their door before disrobing. They will also close the door when talking to their partner or friends about a party or an event where they are expected to show up.

Privacy, when allowed in the right measure can help with fostering the bond with the teen and their parents. They may start to ask for your advice with some personal problems if they think you will show respect in return, and not be too judgmental. They may also seek guidance from you about their plans.

Setting Rules for Privacy – A Beginner's Guide for Parents

Teenagers need space and privacy to do things their way. Therefore, doing things like going through their diary or journal, or checking the pockets of their jeans or school bag without their permission is a big no-no. Unless of course, your concerns are for their safety and they have been acting shady for a few days or weeks. Boundaries allow them to learn about responsibility. Besides, it is highly unethical to go through their stuff without their knowledge because it can damage the trust between the two of you. Imagine, if someone searched your drawers without your permission. Would you not see it as a breach of your privacy?

Since the goal is to improve the relationship between the parent and the teenager, you have to act sensibly and make them feel safe in their house. Some healthy ways to set boundaries and rules for privacy should look like this:

Seek Input

If you are going to set some ground rules for them, the least you can do is include them too. Have a debate over curfew times and how much screen time should be allowed and reach a mutual decision. This will make them feel validated and not make you a strict parent.

Have Important Discussions Frequently

Keep in mind, the term frequently doesn't mean all the time here. Talking to your teens about stuff like drugs, sex, addictions, and bullying from time to time can keep the door open for communication. Don't be too outspoken and inquisitive. Try to blend it into normal conversations to seek their opinions about it.

Watch Out for Them

Keep an eye on their school performance, relationships, and social media without trying to micromanage. Knowing what is going on in their lives can help you understand them better.

Put Limits on Digital Media

From the very beginning, let them know beforehand that you will be asking them about the apps installed on their phones regularly. You can also have them install tracking and monitoring apps on their phones, not to spy, but to always know that they are safe. They should know of your intentions too, so that they don't think you don't trust them.

Knock Before Entering

If you know they are in the room and the room isn't locked, it is still wise to knock before entering without an announcement. That would be an invasion of their privacy and they will make sure to have it locked the next time, even when they weren't doing something suspicious. Therefore, don't let your hastiness take away the trust they have in you.

Leave the Room When at the Doctor's

It is humiliating to have to declare in front of your parents that you have been active sexually when they don't even know that you have a partner. This is why a doctor's visit can be rather unpleasant and shocking. If, as their parent, you sense the uneasiness on their face when asked intimate questions about their sexuality, excuse yourself to leave the room to let them be open with their doctor in peace. They will come to you when they feel confident enough to share something as intimate as this with you.

Conclusion

Teenagers aren't a different breed as we often think. Everyone is quick to judge them for being rebellious, ill-disciplined, and rude. But this isn't the case with all teenagers. Some are just an extension of their former self with a few upgrades. They are still closely connected to their parents, have strong bonds with their friends, respect their peers, and are known to be the most empathetic people in their class and among peers.

The hero is, of course, the parent/parents who instill the right values and morals from the start. They use effective parenting skills to nurture, discipline, and instill responsibility to raise successful and competent kids. They value honesty, trust, and happiness because these seem to be the ethics people care about in the professional world. They teach them to have manners, show empathy and be compassionate towards others which makes them a great and kind individual.

Your job is to impart the same wisdom in them to help them prepare themselves for the next phase of their lives. If you think that they are too old to be taught something new, you are wrong. You can always preach about something if you do it the right way. You just have to be strategic about it in a way that it doesn't come off as a lecture or a demand but rather, a suggestion. You have to let them choose or at least let them have a say.

If we quickly review the book, we notice we have done almost the same. We have put into practice various parenting skills, but left it on them, the teenager, to decide if they want to follow those rules or not. We used different strategic ways to impart that knowledge, such as becoming the prime example, allowing them some space to themselves, lending our time and ears to them to make communication more effective, picking the fights worth fighting and ignoring the ones that aren't, setting reasonable expectations, and helping them find ways to reduce anxiety and depression.

Hopefully, this book will leave you with many new and implementable ways to deal with teen anxiety, foster strong relationships with them, and make communication smoother and easier. If you liked the advice and found it useful, someone else will too. Let us know what you think of it and how you found it helpful.

References

Anxiety in teenagers. (2019, February). Raising Children Network. https://raisingchildren.net.au/pre-teens/mental-health-physical-health/stress-anxiety-depression/anxiety

Any Anxiety Disorder. (2017, November). Nih.Gov. https://www.nimh.nih.gov/health/statistics/any-anxiety-disorder.shtml#part_155096

Coleman, P. K. (2003). Perceptions of parent-child attachment, social self-efficacy, and peer relationships in middle childhood. Infant and Child Development, 12(4), 351–368. https://doi.org/10.1002/icd.316

Damico, P. (2017, November 28). 7 Common Causes of Teenage Anxiety. Paradigm Malibu. https://paradigmmalibu.com/common-causes-teenage-anxiety/

Duineveld, J. J., Parker, P. D., Ryan, R. M., Ciarrochi, J., & Salmela-Aro, K. (2017). The link between perceived maternal and paternal autonomy support and adolescent well-being across three major educational transitions. Developmental Psychology, 53(10), 1978–1994. https://doi.org/10.1037/dev0000364

Eagan, K., Stolzenberg, E. B., Ramirez, J. J., Aragon, M. C., Suchard, M., & Rios-Aguilar, C. (2016). The American Freshman: Fifty-Year Trends 1966–2015 (pp. 1–352). Higher Education Research Institute.

Hall, M. (2013, May 29). How to Set Realistic Expectations for your Teenager. GoNannies.Com. https://www.gonannies.com/blog/2013/how -to-set-realistic-expectations-for-your- teenager/

Joussemet, M., Landry, R., & Koestner, R. (2008). A self-determination theory perspective on parenting. Canadian Psychology/Psychologie Canadienne, 49(3), 194–200. https://doi.org/10.1037/a0012754

Martinelli, K. (n.d.). The Power of Positive Attention. Child Mind Institute. Retrieved June 3, 2020, from https://childmind.org/article/the- power-of-positive-attention/

McCarthy, C. (2019, November 20). Anxiety in Teens is Rising: What's Going On? HealthyChildren.Org. https://www.healthychildren.org/English/he alth-issues/conditions/emotional- problems/Pages/Anxiety-Disorders.aspx

Morin, A. (2017, August 17). The 1 Skill College
     Students Wish Their Parents Had Taught
     Them. Psychology Today.
     https://www.psychologytoday.com/intl/blog
     /what-mentally-strong-people-dont-
     do/201708/the-1-skill-college-students-wish-
     their-parents

Morin, A. (2019, September 23). This Might Be the
     Simplest But Most Effective Way to Prevent
     Behavior Problems. Verywell Family.
     https://www.verywellfamily.com/positive-
     attention-reduces-behavioral-problems-
     1094784

Murray, T. A. (2018, March 30). Picking your battles:
     the core of parenting a teen. Thrive Global.
     https://thriveglobal.com/stories/picking-
     your-battles-the-core-of-parenting/

Paxson, M. S. (2017). Setting Realistic Expectations.
     CHADD. https://chadd.org/attention-
     article/setting-realistic-expectations/

Seifert, C. (2018, November 28). What Effects Do
     Parental Expectations Have on Kids? Hello
     Motherhood.
     https://www.hellomotherhood.com/what-
     effects-do-parental-expectations-have-on-
     kids-9634703.html

Teen Role Models: Who They Are, Why They Matter.
(2011, January 31). Barna Group.
https://www.barna.com/research/teen-role-
models-who-they-are-why-they-matter/

Understanding Adolescence. (n.d.). Skills You Need.
Retrieved June 3, 2020, from
https://www.skillsyouneed.com/parent/unde
rstanding-adolescence.html

Witmer, D. (2020, March 23). Privacy and Trust Go
Hand-in-Hand for Teens (A. Morin (Ed.)).
Verywell Family.
https://www.verywellfamily.com/why-does-
my-teen-need-privacy-2609615

Youth Index 2019. (2019). In Prince's Trust (pp. 1–
11). https://www.princes-trust.org.uk/about-
the-trust/research-policies-reports/youth-
index-
2019#:~:text=Youth%20Index%202019,peop
le%20aged%2016%20to%2025.

Book Description

Is she being over the top about everything lately? Does she give you a hard time with her dressing, food choices, and messy habits? Does she seem to have a mind of her own and disobey you on purpose?

Dear parents,

Welcome to the most dramatic and tough phase of your life.

Raising a teenage daughter is both hard and challenging. However, the right social skill set and parenting techniques can make it less daunting, and in some cases, even wonderful and rewarding.

Teaching our girls on how to communicate better, manage conflicts with their friends efficiently, act like responsible and disciplined adults, regulate their emotional fluctuations well, and remain transparent, and empathetic are all essential skills she needs to learn from you.

Thus, to help you start on the right foot, this book lists the 7 most effective parenting skills to not only understand your teenage daughter well but also be able to communicate with her and form a strong bond.

Written in a rather simple and easy-to-read and follow manner, hopefully, this will serve as a stress reliever for many parents struggling with raising a successful, happy, and confident teenager. It discusses the various changes that happen during adolescence as well as lists strategies on how to cope with them.

7 Vital Skills for Parenting Teen Girls and Communicating with Your Teenage Daughter

Proven Parenting Tips for Raising Teenage Girls with Self-Confidence and Coping Skills

Frank Dixon

been derived from various sources. Please consult a licensed professional before attempting any techniques outlined in this book.

By reading this document, the reader agrees that under no circumstances is the author responsible for any losses, direct or indirect, that are incurred as a result of the use of the information contained within this document, including, but not limited to, errors, omissions, or inaccuracies.

Introduction

"But, mom, you don't know anything..."

One of the most common cries of a teenage daughter. Teenagers, in general, are rebellious creatures. They are also unpredictable and secretive. They will close the door on your face when talking to someone on their phones, lie to you about going to a sleepover at a friend while packing their most provocative dress in their bags. However, they aren't all bad. In fact, as they grow older and steer their way towards entering adulthood, they become the best of friends. A bond between a teenage daughter and a mother or a father and his son is often spoken of. For parents, it is one of the most challenging yet delightful periods of their lives because they finally get to see them grow into these beautiful birds ready to leave the nest in some time.

That growth doesn't come without challenges. In fact, many parents think that living with a teenager is like living with a stranger in the house. The lines of communication are mostly jammed and there is no way to know what they are thinking or doing or thinking to do. If you are a parent with a teenager in the house, you will get the joke.

Since we are going to focus on teenage daughters, the dramas, the self-esteem, and body image issues here, let's try to visualize what daily life with a teenage daughter looks like.

For starters, teenage daughters believe that the parents are the straight-up target for releasing all the pent-up frustration and anger. You will often find yourself being labeled as unconcerned, uncompassionate, and naïve. However, to blame them for all the chaos in the house will be one side of the story. Unlike old times, our daughters don't have it easy today. They have to deal with tons of stressors which lead to unwanted anxiety and depression. They are subjected to bullying for looking a certain way and develop eating disorders because of it. They are also exposed to things like substance abuse, sexual experimentation, harassment, and whatnot. Things weren't always the same before. Friendships nurtured during sleepovers when pals went ghost-hunting. There were fewer secrets and each presented the other with an honest opinion. There was less judgment and more compassion.

It is ironic that although we have more resources than ever to teach girls to cope with the stressors, their life seems too pressure-optimized. On the other hand, this leaves parents to deal with excessive worry and feel incompetent to help them in some way.

As a parent, you might often ask yourself how to help them feel safe and confident, how to make them feel more in control of their lives, how to teach them to carry the world on their backs fearlessly and the answer is simple: you teach them some basic coping, communication, and relationship management skills. When you teach them these, you make this testing phase of their lives easier to pass through.

In this book, we shall look at 7 essential skills to teach teenage daughters to make their lives stress-free and manageable. It will also benefit you to build a deeper and stronger bond with them and become an important part of their lives and experiences. The stronger the bond, the stronger the communication. The stronger the communication, the fewer the secrets. The fewer the secrets, the more the trust between you two. So, you see, it is like a chain that ends with a fulfilling and harmonious experience for the two of you.

So, without further delay, let's begin.

Chapter 1: The Growing Teenager

You can be certain about one thing: Today's teenagers are stronger and more spirited than ever. They will stand up against what's wrong and won't back down when it comes to having their opinions heard. They are generally more empathetic and smarter than previous generations, too. They will have a say about anything and everything and feel things more deeply. The reason can be contributed to their exposure to the world via the internet and social media. It should surely be counted as a blessing, but we also know of its dark side and how harmful it can be for a young adult to cope with the pressures of it.

Most of the time, these changes not only affect them on the whole but also the parents. It leaves you confused about how to respond and react to the situations you find yourself in and no matter how many parenting books or articles you have read online, the reality is too real and difficult to handle. As they try to be more in control and independent, there is sometimes a clash between you two. You are then expected to have a cool head and manage and prevent conflicts before they escalate and you two drift apart.

In this first chapter, we look at the various social, physical, and emotional changes they go through and how they affect their behavior, attitude, and mood. The changes are mostly puberty-related, which means they can't be blamed for all the chaos they create because they are a part of it, too. If it is hard being a parent, it is also hard to be a teenager and go through so many transitions at once without having proper knowledge of it.

Physical, Emotional and Social Changes

During adolescence, it is common to notice many cognitive, social, and emotional changes in young girls. The way their interactions change, the way they form friendships, the way they search for their identities are all aspects of the many changes happening within them. Physical changes being the easiest to decipher and note. However, many emotional and social changes also occur that we must take into account trying to learn about their mood, behavior, and interactions.

Physical Changes

Puberty can start as early as eight or as late as about thirteen. The standard, however, is set at about 10 years of age. Puberty is what leads to the many bodily changes we see in teenage girls. Some of the most common changes in their physical appearance include:

- Breast Development: Breast development or budding is one of the most prominent indicators of puberty. Girls develop nickel-sized bumps under their nipples and their nipples become sore and tender.

- Body Hair: Girls, when they hit puberty notice coarse growth of hair in their underarms, legs, and around the genital area. Pubic hair, according to many, is the first indicator of puberty.

- Periods: Periods is the most important indicator of reaching puberty. The timelines can vary but if we talk about the USA, the average age for a girl to have her first period is about 12 years.

- Increase in Height: Unlike boys, girls have a faster growth spurt and begins before their first period. The earliest signs of height growth are when their breasts start to bud, around six to eight months before their first period. It must also be noted that by the time a girl has her first period, the rate of their height growth decreases, and they only grow one or two inches taller after that.

- Wider Hips: Girls also notice their waist becoming smaller and their hips becoming wider.

- Sweating and Body Odor: Sweating under the armpits is another common occurrence when girls are turning into women. They may need to shower more often and apply deodorant in their armpits to avoid smelling bad.

Emotional Changes

Now that she is turning into a beautiful young adult, you may notice the show of strong feelings and intense emotions. Their mood becomes unpredictable and they demonstrate many ups and downs at varying times which makes it harder for parents to interpret and respond accordingly. Thus, the increase in the number of conflicts at home because they feel unheard, misunderstood, and unvalued. Most of the blame can be put on the different chemicals in their brain and their lack of emotional intelligence. They are unable to process and express their emotions like grown-ups and it leads to an increased amount of frustration. Some other significant emotional changes include:

- Increased Sensitivity: With time, they become better at processing other's emotions which in turn, makes them empathetic. However, they may still have a difficult time reading or decode facial expressions and body language.

- Become Self-conscious: Suddenly, the way they look is all that matters. They become conscious about the many physical changes they are going through and it affects their self-esteem. With little knowledge about their unique stature, they start to compare themselves with other girls in their school and feel insecure.

- Lack of Decision-making skills: many teenage girls think that they are invincible. They think that they are queens of the kingdom and thus want to rule. However, this often leads to bad decision-making such as dating the wrong boy or using unhealthy and damaging products for their skin, face, and hips without the knowledge of their parents, to become more desirable.

Social Changes

Young girls are so worried about where they fit into this world that they are always searching to associate themselves with someone or something. This is the age when they begin to idolize their teachers, celebrities, social influencers, or their parents. They try to put themselves into a certain box. Either they are hot or they aren't. Either they are thin and skinny or fat. Either they are popular or unpopular etc. they will put on different clothes, get their hair dyed after crying for a week in front of their parents or start dieting. As parents, you must know that this is just a normal phase in their lives. They are just trying to figure out their standing. With time, their sense of identity becomes stronger and they get a better sense of who they want to be like when they grow up. Other than that, you can expect them to depict the following changes.

- Seek Independence: their need for independence increases. They want to decide for themselves or at least have a say in matters concerning them.

- Develop a Sense of Morals: They will start to differentiate between right and wrong. They will start to take responsibility for their actions and be ready to suffer the consequences of a bad decision. They will also be inquisitive about the right morals and values.

- Seek More Responsibility: They will start to own up to their actions, both at home and in school, and be more willing to work on their strengths and weaknesses.

- Seek New Experiences: As they learn to gain control of their impulses, you can expect them to indulge in some risky behaviors such as self-harm over a heartbreak or driving while intoxicated. This is the doing of their brains that encourages them to try new things and seek more out-of-the-world experiences.

- Become Influenced Easily: They also seem to be easily influenced by their peers, role models, and other influencers they follow on their social media accounts. They will try to be like them, do what they do, or just be inspired to grow up to be like them one day. Most girls this age, fantasize about TV celebrities, movie stars, and the "bad boys" in their school, and have imaginary romantic relationships with them.

- Explore Sexual Identify: Talking of romance, the hormonal balances, and the puberty-related changes also make them want to try sexual things with a partner. Most teenagers do it out of curiosity or because others are doing it, too. They may also have intimate relationships early one which is why it is highly critical that you discuss with them the topic of safe sex in detail. You must also tell them that they shouldn't feel pressured to do anything they don't want to do and report to you if anyone forces them, too.

Mood Swings, Social Media, and Independence

As stated, puberty brings along a new set of challenges and changes. The physical changes young girls go through during the first three to four years can trigger many body-image related issues. The less confident they are, the poorer their self-esteem. Hence, you can expect them to be always a little self-conscious about what they are wearing especially during the days of menstruation or looking like with pimples and acne breakouts on their face. The onset of the discomfort can have a significant impact on their mood. They may seem anxious, angry, or depressed.

Moreover, their brain is still in the process of developing with the prefrontal cortex as its main candidate. This region of the brain is responsible for decision-making and judgment, which is why we may notice some poor decision-making on their part about their choices and preferences. However, since it is just a phase, their choices change with time, and their capacity to make sensible decisions improves, too.

Mood Swings and Teen Girls

We have often seen a stereotypical image of a difficult daughter in movies and TV shows where the parents feel helpless when it comes to knowing how to handle them. They can be seen fighting with their siblings over insignificant things like a TV's remote or sitting in the front seat of the car when driving to school. A lot of times, this anger is a way of releasing the pressure and frustration they feel within.

According to one study, teenage daughters do suffer from mood swings when they are growing

(Maciejewski et al., 2015). Some 500 adolescents were called in for experimentation. Their ages ranged from 13 to 18. The teenage girls were told to keep an online account of their daily happiness, sadness, anger, and anxiety for the next five days. After reviewing the individual responses, the researchers found that mood swings were quite prevalent in early adolescence. The girls showed extreme variations in their level of happiness and sadness.

For a parent, it can be hard to deal with the ups and downs they go through. They are unable to know what to do and can be quite confused. Therefore, to make sense of the situations, they label them as disrespectful or difficult which isn't the case.

Social Media, Body Image, and Teen Girls

Body-image is a critical issue with young girls. As they start to sprout, they become extremely concerned about the way they look and feel. They become insecure about their looks and the pressure to look good and healthy on social media just adds to that pressure.

During an interesting online survey by Common Sense Media, 35% of the teenagers (girls) are worried about being tagged in unattractive photos and videos by their friends without their consent. Another 27% of them feel stressed whenever posting a picture of themselves on their social accounts, uncertain about how it will be received. Further, 22% of them feel extremely sad and worried when they don't receive any likes or comments on them (Rideout & Robb, 2019).

On one hand, social media helps us to stay connected and be aware of everything happening around the world and on the other, it is raising a generation of self-conscious young men and women who go to extreme lengths to look 'beautiful' According to one study, the use of Facebook is linked to an increased risk of eating disorders among young girls (Mabe et al., 2014).

Not to mention, social media also gives rise to incidents of cyberbullying (Anderson, 2018). Some people feel bad because they are mocked for being different while others feel left out and unnoticed. It is wise to say that the cons outweigh the cons when it comes to one's mental health and peace of mind. During a TV show called #Being Thirteen: Inside the Secret World of Teens, a group of thirteen-year-olds was called in for a survey. The researchers found that those who spent/checked in on social media 50 to 100 times a day were less happy and satisfied with their lives than those who checked it only a few times per day.

Independence and Teen Girls

The growing need for independence is another sign of adolescent development. Teen girls become more responsible, figure out their values and morals, and express themselves through their fashion choices, friends, the music they listen to, or hobbies they are interested in. they may not always be in line with the ones made by their parents and thus, conflicts may arise.

They want to be able to make decisions for themselves. However, they aren't always the right decisions and you might want to save them from the hurt and damage early on. However, because it isn't coming from them, they might not take those opinions too well. Again, no need to worry as failure is the best teacher. The more times they fail, the more valuable lessons they learn. This also helps them develop resilience i.e. coming out of a bad experience with their head held high. For you, it mustn't be easy to know that they are going to fall and still not lend a hand. Don't! Or else, they may see it as a conflicting opinion and deliberately attempt that thing just to prove you wrong.

Chapter 2: A Parent's Essential Toolkit

Many parents believe that raising a teenager is a nightmare. There is so much you want to do for them but they don't let you. They choose their paths, fight to get their way, make friends you don't approve of, keep secrets, and go behind your back on several occasions, and whatnot. This can take a toll on the parents as there is nothing that prepares them for this kind of attitude. Although not all kids behave this badly, it can be said for most of them. They find their parents a little old-fashioned. The last time they checked, you had scolded them over a joke they cracked and given them a full 10 minutes lecture over it. So, you can understand their hesitance to come to you with their problems. Also, in many homes, the relationship between a parent and a daughter is more dictatorial and less friendly. So, what to do and what not to do, can be rather tricky. Thus, to get you started on the right foot, here are seven essential skills to teach them right from the start.

A Guide to the 7 Essential Parenting Skills to Teach Teenage Daughters

Isn't it odd that your once lovely, smiley little one is fuming with anger, hiding things from you, and doing things their way just to push your buttons?

Whatever suggestions you make are wrong and everything you do or say is old-fashioned.

As children grow older, parents need to adopt new parenting techniques. Yesterday, they needed to be shown how to eat, chomp on their food, go potty, and dress but today, they need to be told how to behave, resolve conflicts, express themselves, be transparent and listen. You may think that they no longer need a parent-figure in their lives now that they act all grown-up. You are mistaken. They need you more than ever to teach them some essential skills to make this phase of their lives easier. They need you to guide and mentor them by instilling good habits as well as teaching them some basic communication, coping and conflict resolution skills to feel confident in their skins and have high self-esteem. You need to implement strategies that will enable them to own up to their mistakes, stay disciplined, and not give in to the pressures of social media and cyberbullying.

Thus coming to the 7 essential skills this book is all about, take a look at the skills we think to cut and are deemed most valuable to teach.

Essential Parenting Skill #1: Communication and Listening Skills

She needs to learn to talk. Period. She must know how to make herself heard, listen without judgment, and express herself in a disciplined and consistent manner. Good communication skills from an early age also make children more empathetic and compassionate towards others and their feelings. She must also learn to carry herself respectfully in social gatherings, and with people of different ages, manage negative emotions, and prevent arguments from turning into bigger disagreements. Therefore, as a parent, be concerned if she isn't picking up these skills as these are what sets the foundation for the rest.

Essential Parenting Skill #2: Values, Discipline, and Responsibilities

All teenagers must know what is expected of them. They must know to adhere to the rules set by their parents and teachers and avoid misbehaving. Teaching them how to be responsible, own up to their shortcomings, and be disciplined is a parent's job. Again, these are things whose foundations you have to lay early on as most children when they hit their tweens and teen years begin to demonstrate a lack of empathy and discipline. They start to take others for granted, including their parents, and make it harder for those parents to parent.

Essential Parenting Skill #3: Conflict Resolution and Management

Conflicts arise when there is a disagreement of some sort between people. They can be minor and resolved with both the parties sitting together and sorting it out or major where adults have to intervene. Teenage daughters face tens of conflicts, if not more, daily. Conflicts can be highly stressful for her and can lead to depression and panic attacks. Many teens don't do well with it, and thus, as parents, we have to teach them how to cope with the emotions that arise as a result and healthily deal with them.

Essential Parenting Skill #4: Combat Body-Image Issues and Cyberbullying

With the advancement of technology, social media addiction is becoming a real and scary thing. Children, especially teenagers spend more time online than they should, exposing themselves to all sorts of heinous, obscene, and self-destructive things. Social media has also given rise to cyberbullying, in which many teenage girls become the victim. They are laughed at, mocked, and made fun of online by their classmates and friends all the time which can lead to some serious self-esteem issues in them. Therefore, as a parent, it is your job to limit the amount of time she spends browsing the internet and control the type of content she exposes herself, too. This accounts for setting some ground rules that you must teach her about as well as how to cope with the pressures that come with it.

Essential Parenting Skill #5: Empathy, Compassion, and Emotional Intelligence

With her ego taking over her life, she hardly shows an ounce of compassion and empathy. She also has a troubled time dealing with the many new emotions and feelings they go through. Therefore, she must be taught how to manage the onset of difficult emotions, behave, and act well-mannered and show compassion towards others.

Essential Parenting Skill #6: Honesty and Transparency

Honesty and transparency mean that no lies are told and no secrets are kept. As our girls start their journey towards becoming a woman, they encounter many challenges. They become distant from their parents and they form more intimate bonds with their partners and friends. They start to slam doors in the face, yell, and roll their eyes. However, this shouldn't stop parents from teaching them to remain honest and transparent. They must feel comfortable sharing stuff with you and express themselves without feeling judged.

Essential Parenting Skill #7: Relationship Management

Relationship management refers to the art of maintaining and supervising different relationships one forms with another. It entails the building of strong interpersonal communication skills as well as the ability to form bonds that help you and your partner nurture, grow, develop, and resolve conflicts. Since young girls start to look up to others and form bonds with their peers, it is important to teach them how to maintain strong friendships and learn to resolve any conflicts that arise.

Chapter 3: Essential Parenting Skill – Communication

Communication is one of the most essential life skills. Humans have used it as a means to express themselves, have their needs fulfilled, and form bonds. If we think about it, we have been communicating from the minute we were born. First, we cried to demand food and a diaper change, then picked up a few words and then started to speak full sentences at the age of three or four. So, you might wonder, if we have been doing it for so long, why do we still need to learn it? Why do we need to teach our teenage sons and daughters to do it? It is because if we don't, we will not be able to pick up the meaning of what has been said. Ask yourself this, if you don't know the meaning of a specific word, how can you use it in a sentence? Similarly, if you don't understand what has been said to you, you can't form a proper response or reaction. You can't communicate back until you understand the context and meaning of it.

Therefore, it is an essential social skill all parents must teach their children so that they can be raised as knowledgeable, smart, and vigilant. They can read between the lines, i.e. pick up the context of something using non-verbal cues such as facial expressions, body language, physical action, the tone of voice, etc.

Importance of Building Effective Communication skills in Teenage Daughters

Everything we say or do sends a message. We may not even realize but our body language may communicate on behalf of us. Such as, if we are sitting through a three-hour workshop session, we may not even realize we are sleepy until we have yawned at least twice. If we are caught, what does that say about us or the speaker? This means that it is easy to form judgments even when one isn't actively communicating.

Good communication skills are like that icing on the cake that makes it all the more delicious and tempting. It allows us an upper hand over the receiver. The more sound and sensible we are, the easier it is for the receiver to understand and form an opinion.

For teenagers, effective communication skills allow them to be perceived well. It adds an element of awareness and confidence. When they depict good communication skills, it makes the message more meaningful. Moreover, it allows them to be as expressive or impassive as they want to be. When teenagers can hold conversations with others, it also boosts their confidence and self-esteem. It allows them to speak their minds which helps them cultivate meaningful relationships with everyone.

Teaching Her to Listen, Talk, and Connect

Since the book is about encouraging communication in young girls, we must know that most of them look up to their moms for guidance and mentorship. From an early age, they have been imitating your actions, behaviors, and moods. Remember the time they would want to dress up like you, wear your shoes, and apply your makeup... Since they look up to us as their role models, it is time we become one. The point being: if you want to teach her effective communication skills, you have to model it yourself. How you resolve conflicts, hold communication, express yourself, demonstrate happiness or anger are all ways that she is going to pick up.

Therefore, to emphasize the importance of learning how to communicate, you have to be her teacher. You have to be smart about it, too. Because chances are, if you come onto her as if giving her a lecture or ordering her, she is going to misbehave and disobey. You have to act and think like a teenager and mold your words in such a manner that it reaches her head as well as her hearts. So, what else can you do to help her learn how to communicate? Take a look below!

Spend Time With Her

The most effective strategy to boost their confidence in their ability to converse well is by providing them the opportunities to do so. Seek their opinion over things, ask them about their day, discuss the days' activities, talk to them about their friends, read, eat, and watch TV together.

Praise Her

Constant nagging creates distance. You don't want that. You want her to come to you with all her problems no matter how naïve or complicated they are. They will likely roll their eyes or slam the door on you if you are a harsh critique and keep finding faults in her. On the other hand, if you use praise, appreciation, and recognition to your advantage, you might get through to her. She might open up to you when she notices that you don't judge her choices, values her opinions, and praises her for the good she does.

Use Social Media to Your Advantage

If you feel you are incapable to find something interesting to talk about, you can always use social media as a tool to help you bond. If you are friends with her on Facebook or Instagram, you must be able to view the type of content that interests her. Take a look at what she likes and comments on. You can always talk about it with her over dinner or during her free time to encourage communication.

Be the Parent

Although you might want to give her some space and privacy, this shouldn't mean that she can get away with whatever she likes. You have to lay some basic ground rules such as when she is and isn't allowed to close her door, until what time she can stay out with her friends, who can/can't be invited over, etc. Having these in place will prevent conflicts later. Also, it will make her grow up to be disciplined and value rules and regulations in the professional world.

Teach Her How to Express Herself

She must know how to express herself efficiently. This means she must know how to stay calm in panicking situations, use words instead of anger to articulate it, and practice good communication etiquette when speaking to an elder or a toddler, etc.

Enforce Effective Listening Skills

Teach her how to listen attentively without being distracted when talking to someone. An essential part of effective communication is good listening which involves devoting your complete attention to the speaker. When undivided attention is given to someone, it shows strong character and genuine concern. She must also know how to ask or probe questions in a polite manner when she isn't able to comprehend something.

Teach Her to Notice Body Language

Sometimes, you don't need words to express yourself. Your body language does it for you. However, teens may have difficulty picking up non-verbal cues and making wrong assumptions. Therefore, encourage the art of observation. Additionally, make her notice her body language when she is in different states of mind such as happy, angry, sad, or distracted. You can make a video of her depicting any of these and then watch it together to put forward some suggestions on how to improve.

Get Together to Critique

If you want to teach her how to open up to you and others, one of the best ways to do is by getting on board with her to read or watch a book or film together and then critique it. You can also create a YouTube channel together and upload reaction videos where you share your thoughts about something you just reviewed. You can discuss the things you liked or disliked, things that could have been improved or taken out, etc. This encourages storytelling in kids, which again, is a great form of communication.

Encourage Blogging or Journaling

Journaling or simply keeping a diary has been proven therapeutic for teenagers. It allows them to vent out their emotions on a paper in a healthy and low-stress way. They can be who they are when they are writing a diary and express feelings they have kept bottled up. Encourage your teenage daughter to keep a diary and record day-to-day events in it. If she isn't old-school, you may also suggest turning to the internet and starting a blog. With the whole world online, she will surely find someone going through the same and be able to connect with her and improve her communication skills in the process.

Chapter 4: Essential Parenting Skill – Conflict Management

During the teen ages, we have more clashes with our kids than we ever had in the past. For instance, when they were young, they would mostly wear things you made them wear but now they might have a difference of opinion. They may want to pick their dresses and wear something you don't approve of. You may also have differences of opinions on whether they should own a car or not before they turn eighteen, whether they should have sleepovers or not etc.

These types of conflicts are healthy and normal as it tells us about each other's expectations. You understand her need for independence and she understands your need regarding her safety. However, sometimes, conflicts can turn nasty. They may become so big that all channels of communication between the two of you get blocked.

Thus, you both need to know of some good conflict management and resolution strategies to deal with them, resolve them, and then move on. When you and your children are on the same boat, aka living in harmony, it reduces the family's stress levels. It can also result in a healthy and strong relationship with your child. Knowing how to deal with conflicts effectively is yet another essential skill to teach your teenage daughter. With her hormones raging and mood swings taking over her better judgment, she will be making many enemies, too. She will probably go through heartbreaks, end ties with lifelong friends, and deal with the pressure-inducing demands from her school. Equipping her with the right skills to deal with all of these things can be rewarding shortly when she graduates and enters the professional world.

Importance of Teaching Conflict Management Skills

All-day long, she confronts conflicts when she has a disagreement with you over something, with her best friend about not replying to her texts sooner, or with her boyfriend who seems more interested in playing ball with his friends than talking to her. It is almost impossible to protect them from conflicts and thus, they must know how to deal with them respectively.

After all, she can't avoid people all her life. She must know how to make confrontations less scary. She must know how to deal with a differentiating opinion and hear what others have to say. Learning to deal with conflicts allows us to get along with others better. We feel more control of the situation when we successfully handle any issue that may have led to becoming a conflict.

Therefore, you must teach your daughter how to manage them.

Teaching Our Girls to Resolve Conflicts

For centuries, women have been expected to be the paragons of inclusivity and acceptance. They have been told to be like Mother Teresa, selfless, and forgiving. They have been told to model acceptance and embrace compassion. This school of thought has done some drastic damage to the making of a woman who views these values important and chooses to remain in unhealthy and toxic relationships. This has to stop. We mustn't raise our teenage daughters to such injustice. We need to set better values and instill better and empowering skills in them to not bend at the face of a conflict but rise and hold a sword. We have to read with them stories about women who became the heroes of their own stories instead of telling them to rely on their counterparts for everything. We have to tell them that it is completely okay to not want to be friends with everyone.

We have to teach our girls to navigate through conflicts with confidence without bowing down their heads and taking the blame for everything.

So how can we, as parents, help them manage conflicts in a non-toxic and healthy manner? Let's learn below.

Plan in Advance

Teen girls tend to be impulsive. They rarely take the time out to think things rationally before speaking them out like venom on others. Chances are if she doesn't know what to say and when to say it, she will have many regrets to cry over, later. Therefore, encourage her to seek advice from someone older and wiser than her, such as you, when she finds herself in a conflicting situation. When she knows she can look up to someone for consultation, she will avoid being rude and unreasonable.

Don't Call in an Audience

Sometimes, teenagers believe that having an audience or support system behind them during a confrontation makes them appear stronger. True, but it can also escalate things further, when more secrets are out, feelings are hurt and emotions run high. Therefore, if she has a problem with someone, say a girl from her class, she must choose to talk to her directly in a one-on-one conversation. This will prevent the confrontation from becoming a fight scene from the Mean Girls.

Use 'I' Instead of 'You'

Using statements starting with 'I' are less conflicting. They are less provoking and yet direct. Statements starting with 'you,' on the other hand, blamed others. Take a look at what we mean by this:

- "I feel sad that you told everyone about that incident after school."

- "You are so mean. You told everyone about that incident after school."

Notice the difference in the tone and emotions in each of these sentences. The first one seems less disputable than the second one.

Admit Mistakes

Another important thing to teach your daughter is to admit when she is wrong and apologize. Doing so diffuses the situation instantly and prevents the escalation of the conflict. She must know what genuine apology sounds like and how to make the other person understand her situation without being loud, or angry. A good apology must list the amends she is going to make to dissolve the situation and prevent further conflict.

Breathe In and Breathe Out

Sometimes, while discussing a friend, she may get all riled up and fumed. Teach her some basic breathing skills to not lose her temper and stay calm. Breathing in and out for about a minute when she feels too overwhelmed with her emotions can help her relax and think rationally.

Calm Her Down

Just because they have broken up with a friend doesn't mean that friend automatically becomes an enemy. Your daughter should know that it is okay to move on and not hold onto a grudge forever. Easier said than done, teach her to let go and move on. Tell her that friendships end for a lot of reasons and it doesn't mean that they will never have a friend again or trust someone so deeply.

Chapter 5: Essential Parenting Skill – Coping with Body-Image Issues and Cyber Bullying

Did you know, kids form an opinion about their bodies from an early age, as little as three? It is the time when their tiny brains begin to understand the concept of thin and fat and also the age where they actively start to seek idols and role models. They want to look like them and when they don't, they feel disheartened. A lot of young girls who see ballerinas and models on TV want to be like them when they grow up and in their little mind, it all starts with looking petite.

Here, the role of the parents is a crucial one as they have to save them from succumbing to the ideals they think are normal when they aren't. It is our job to implant the right ideas about body image and self-esteem.

Although it is very difficult in this age and time to escape the idea promoted by social media and advertising companies, it is still imperative that we teach our young girls to not fall into the traps they lay. We must ensure that they take the right message from an ad they see and not just want to blindly follow others like a herd. Still, how much can you shield them from? She is going to school, on social media, and looking at hot girls dating the hot guys.

It's simple math. So, whenever she looks at herself in the mirror, she sees all the flaws instead of the things that make her stand out. She focuses only on outward beauty and not what lies within because in her naïve mind, that is what matters. She thinks her body has to be perfect. She thinks having the perfect body will earn her acceptance, love, and admiration from others. She thinks it will make her happy.

The only problem is that there is no absolute definition of beauty. Not long ago, being petite and a size zero was considered the epitome of beauty but today's research reveals that men like to date women with curvy bodies. They admire rounder hips, a blossomed chest, and thick legs. So, chasing after something that may change tomorrow doesn't make sense, right? Besides, let's not even get started on how much editing and photoshopping goes into making models and celebrities look perfect on cover magazines.

Young girls want to look like them and when they don't their self-esteem suffers (Huebscher, 2010).

You can't let your daughter go through the same mental torture or allow her to be bullied online by her mates and friends. The damages done may be irreversible. Since it is harder to shut down the haters and move on with our lives, why don't we teach our girls to be happy in their skin? Why don't we teach her that she doesn't have to starve herself to lose weight and instead, have a healthy and balanced diet? Why don't we teach her that she has to accept and appreciate the beauty that she is and not try to compare herself with every single person she goes to school with?

Teaching Her to Own Her Uniqueness

We know, as their parents, the importance of nurturing a positive body image, however, it isn't us that we have to convince, it is our teenage daughters. We have to make them understand that to grow into healthy and well-rounded adults, they can't continue to starve their bodies and deprive it of the basic nutrients. We have to brainwash them about the idols they fixate on and introduce to them inspiring personalities like Oprah Winfrey, Michelle Obama, Hilary Clinton, Serena Williams, and more who are more than just pretty faces we see on our TV screens. These are the kind of powerful women your daughter should look up to. She must follow in their footsteps and aim to become great and inspirational, not just someone everyone calls pretty.

It is sad to see girls, who get the best grades in school and have terrific talents and yet, feel like they aren't good enough. So, what can we do to disregard such a mindset and encourage them to own their uniqueness?

Focus on Inner Beauty

The first thing you need to tell your daughter is to focus on being a good person instead of being a pretty person. It is one's character and personality that makes them likable, not their looks. Start by praising her for her positive attributes such as how calm she is all the time, how honest she is, how sincere she is towards her friends, how much she values her family's values and traditions etc. She needs to see that it is these things that make a person appear beautiful in the eyes of others and not their outer beauty.

Promote Healthy Eating Behaviors

Children take up most behaviors from their parents. If they see you snacking on unhealthy snacks all the time or eating at abrupt hours, she will pick up the same habit. Your job is to not normalize such behavior for her, but rather encourage good eating habits. Introduce to her a variety of fruits and vegetables to snack on when she feels hungry. Indulge in low-fat dairy products lean meats and processed cereals and, avoid processed meat, high in sugar content, and fizzy drinks. She can always snack on some junk food occasionally but don't allow too much of it.

Discourage Dieting

Never encourage your child to diet as it can lead to worrisome symptoms like low blood pressure, fatigue, nausea, weakness, constipation, dehydration, and headaches. Too much dieting can turn into an eating disorder like bulimia or anorexia. Besides, some studies prove that those who diet regain the lost weight in less time than what they spent dieting (Mann, 2018). Therefore, talk to her about the dangers of it and why she must never do it.

Avoid Negative Body Talk

When around her, don't point out her flaws. You are the last person she wants to be criticized by. This also goes for your own body. You have to feel confident in the way you look so that she picks up that, too. You must work on modeling a healthy acceptance and not complain about the ugly parts such as the sagginess of your skin, muffin top on your belly, or the loose skin on your thighs. Also, don't emphasize physical appearances. If she is suffering from low self-esteem due to it, you have to uplift it by talking about the different aspects of what makes her beautiful.

Exercise But Not to Lose Fat

There is a difference between exercising to stay healthy and exercising to lose weight. Make exercising a fun activity without focusing too much on the losing weight aspect of it. it is more important that she feels healthy than pretty. Plan events like hiking trips to the beach, or to the farmer's market where more walking is involved. You can even go to parks near your house for a jog or rent bikes to go cycling on the weekends.

Chapter 6: Essential Parenting Skill – Empathy

Have you ever noticed how your teenage daughter has no compassion for others? You give her some bad news about a relative's illness and she rarely nudges with discomfort or apology. Does it also have a hard time looking at things from a different person's perspective and always focusing on herself? Does she find herself struggling to engage in activities that only benefit others, say like volunteering?

She isn't trying to be mean on purpose, she just lacks the basic empathy skills, that's all!

For most parents, it is easier to just jump to the conclusion that their child isn't empathetic. They don't shed a tear when a butterfly they spent caring for after it injured one of its wings, dies after a week. They don't feel guilty when proving someone wrong. They don't feel ashamed when they don't give up their seat on the bus to a handicapped kid in their school. Although it does seem like they lack the caring nerve, it isn't true. Luckily, empathy can be nurtured at almost every age.

Your teenage daughter may also have some issues with emotional intelligence. You may have a difficult time trying to understand her or her odd behavior.

According to one study, it isn't her fault, but her brain's fault.

The research suggests that the way a teenager's brain develops during adolescence may affect empathy (Graaff et al., 2014).

Most people master concrete thinking skills when they enter secondary school. However, our executive functioning skills like organization, planning, self-control, decision-making, and other such areas can take longer to establish themselves. Research suggests that our affective empathy and cognitive empathy skills also develop during the teen years. Affective empathy refers to the ability to recognize and respond to the feelings of others appropriately whereas cognitive empathy refers to the ability to see things from a different person's perspective and think mentally. Both of these skills hold importance in helping teenagers cope with the social pressures they face, manage their and others' emotions, and prevent conflict.

However, different regions of the brain are responsible for affective and cognitive empathy. Affective empathy relates to the limbic region whereas cognitive empathy is grounded in the medial prefrontal cortex of the brain. Since these two are linked, it shows that a child's affective empathy can be a predictor of the level of cognitive empathy as teenagers. In girls, affective empathy remains stable and relatively high throughout adolescence whereas cognitive empathy begins to rise by the time they turn thirteen and above.

Importance of Teaching Empathy

Research reveals that empathy is something children learn throughout their childhood and teen years (Overgaauw et al., 2017). It has proven to be an essential life skill as it promotes the building of healthy and stable relationships. Young girls need it more because their interactions are varied. They have to deal with their parents, siblings, friends, and teachers. They are interacting with people of all ages all the time. Ask yourself this, if given the choice, would you have worked with someone inconsiderate, unkind, or hard-hearted? Or would you have preferred to work with someone kind, compassionate, and respectful towards your feelings, and emotions?

Another compelling reason to foster it in children, especially young girls because they get bullied, too. They are mocked for being fat, dark-skinned, or from a different race. Knowing what empathy is can put an end to bullying as every child is aware of how it feels to be in someone else's shoes. When they know how it feels like to be bullied, they are less likely to do it. They can place themselves in the situation the bullied is in, and comprehend how destructive it can be. Therefore, we believe that schools should focus more on building empathetic skills in kids than organizing redundant events all the time. However, for your daughter, it has to start at home.

Be Her Rock

For her to feel empathetic towards others, you have to fulfill her need for emotional support. If her own needs feel unfulfilled, she may not be able to show empathy towards others, she will be so consumed in her own set of problems that she would have no time to look at the problems of others and offer support.

Give Feelings a Name

Your teenage daughter is now at an age where she is introduced to several emotions and feelings. It can be hard for her to deal with them if she doesn't know how to identify them. For instance, many people, even adults, are unable to differentiate between frustration and anger. Giving feelings and emotions a name or label makes it easier to deal with it. Help her navigate through each negative emotion healthily.

Teach Her to Cope with Negative Emotions

Now that she is entering a new phase of her life, she is bound to get introduced to several new emotions such as anger, jealousy, rage, envy, melancholy, etc. Not knowing how to cope with them when she feels overwhelmed can lead to self-damaging habits. If she feels out of control or too much in pain over a breakup, she might try to deal with it in unhealthy ways. Each year, approximately 14.45% of young adults and adolescents try to end their lives by committing suicide. The rates are both shocking and alarming for parents. Therefore, from an early age, you must teach your children how to deal with emotions that make them feel out of control, in a positive and problem-solving way.

Ask Her How She Feels

Repeatedly asking her about her mental and emotional state can also prevent any attempts at suicide or self-harm early on. Kids are geared toward empathy naturally. Even if a toddler notices someone crying, they go up to them and hug them to make them feel better. However, as they grow older and become young adults, their focus becomes self-centered. They also start to hide stuff from their parents, which is why you have to keep probing questions about their mental and emotional state and keep a close eye on what they are up to. You can also role-play scenarios where you ask them how they would feel if someone did something bad to them and didn't show empathy.

Teach Her the Difference Between Good and Bad

Every day, we expose ourselves to several types of behaviors. Some are good, such as someone helping a homeless guy by buying them a meal from a restaurant. Some are bad, such as watching someone bully someone or making them sad. As a parent, you have to show her the difference between the two and talk about the effects each can have on someone. For instance, the homeless guy will be joyous whereas the guy who was bullied won't be.

Be a Good Role Model

Again, she is going to learn behaviors from you. If she notices that you are kind, considerate, and compassionate towards others, don't judge others and are always lending a helping hand, she will learn it, too. Show her how being charitable and selfless can be so rewarding. Show her what happiness and satisfaction it brings into your life.

Chapter 7: Essential Parenting Skill – Honesty

Teens and adults want the same thing from one another: transparency and honesty. They want to be able to say things to them without having to hide or manipulate it. They want open communication, empathetic support, and emotional comprehension from one another so that secrets and lies can be avoided. However, as your girl grows up to become a teenager, she starts to hide stuff from you, say lies to your face and act as if you are the one making a big deal of everything. Years of research have revealed that teens want to be honest with their parents only if they feel like they will be heard and not critiqued (Yau et al., 2009). They are more likely to be honest when they feel close to their parents and trust them to make decisions on their own. They expect parents to offer them some room to grow and not have to hide stuff.

On the other hand, another research, aimed to look at lying behaviors in different age groups ranging from 6 to 77, found that people are most dishonest when they are in the teen ages (Debey et al., 2015). So, what to believe and what not to?

Our suggestion, it doesn't matter. Your goal, as a parent, should be to raise honest children. Your goal should be to teach them about the importance of being transparent.

Lying is considered as one of the many developmental milestones that kids reach when they are about three years of age. Yes, it can be shocking to some but kids begin to lie by the time they turn three. As they grow older and comprehend the consequences and depth of it, they become less likely to lie unless they fear punishment, want to please others, to save face, get away with something or preserve others' feelings.

Everyone lies but it can be hurtful to be lied to. As a parent, you have to teach your girl about the dangers of it, so that she doesn't grow up to use lying as a means to get away with things or hide things from you. She needs to know that lying breaks trust, adds stress, compounds the problem but doesn't make it go away, ruins healthy relationships, and can always backfire.

How to Teach Her to Be More Honest?

As she grows up to become this amazing woman right before your eyes, you may want to be an active part of herself. However, you notice that she keeps to herself, only replies when questioned about something, and keeps secrets. For instance, you may find the light to her room open in the middle of the night and when you question her about it the next day, she says that she had fallen asleep way before that. It may get you curious as to why she is lying about it and not stating the truth. You may get suspicious and pry into her private space more. You may check her phone for messages to friends, read her Facebook chats, or go into her DMs on Instagram, all because of one small lie. You start to see her like some culprit and not trust anything she says. Do you see where this is going? It is turning you into a madwoman looking for some clue to prove her daughter wrong. Who will benefit from it, even if you prove her wrong?

All this inconvenience could have been avoided had she told you the truth in the first place, right?

So, what is the first thing you need to do here? Encourage her to be honest with you. How can you do that? By modeling honesty yourself. She shouldn't find you lying about being sick to skip work or lie to your partner about being late at work when you were celebrating the signing up of a new client at the bar with your colleagues. She doesn't need to see you making excuses to skip a family dinner on your partner's side because you have the flu or because you just don't want to go. Once she notices you taking the plunge for being late or going to dinners even when you don't feel like it, she will learn to do the same. She will learn to be accountable for her shortcomings and own up to her mistakes, even if she lands her in the pit. Other than that, you can:

Tell her How Hurtful Lying Can Be

She needs to know about the consequences of lying and how it can hurt people. She needs to get out of her little bubble and learn to care for others. To implant this wisdom in her, you have to sit her down and calmly discuss the dangers of being dishonest and why she shouldn't lie. Offer her your unconditional emotional support so that she knows she can turn to you with all of her problems instead of hiding them.

Reward Honesty

Rewarding or praising honesty is another way to nip the habit of lying in the bud. If she notices how happy it makes you when she tells the truth or how she doesn't get punished even when she comes up to you with information about something wrong that she did, she will start to do it more often. She will see it as a much easier way to deal with her problems because she knows that one lie can lead to another hundred and then another hundred to keep up with the previous ones.

Seek Reasons Behind Lying

Why is she lying to you? What could be the reason? What could she possibly be trying to hide? These are all questions you may want to ask yourself first and then her to know what's going on in her head that is compelling her to lie. Sometimes, teenagers lie when they are trying to protect someone or themselves from something inevitable. You must also know that kids don't lie out of habit; at least, not most of them do. They fear disappointing you and don't lie just for the sake of it either. Therefore, have a chat with her about why she feels the need to hide the truth and keep secrets and not come clean.

Don't Shame Her

If you notice that she has been frequently lying to you and others just to get away with things, talk to her instead of accusing or shaming her. Ask her about her fears and why she finds lying as her 'go-to' way to cope with things. Shaming her or accusing her when she gets caught red-handed will only make her sneakier with her lies and not address the issue.

Be a Good Listener

All children know the right thing to do but they just want to make things easier for themselves. Lying or cheating are things that allow us to get away with things in an easier manner. You have to allow her the freedom to choose for herself whilst ensuring her safety. You have to learn to listen and talk her through things in a compassionate manner so that she avoids taking the easy way out the next time. Keep in mind that you just have to guide them, not try to fix anything.

Chapter 8: Essential Parenting Skill – Responsibility

The teen years are the time when freedom looms large but family comes in between to prevent them from achieving that much-wanted independence. Parents want to raise their kids to become responsible adults whereas adolescents want to explore new things, go on adventures, and engage in risky behaviors and whatnot. Teaching kids to be accountable for their actions and grow up to become trustworthy and responsible adults is the job of every parent. To get started, they need to set some ground rules and guidelines that list their tasks, responsibilities, and commitments that are expected of them and also, age-appropriate. Of course, it isn't going to be an easy take and they may face resistance from their teenagers but they have to stand their ground.

Like most parents, you must dream of raising a responsible yet independent woman to one day. Someone that knows how to manage herself her emotions, friends, and family, follows her passions religiously and doesn't embarrass you or herself by falling short. No matter what, you have to continue to try in shaping her personality so that she is prepared to deal with the realities of adulthood.

Therefore, in this chapter, we look at how parents can teach their girls to become responsible adults, account for their behaviors and actions, and present themselves as civilized adults.

Teaching Her to Be Responsible

You may expect her to act like an adult but she is still too young to understand numerous things. After all, she is still growing and yet to face the many challenges life will throw at her as she enters another phase of her life: adulthood. Her social behavior is changing, thanks to the many hormonal changes inside her. She is confused, crying, yelling, running from chores, not owning up to her mistakes, and lying to you. What she needs is some guidance about accountability and responsibility. She needs to comprehend why some things must be done or owned up to even when she doesn't feel like it. It is your job to shape her behavior and you have to do it now. Below are some tips that will hopefully help you to raise her as a responsible adult.

Set Realistic Expectations

Start with setting some expectations for her to see if she complies or not. Don't leave her in the blind, thinking she will learn things through experience. When children know what is expected of them, they are more likely to live up to them. If the expectations are abstract or vague, they will avoid them. Setting realistic expectations is the first step in teaching her about responsibility. She must know what chores she has to do, why you expect her to clean her room and washroom, why she must dress modestly etc. she must also know what kind of behavior is expected of her, how she must remain disciplined and behave well.

Create a List of Chores

Doing chores is one of the most hateful things to a teen. No, she doesn't want to help you clean the fridge, wash the windows with soap and water or mop the floors. She wants you to do it. However, if she doesn't learn these things now, she will have a hard time adjusting to it when she leaves for college and gets a place of her own. Therefore, make a chores list and hang it on the fridge. Chores are an ideal way to teach about responsibility and the important role it plays in building discipline. She may resist doing them in the beginning but will eventually start to follow them out of habit soon. If she doesn't do them on purpose, let her know that there will be consequences.

Allow Her to Choose

Now that she is all growing up, make her see the importance of responsibility by allowing her to have a say in things concerning her and the family. For instance, if you are planning a trip for the summers, or planning to change houses, ask for her input on the matter. This will make her feel an important part of the family as well as give her a sense of responsibility. You can do the same with the chores. You can offer her a choice between doing the dishes and folding the laundry instead of asking her just one of the things. Whichever choice she picks, she is likely to get it done.

Have Consequences

If she deliberately avoids doing something and expects you to cover up for her, don't become a partner in it. She needs to learn about the consequences through experience. For example, she may want you to make up an excuse as to why she didn't finish her homework over the phone with her teacher. If she wasn't ill and purposely put it off, then don't be a part of the crime. Let her be punished. Let her be shamed in front of her classmates. She should know what punishment awaits her if she puts things off out of habit. Tell her that you reap what you sow.

Set Rewards for Achievements

If she does something good or something that was expected of her, reward her for it. It doesn't have to be a bribe or something tangible. It can be kind and appreciative words that boost her confidence and makes her more likely to repeat the same behaviors she got rewarded for. Besides, a little pat on the back or a little gift of appreciation doesn't require much work.

Engage Her in Volunteer Work

Volunteering broadens our minds and makes our souls delighted. It allows us to help others without expecting anything in return. For your daughter, it is a great way to see that the world has other people in it, too. It doesn't revolve around her only. When she will feel a part of an important cause, she will realize the privileges she has had and become responsible.

Set Goals with Her

If she has a passion or dream that she wants to follow, sit down, and draw out a roadmap together. Identify the steps she needs to take to reach her long-term goals. However, that is all you need to do and step back. The rest lies on her shoulders. Your job was only to help her navigate her options and paths. It is now her responsibility to make it happen. Sure, you can offer help if she asks for it but not before that!

Chapter 9: Essential Parenting Skill – Relationship Management

For most parents, navigating a teenager through adolescence is the most intimidating chapter of parenthood. They find them hard to discipline, set rules, and set expectations. They have trouble knowing when they can intervene in their lives and when they can't.

When it comes to relationships, things can be even harder because then you don't know how much they are sharing with you and keeping a secret, what activities are they involved in, are they being safe or not, etc. However, even a more thought-provoking question if they are practicing consensual sex or not. Sometimes, young girls are unaware of what touches and actions are appropriate. They end up complying with things they aren't ready for and give into abuse without even knowing that it accounts as such. Therefore, she needs to know the difference between a healthy and toxic relationship as well as the many types of abuses she may be subjected to, without proper knowledge.

A healthy relationship is one where respect, trust, communication, mutual understanding, and support prevails high. There must also be healthy boundaries between both partners and respected by them accordingly. An ideal partner mustn't want you to change and accept you for who you are. They should respect your personal choices and support you in your passions. The sex or any such activity leading to it must be consented upon by both partners before and none of them must feel obliged in some way to please the other.

Different Types of Abuses and Why She Should Know How to Distinguish Between Each

As stated earlier, she may be subjected to one or more of these abuses without knowledge. Therefore, as a parent, it is your job to introduce these to her and inquire if she feels like the relationship with her partner is abusive or not.

- Physical Abuse: This type of abuse occurs when one partner uses physical force to harm the other but the injuries incurred aren't visible to quality as such. This can include, kicking, choking, biting, and hitting, etc.

- Sexual Abuse: This type of abuse occurs when one partner tries to force themselves on to others without their consent or create surroundings where they feel helpless to save themselves from their partner. It can include restriction to use condoms or birth control, forced sexual activity, or pressuring the partner into doing something non-consensually.

- Emotional Abuse: This type of abuse occurs when one partner degrades, insults, manipulates, humiliates, or intimidates the other into doing things they don't want to do. They warn to leave them or tell lies about them if they don't agree with them.

- Digital Abuse: This is bullying your partner using technology. This can include taking pictures of them and making videos in a compromising situation and then using it to manipulate and blackmail them.

Teaching Her the Meaning of Healthy Relationships

Now that we have discussed the different types of abuses she may experience, she must know how to proceed with new relationships and approach sex when she feels ready for it. In this final section of the book, we discuss the many ways you can help her understand the different ideas, beliefs, and expectations regarding healthy relationships so that one day she can have one.

Talk Credibly

No need to skim through the conversation without going into the details. When giving her the talk, you have to answer all the questions she may have in her mind so that she stays safe and practices safe sex, too. If you aren't the talking kind, you can always send her links to websites that answer the questions well or send her to one of your friends or relatives she feels close to, to open up.

Set Boundaries and Expectations

Setting expectations and boundaries early on, such as expecting her to dress modestly when going or setting boundaries like, obliging to the time of the curfew, can help you both stay in your lanes. She will try not to break the rules and you won't have to spend all night worrying about whether she is safe or not. Some parents also put restrictions on who they can date and what qualities they should have to qualify to date her, but that is a far stretch.

Offer Support

She must, at all times, know that she can count on you for your support when she needs some help with her relationships. Lend her a compassionate ear and help her pick her options for birth control. You can also discuss the pros and cons of becoming a parent at an early age but not give her any idea that you are trying to intrude and decide for her.

Stay Neutral When Discussing Preferences

This heading wouldn't have made much sense had this book been written in the 80s or 90s but it matters now. When discussing with her about relationships and dating and how to involve in safe sex, don't assume that she must want to date a guy. You have to use gender-inclusive language and stay neutral without imposing a certain gender preference. If you do, she might think you won't understand or accept her if she chooses differently. This way, when you open up the possibility of her preferred sexual orientation, you will make it easier for them if they choose to come out of the closet someday and continue to find out where they fit in this world.

Be Respectful

Above all, show respect when talking to her about such things. You have to respect her individuality, beliefs, and opinions and come on to her in a non-obstructive or judging manner. This will open the line of healthy communication for you both and also get the job done.

Conclusion

Parenting isn't only about fulfilling the basic needs of our children. It is also about instilling good habits, imparting high values and morals, and preparing them for a life to be lived by them on their own. All of this is possible when we find a way to connect with them and keep the channels of communication open to cultivate strong relationships. With teenagers, this becomes a struggle because they start to have a mind of their own and view things differently. They are quick to judge and don't focus on the long-term aspects of things.

Your growing daughter may depict the same and want more privacy and independence. She may want to lead her life according to her rules. She may want to feel more in control of her decisions and preferences. She may no longer need you as a guide to problem-solve things for her.

But as any sane parent, you know what to do!

You know this isn't the time to sit back and watch her make a mess of her life. This is the time to be proactive and help them navigate their way towards success. This is the time to help her with her relationships. This is the time to teach her about compassion, responsibility, discipline, conflict management, and the need for transparency and good friends in her life so that she can lead a prosperous, confident, and successful life.

References

Anderson, M. (2018). A Majority of Teens Have
     Experienced Some Form of Cyberbullying. In
     Pew Center Research (pp. 1–19).
     https://www.pewresearch.org/internet/wp-
     content/uploads/sites/9/2018/09/PI_2018.
     09.27_teens-and-cyberbullying_FINAL.pdf

Body image – tips for parents. (2012). Vic.Gov.Au.
     https://www.betterhealth.vic.gov.au/health/
     healthyliving/body-image-tips-for-parents

Chhandita Chakravarty. (2014, December 19). 10
     Handy Tips On How To Make Your Teenager
     Responsible. MomJunction.
     https://www.momjunction.com/articles/han
     dy-tips-make-teenager-
     responsible_00118480/

Debey, E., De Schryver, M., Logan, G. D., Suchotzki,
     K., & Verschuere, B. (2015). From junior to
     senior Pinocchio: A cross-sectional lifespan
     investigation of deception. Acta Psychologica,
     160, 58–68.
     https://doi.org/10.1016/j.actpsy.2015.06.007

GoodTherapy.org. (2015, February 27). 9 Tips for Talking to Teens about Dating and Relationships. GoodTherapy.Org Therapy Blog. https://www.goodtherapy.org/blog/9-tips-for-talking-to-teens-about-dating-and-relationships-0227157

Graaff, J., Branje, S., Wied, M. D., Hawk, S., Lier, P. V., & Meeus, W. (2014). Perspective Taking and Empathic Concern in Adolescence: Gender Differences in Developmental Changes. Developmental Psychology, 50(3), 881–888. https://doi.org/https://doi.org/10.1037/a0034325

How to Help Teenagers Develop Empathy. (n.d.). www.melbournechildpsychology.com.au.https://www.melbournechildpsychology.com.au/blog/help-teenagers-develop-empathy/

Huebscher, B. (2010). Relationship Between Body Image and Self Esteem Among Adolescent Girls. In Search Results Web result with site links CiteSeerX (pp. 1–21). http://citeseerx.ist.psu.edu/viewdoc/download?doi=10.1.1.390.333&rep=rep1&type=pdf

Lee, K. (2019, June 29). How to Nurture Empathy and Emotional Intelligence in Children. Verywell Family. https://www.verywellfamily.com/how-to-nurture-empathy-in-kids-and-why-its-so-important-621098

Lindholm, M. (2018, May 10). 10 Rules for Living with a Teenage Daughter. Psychology Today. https://www.psychologytoday.com/intl/blog/more-women-s-work/201805/10-rules-living-teenage-daughter

Mabe, A. G., Forney, K. J., & Keel, P. K. (2014). Do you 'like' my photo? Facebook use maintains eating disorder risk. International Journal of Eating Disorders, 47(5), 516–523. https://doi.org/10.1002/eat.22254

Maciejewski, D. F., van Lier, P. A. C., Branje, S. J. T., Meeus, W. H. J., & Koot, H. M. (2015). A 5-Year Longitudinal Study on Mood Variability Across Adolescence Using Daily Diaries. Child Development, 86(6), 1908–1921. https://doi.org/10.1111/cdev.12420

Mann, T. (2018, May). Why do dieters regain weight? Https://Www.Apa.Org. https://www.apa.org/science/about/psa/2018/05/calorie-deprivation

Miller, D. (2018, February 28). Enough. It's time to stop using the "mean girl" label for teenagers. Women's Agenda. https://womensagenda.com.au/leadership/advice/steps-help-teen-girls-resolve-conflict/

Overgaauw, S., Rieffe, C., Broekhof, E., Crone, E. A., & Güroğlu, B. (2017). Assessing Empathy across Childhood and Adolescence: Validation of the Empathy Questionnaire for Children and Adolescents (EmQue-CA). Frontiers in Psychology, 8. https://doi.org/10.3389/fpsyg.2017.00870

Rideout, V., & Robb, M. B. (2019). The Common Sense Census: Media Use by Tweens and Teens (J. Pritchett (Ed.)). Common Sense Media.

Saltz, G. (2016, February 16). How to Help Your Daughter Have a Healthy Body Image. Child Mind Institute; Child Mind Institute. https://childmind.org/article/how-to-help-your-daughter-have-a-healthy-body-image/

Yau, J. P., Tasopoulos-Chan, M., & Smetana, J. G. (2009). Disclosure to Parents About Everyday Activities Among American Adolescents From Mexican, Chinese, and European Backgrounds. Child Development, 80(5), 1481–1498. https://doi.org/10.1111/j.1467-8624.2009.01346.x

Young, K. (2016, June 1). When Children Lie – How to Respond and Build Honesty. www.heysigmund.com. https://www.heysigmund.com/when-children-lie/

Book Description

Does your child have a hard time sitting still? Do they have little to no patience when it comes to waiting their turn? Are they always seeking attention using negative behaviors like crying, whining, or throwing temper tantrums? Does their teacher complain of poor focus and attention in class? Are they always interrupting you and others in a hurried manner?

They could have attention deficit hyperactivity disorder (ADHD).

Children with special needs, such as those with ADHD require more love, care, and time. Parents have to be more patient with them as, most of the time, they exhibit behaviors that are out of their control and need to be disciplined. However, that discipline doesn't come in the form of punishment, rather in the form of some helpful, yet effective, parenting rules and skills.

In this brief guide, we review 7 vital parenting skills that have been proven effective when dealing with children who have ADHD. We explore the various means to implement these skills and put them to the test for their effectiveness. We also discuss why parents need to learn and practice these skills. Some of the principal topics discussed include the following:

- Offering children with ADHD structure and its role in behavior modification

- Setting clear expectations to instruct, explain and follow

- Understanding why some mild misbehavior must be ignored

- Introducing the idea of consequences to improve behavior

- Need for positive attention and its impact on children with ADHD

- Learning to block out distractions to improve focus

- Establishing reward systems and knowing their effectiveness etc.

Written to inspire every parent and facilitate them in modifying behavior in their children, this book comes packed with science-backed research and implementable strategies to offer readers some support when dealing with a child with ADHD.

7 Vital Parenting Skills for Teaching Kids With ADHD

Proven ADHD Tips for Dealing With Attention Deficit Disorder and Hyperactive Kids

Frank Dixon

licensed professional before attempting any techniques outlined in this book.

By reading this document, the reader agrees that under no circumstances is the author responsible for any losses, direct or indirect, that are incurred as a result of the use of the information contained within this document, including, but not limited to, errors, omissions, or inaccuracies.

Introduction

Young children are active and impulsive in general. The world is their oyster - they are only discovering more and more every day. That leads to them acting rambunctious, often. When they are joyous, nothing can stop them from climbing the stairs, jumping around the house, and running inside and out. They won't listen when told to sit properly, they fidget and squirm. They prefer going out to explore all that their mind hasn't yet processed, and will cause chaos wherever they go. The point being that it isn't unusual to have hyperactive kids who have trouble remembering things, obeying orders, or listening.

Parents all across the globe go through more or less the same difficulty when raising a child. Sometimes, their kids simply forget to do what they have been told and sometimes, get distracted while doing so. They will drop things, be careless, and get anxious waiting for their turn when playing collaboratively with other children. It is safe to say that this is a normal part of childhood.

The main difference between a child who has ADHD and a child who doesn't is the frequency of these behaviors. A child with ADHD will exhibit these behaviors as the norm, and a child who doesn't might exhibit these behaviors from time to time. The challenges for parents amplify as the symptoms are rather chronic, pervasive, and disruptive. Children with ADHD have trouble at school, have an even harder time making friends and socializing, and need to be reminded of things frequently. The symptoms must be present for at least six months to be diagnosed as a disorder. If diagnosed, it can impair a child's normal development and make it harder for parents to parent them.

Some of the most commonly-associated symptoms and behaviors a child with ADHD exhibits are frustration, becoming easily overwhelmed, trouble regulating emotions, and struggles with cognitive functions. For instance, you may notice some lagging on their part when it comes to tasks such as planning, organizing, staying focused, and remembering details. Their development also takes time to mature. But that doesn't mean that life for them is dull or boring. They can also be some of the most charismatic, popular, and personable people to hang out with.

Caring for a child with ADHD can be draining for both parents. They need extra attention, extra love, and extra explaining for everything they have been told, so you can imagine the amount of time and energy needed to tend to one. Their impulsiveness, chaotic behavior, and fearlessness can make everyday activities such as eating, bathing, or sleeping stressful and exhausting.

But it will be less stressful if you use the 7 vital parenting skills discussed here. To help parents deal with a child with ADHD, our essential parenting skills will come in handy to plan, organize, engage, and improve performance as well as behavior. It will help them teach about discipline, responsibility, and how they can regulate their emotions themselves, giving their parents a little air to breathe.

Let's begin to explore these in detail and learn of ways in which these parenting skills can guide parents.

Chapter 1: Life With an ADHD Child

A ll kids, especially toddlers, behave out of the norm occasionally. You have run after them to feed them a spoonful of their lunch, and then do the same at dinner. You have ignored their screams as they try to get away with not taking a bath. You have told them to sit tight in the car as you drove down a busy road, but they have ignored the order without a care in the world.

But for some parents, it is much worse. What they have to deal with is constant. This means they don't just have to run after their toddler during meal times but always, just to ensure they don't hurt themselves. They have to repeat their orders several times in a minute to get their child to respond. These instances are so frequent that they begin to hinder the family's ability to lead normal lives. Other children in the house also feel neglected, parents are shamed for having an ill-mannered child and it is difficult to have a peaceful evening out with the family without having everyone staring back in disgust or judgment.

Understanding ADHD

Attention deficit hyperactivity disorder (ADHD) is a chronic condition in the brain which affects a child's ability to control behavior. Unlike other kids, they are unable to process information or stop thinking about something in a jiffy. Children diagnosed with ADHD have trouble controlling their actions and have a hard time mingling and befriending kids their age. They also report trouble getting along with their teachers, siblings, and parents. They have a difficult time learning and grasping new knowledge and have a poor attention span. If there is anything they don't understand or are unable to process, they move onto another thing, without giving it much attention. They are impulsive, which puts them in physical danger. If you are a parent of a child with ADHD, your child may have been labeled as bad or ill-mannered by those who don't know about their condition.

If we look at the statistics, national data reveals that almost 9.4% of children aged 2-17 in the US are living with ADHD. The data also suggests that boys are twice as likely to develop ADHD as compared to their counterparts. The biggest fear most parents have is whether their child will ever be accepted as a normal kid in the world or not. It is natural for them to want to give their kids the best of the best. However, when one kid aces everything and the other lags to grasp even the basics, it can be hard to parent them both at the same time.

To further understand what it looks like to raise a child with ADHD, we must look at the various behaviors they depict and how they differ from those demonstrated by another child without ADHD.

These behaviors are divided into three categories – inattention, hyperactivity, and impulsivity.

A child with inattention behaves in the following manner:

- Daydreams

- Doesn't listen

- Gets distracted easily

- Doesn't follow through the instructions given to finish a task

- Makes careless mistakes

- Doesn't care about the details or steps of things

- Forgetfulness

- Poor organizational skills

- Misplaces or loses items

- Avoids doing things requiring mental effort frequently

A child with hyperactivity behaves in the following manner:

- Is always moving around as if driven by a battery

- Has trouble staying seated

- Talks too much

- Fidgets and squirms

- Can't play in peace and makes noises

A child with impulsivity behaves in the following manner:

- Speaks and acts without thinking

- Running around without an awareness of their surroundings

- Has trouble waiting for their turn

- Doesn't like to share

Although the exact cause of ADHD is still under scrutiny, research suggests that it is due to neurological and biological factors. Some risk factors, however, put your baby at risk of developing the disorder. These include the following:

Biological: It can be caused by biological factors when there is a chemical imbalance in the way neurotransmitters function. Neurotransmitters regulate behavior. An imbalance may cause a child to develop ADHD before or after birth.

Hereditary: Your baby is also at a higher risk of developing ADHD if one or both the parents are diagnosed with ADHD.

Prenatal exposure: Although there isn't any direct link or evidence to prove this, smoking and drug abuse during pregnancy can also be linked with ADHD in children.

Environment: If the child has been exposed to poisons or harmful toxins in the environment such as exposure to lead, they may also exhibit signs of ADHD.

Common Challenges With a Child With ADHD

According to research published in the Journal Pediatrics, 70% of diagnosed children with ADHD suffer from at least one other physical or mental problem such as anxiety, learning disability, depression, and speech or hearing disability (Law et al., 2014). Also, one in five of these kids with ADHD have more than three or more mental or physical problems, increasing their chances of lagging behind in school and professional life.

Parents who are raising a child with ADHD along with others, experience enormous stress and struggle to cope with the symptoms while being stigmatized by their friends, family, and community. Even they experience burdensome emotions and resort to social distancing and isolation from gatherings to feel normal. Before we move onto revealing the 7 vital parenting skills that help parents cope with the symptoms associated with ADHD in their child, we must look at the challenges they have to face being a parent.

One study suggests that approximately 23% of married couples raising a child with ADHD under eight years of age get divorced as opposed to nearly 12% without an ADHD child (Wymbs et al., 2008). It is easy to imagine how this must look for couples who are unable to spend time by themselves as a couple and bond because they have to attend to their child with ADHD constantly.

Boredom is another common, yet neglected, drawback of living with an ADHD child. As they need to be tended to 24/7, and need instructions to be repeated often, it leaves parents with little time to do the things that interest them or that they enjoy. Due to a low attention span, the child also needs regular doses of entertainment to stay engaged, which means that parents have to come up with new and interesting things to keep them engrossed in one thing. Consistency and the need to repeat instructions can also become monotonous and tiring.

Isolation is another challenge that parents have to deal with, especially when they are a single parent and raising a child with a learning or attention deficit disorder. It becomes hard to raise them with empathy and love. When they feel constantly criticized by others for their poor effort to have a hold on their child, they start to feel like they are the only ones going through it, and begin to feel hopeless about the situation getting any better in the future.

And finally, they feel guilt. They think that it is somehow their fault that they gave birth to a child with ADHD. They also feel depressed when they notice that their other kids are being neglected of the attention and love that they deserve. They blame themselves when they are out of control. They blame themselves for not doing enough to keep them calm and help them get better. They feel disheartened when they see them miss out on all the wonderful experiences kids their age generally have.

Nonetheless, here's the thing. There is not much they could have done to prevent it. It isn't their fault and whatever they are doing, the many hours they are putting in and the extra love and affection they are bestowing on them is commendable. However, they can modify things a little bit and develop skills to deal with your unique circumstance better. The changes required aren't much and just offer a new perspective to view things differently and stop feeling helpless and depressed and be prepared to give them the best life and future possibilities.

Chapter 2: The 7 Vital Parenting Skills to Deal With an ADHD Child

I t isn't a secret that children diagnosed with ADHD need extra attention, time, and love. We want to see them as successful as our other children or as their peers. We fear that if we don't do enough, they might lag behind and never be able to achieve success.

This isn't true. Did you know some of the most successful people of their time have this neurological disorder? For example, Michael Phelps, the international Olympic swimming champion, battled with ADHD during childhood and a significant part of his adolescence (Celebrity Spotlight: How Michael Phelps' ADHD Helped Him Make Olympic History, n.d.). Recipient of 28 gold medals and one of the most successful and celebrated American heroes, he had a difficult time in school and was known to act out and disrupt the class. It was in the pool that he found some calm and relaxation which allowed him to let this mind and body stay on track and focused. He once had a teacher in his class who told him that his misbehavior will ruin his adult life and he will never amount to anything significant.

Another well-known individual, parenting more than 400 companies under the name Virgin Group, Sir

Richard Branson also dealt with ADHD during his childhood. Richard, as recalled by his teachers and peers, was always erratic and a misfit (LaMagna, 2018). Richard himself wrote that school was the most dreadful time in his life as he had no understanding of what was being taught. Today, the world knows him as one of the smartest business magnates and investors.

If we look at some celebrities, we come across big names like Jim Carrey, Adam Levine, Paris Hilton, Channing Tatum, Howie Mandel, and Justin Bieber, who have all struggled with attention deficit or hyperactivity disorder.

Although their success is their own doing, a major behind-the-screen role is played by the family, especially their parents. They are the ones who raise them, encourage them to dream big, help them navigate through their dreams and passions, and watch them with pride in their eyes as they soar higher and higher.

When raising a child with special needs, parents are expected to do more. They are expected to stand up for their kids, protect them from the world, and raise them as confident, resilient, and self-reliant adults.

To do so, you need the right resources and rules to live by.

To get you started on the right foot, we are now going to reveal the 7 vital parenting skills to understand, help, and raise children with ADHD. The 7 parenting skills aren't just tools for you but also for your child to learn from so that when they grow up, they learn to manage their behavior themselves effectively.

The 7 Vital Parenting Skills for Teaching Children With ADHD

Parenting Skill #1: Provide Structure

Structure and routines are an essential part of raising a child with ADHD. Structures and set routines have proven to be helpful in minimizing negative or hyperactive behaviors, thanks to their predictability.

Parenting Skills #2: Set Clear Expectations

Clear expectations from the start is another smart way to discipline children with ADHD. It helps them comprehend what is expected of them and what tasks and chores they need to perform. This eliminates confusion and frustration.

Parenting Skill #3: Establish Reward Systems and Praises

The reason rewards and recognition work wonders for children with ADHD is because it keeps them motivated and driven. Rewards, when they come in the form of privileges, can be appealing and even limit misbehavior.

Parenting Skill #4: Eliminate Distractions

Distractions are our biggest enemies and it is only more threatening and scary for a child with ADHD. They seem so tempting that the child is unable to hold back, and gives in to its instant gratification. Thus, we must keep distractions at bay and help children not fall prey to them.

Parenting Skill #5: Set Reasonable Consequences

Reasonable consequences, like expectations, also work in the same manner. When kids know which behaviors will be rewarded and which will lead to punishments, they are in a better state of mind to modify their behaviors. Thus, as parents, we have to let them know the consequences of their actions beforehand so that they abstain from them.

Parenting Skill #6: Ignore Mild Misbehavior

Most of the time, children with ADHD act out of character to seek attention from their parents. They want parents to stay engaged with them constantly, and when they don't, they often resort to negative behaviors so that the parent has to attend to them. This can make a parent mad and stressed out. However, instead of letting them win and gaining that attention, as parents, we have to choose our battles wisely. We have to learn to ignore some misbehavior so that they aren't encouraged and repeated.

Parenting Skill #7: Give Positive Attention

Positive attention improves interactions. When children with ADHD feel valued and cared for, they are more likely to behave and curb bad behaviors. Receiving positive attention from parents, whether in the form of rewards, quality time, or praises can encourage them to abide by the rules set by the parents and learn to regulate their emotions efficiently.

Chapter 3: Vital Parenting Skill – Provide Structure

I f you have a child with ADHD, it mustn't be the first time you hear people tell you that to make your life a whole lot easier, you need to have some structure in your child's life. This comes up as the first piece of advice given by child specialists and healthcare professionals because its effectiveness is, indeed, a life-saver. A structured environment in the house, and routines they can follow-through with easily makes them more efficient and easy to handle. But what does it mean to have structure in life and why is it so important for them?

Being the first vital parenting skill, we are going to explore the idea of what it means to offer children with ADHD a structured environment, how it helps them and how we can create one.

In the simplest of terms, a structured environment is one where there is predictability and organization. The day-to-day routines and tasks are defined in details that are simple to pick up and easy to follow. It involves consistently doing the same things without any unpredicted changes in the sequence or transition. For instance, if your child is expected to have breakfast first and then get dressed, you can't change it without prior notice as it may cause chaos. Similarly, expectations must also be clear from the start (more on this in the next chapter), and the child must also be clear about the consequences of their actions. When these conditions are met, it allows for a predictable and structured environment to be created.

In structured environments, kids are aware of the expectations others have of them. They know what they need to do to finish a task. This further creates a sense of security.

The Importance of Routines and Structure

Children need routines and structure because they are unable to control their impulses otherwise. They have a hard time regulating themselves and their behaviors. With structure comes predictability and focus. When things follow an order, it is difficult to get off track and thus, helps with the elimination of distractions.

With properly enforced routines, children with ADHD can set aside a chunk of time for something, say their homework, every day with consistency. It also helps them get a sense of "what's to come next." For example, if they have the habit of taking out their school clothes, polishing their shoes, and organizing their school bag the night before school, it makes them ready for the next morning. This also sets a clear explanation of what will happen the next morning and make it less chaotic.

Routines in the life of an ADHD child helps them in two ways. First, it improves their daily functioning and efficiency. Their impulsive behavior also remains under control and things start to become manageable.

Second, it eases off some pressure from the parents and other family members as they benefit from it psychologically too. You can expect less drama and decreased stress during family times such as when eating out or doing something together at home, such as watching a movie or doing homework. This leads to a relaxed environment for everyone in the house and helps strengthen the bond in the family.

How to Implement Structure in an ADHD Child's Life

In times when our routines are getting more hectic, it becomes impossible to provide our children with a structured routine. Work keeps us occupied even during off-hours, social media browsing has become a requisite we can't escape from, and competition is only increasing day by day, demanding that we do more and more for our kids to ensure they are raised with the best values and skills possible. You drop your kids off to school, rush to work, then pick them up from school during lunch hour and then drop them off to their practice and then go home, cook, clean, and spend time with your children, and help them with their homework.. So how can you possibly set a routine to be followed? Well, that is debatable, but here's the thing: if you do offer them structure and routine, it will improve their productivity, mental health, and family relationships as well as make them feel confident.

To help you get started, we have created a basic schedule for what a day should look like for a child with ADHD. Keep in mind, not all activities are to be incorporated in the checklist you draft for your child. However, the more elaborative and simple-to-read it is, the better.

Starting with the morning routine, it should look something like this:

Waking up: Stick with the same wake-up time to make mornings easier, every day. If your child is old enough to understand the concept of an alarm clock or timer, they can set one for themselves. If your kid is a toddler or below the age of five, you can wake them up gently with singing or calling their name.

Bathroom routine: This can come in the form of a checklist that contains tasks like taking a shower, using the loo, brushing their teeth, brushing their hair, and putting on school clothes. You can have these written on a piece of paper and stick it on the door of the washroom as a friendly reminder.

Breakfast: They should be offered no more than two options for breakfast, as more choices can be confusing and time-consuming to pick from. Ensure that you cook something nutritious and healthy to make them feel energized. If they are expected to take their medicine, make sure to keep it on the table within their reach to remind them to take it.

Additional chores: If it is the weekend and the child has no school, you can create a list of chores you expect them to finish before lunchtime. It can involve helping you with laundry, doing their homework, cleaning their room or going grocery shopping. Ensure that all these tasks are planned and agreed upon a day before so that they don't come as a surprise. If some tasks involve more than one step that needs to be done in a specific order, then make sure that it is communicated before they start.

An after school routine should look something like this:

Cleaning up: If they have just returned from school, have a list of things they need to do before they come to the table for lunch. This can include changing into clean clothes, washing their hands and face, placing their bag, dirty clothes, shoes, and water bottle in its place.

Homework time: Once they are up or done playing, they must take out their books and study material, and start studying or completing their homework. You can plan a few breaks in between like a fifteen minutes break time after studying for forty-five minutes.

Relaxation or playtime: Set some time aside for unstructured play every day after they are done with their homework. It is up to them to utilize that time.

They can watch TV, play board games or with their toys (if they are young).

Clean-Up: Once they are done playing, take out half an hour to clean-up. If they played with their toys in their room, tell them to put them in the basket and clean their room before coming to the dinner table.

The bedtime routine should look something like this:

Getting ready for bed: Again, this should comprise several tasks to be completed before getting into bed. This can mean washing their face, brushing their teeth, changing into pyjamas, etc.

Prepping for tomorrow: They should also pick out the outfit for the next day, organize their school bag, set their dress, help their parents pack lunch, and organize any clips or accessories

Sleeping time: Many children with ADHD have trouble sleeping. A ten minute massage or back rub, as well as reading a short story before tucking them in bed and kissing them good night can help calm them down.

This is just a guide of what a day in the life of a child with ADHD can look like. You can always add or subtract activities and chores based on their age, the intensity of hyperactivity, or inattention.

Chapter 4: Vital Parenting Skill - Set Clear Expectations

T he second most important parenting skill that parents today must become pros at is setting clearly-defined, step-by-step, and well-guided expectations. Kids, in general, need to know what is expected of them. They need to know what others expect of them in terms of respect, empathy, and discipline. They need to know what behaviors to model in different settings such as when going to a playground versus a library. They need to know how they must present and carry themselves.

Expectations also serve as a motivating force. When expectations are high and promise great rewards, children give their best shot and try to do better. They excel when they know that what is expected of them is reasonable and attainable. However, when expectations aren't realistic, such as expecting a child to do math problems at a sixth grade level when they are only in the third grade, they will get discouraged. Expectations must be achievable. Sure, they should push children to give their best, but shouldn't be too high, or they will end up feeling like a loser when they fail to live up to unrealistic expectations.

When setting expectations for ADHD children, parents need to be a little more patient and elaborate. They can't just write something on a piece of paper and expect their child to follow it. No, they need to lay out, in clear terms, what is expected and in what capacity, what resources are to be used, and what know-how they will need to accomplish the task. Only then, can the desired outcome be achieved.

The best way to communicate expectations is via rules and routines. When creating rules and routines for kids with ADHD, parents and teachers need to account for the developmental delay and lagging in cognitive functioning skills. They need to treat them as special and offer extra support, encouragement, and details. The goal should be to accommodate the challenges they face and help them polish their skills and talents to be able to achieve success.

This all begins with breaking the tasks into smaller bite-size chunks that are easy to understand, process, and follow.

Importance of Breaking Tasks Into Digestible Chunks

The benefits for breaking tasks into sizable chunks, are various. For starters, kids with ADHD have a hard time concentrating or staying engaged in a single activity. So when things are broken into smaller tasks, it becomes easier for them to focus and stay attentive and engrossed. This makes the accomplishment of tasks easier and more manageable for parents. This trick isn't only applicable to children with disorders or disabilities. It applies equally to kids and adults, both without any disabilities, as it prevents another critical problem i.e. distractions. With a short attention span, as little as three seconds, children with ADHD have a hard time staying put both physically and mentally. One can't do much about the wandering of thoughts which hinders task or chore completion or at least, impairs its efficiency. But when tasks are broken into digestible and clear sub-tasks, they become easier to handle and the fear of becoming distracted goes away.

Not to mention, clear instructions and step-by-step guidelines allow children with ADHD to accomplish things that they would never otherwise. Be it wearing the right shoe on the right foot or putting their toys back in the toy basket, everything becomes possible when parents give them the knowledge that they need in a way that is easy to understand.

Finally, when tasks are laid out in stages and expected to be completed in a sequence, they become doable, which results in a boost in their confidence. Everyone, not just kids, feels accomplished and motivated to take on another bigger challenge when they accomplish something they didn't think they could. They feel confident in their abilities and proud of themselves to have made it this far. They are more willing to step out of their comfort zones and do more than what they initially thought of doing. The same happens for children with ADHD. When they complete a task successfully, they feel more driven and confident. They want to experience the happiness and peace that comes with their achievement more often, and thus are more determined to behave and carry themselves better. Therefore, you can expect this breakdown to help them gain more confidence in their abilities, as well as boost their self-esteem which leads to increased happiness and satisfaction – things they desperately crave.

How to Do It?

When the aim is to set clear expectations, there are many essential things you need to do first. For instance, you have to ensure that while you are briefing them about your expectations, you have their full attention. This calls for the elimination of any distractions that may make their mind wander. Second, you have to be strategic with the way you instruct them. You can't expect them to follow chain commands where you direct them to complete several tasks in one sentence and believe that they will remember all of them to a tee. For example, you can't tell them, "Get dressed, comb your hair, brush your teeth, and then come downstairs to put on your coat and shoes before getting in the car." They are bound to forget a few of your instructions, as the developmental delay and slow cognitive functioning will make it difficult for them to follow through all the commands. Therefore, you have to make them simple, understandable, and singular. You can ask them to get dressed and wait until they complete that task, before ordering them the second thing. Other than that, you can:

Make a Chores List

A chores list is a form of a to-do list used by professionals and adults to mark important events, tasks, and assignments. To make expectations more clear and comprehensible, you can write them on a piece of paper and stick it in a place with maximum exposure. If you expect them to complete their homework first before playing, have it documented so that they know what is expected of them at all times.

Watch Out for Good Behavior

The reason you need to do so is so that you can praise them the minute it happens. Being praised feels good and happiness is only multiplied when a child with ADHD experiences it. Therefore, always look out for the behaviors they do well and appreciate them for it. This will increase the likelihood of those behaviors being repeated and transformed into a habit later on.

Show Empathy

For parents, listening to their child with ADHD with empathy and compassion is another excellent way to promote communication and strengthen the bond. The more communicative you two are, the more likely you will be able to discipline them. Children with ADHD are often belittled for being different than other kids their age. When they fail to do well in school like their peers, they feel demotivated. They start to think that there is something wrong with them and thus, may become depressed or anxious. If you lend a compassionate ear to listen to them and empathize with them to make them feel normal again, it can help manage their behavior. Listening with empathy also opens the door for collaborative problem-solving and skills development whilst ending in many teachable moments.

Provide Redirection

Sometimes, despite having been told repeatedly what is expected of them, they forget or become distracted. If such is the case with your little one too, redirection and gentle reminders are a great way to get them back on track and complete the tasks at hand. They may need some more explanation and time, but they will eventually finish it.

Set Timers

Another way of keeping track of the time required for a task is by using timers to keep them focused and attentive. When they know that time is running out, they are more likely to stick to the task and not procrastinate or get distracted.

Chapter 5: Vital Parenting Skill – Establish Reward Systems and Praise

W hatever the goal, appreciation, praise, and rewards can be highly uplifting and motivating, not just for children with an attention or focus problem, but for everyone. Whenever we try to achieve something or take up a new goal, it is the rewards and the result that serves as the motivation to keep going. Take getting slim for instance. When you are trying to lose weight, what is it that drives you to the gym every day or makes you jog for several miles? The fact that you will lose weight, and feel good about yourself. The image you have in your mind of a slimmer you is what drives you to keep pushing and doing another lap.

Even our pets seem to take note of this. When they know they will be rewarded with their favorite treats, they behave well. So how can our little ones be any different? Besides, they have always wanted to impress us and when we reward their effort, it just fills their heart with joy and a sense of pride. They feel confident in themselves and in their abilities, making them more likely to aim for more challenging things.

Since the goal with ADHD children is mostly behavior improvement, a reward system and frequent praise can help a lot. It can be the difference between positive and negative behavior. To them, recognition for a job well done means more than what it means for kids without an attention and hyperactivity-related disorder.

The Role of Positive Praise and Appreciation

But do positive incentives work? According to one research study published in the journal Biological Psychiatry, it does!

Researchers from Nottingham University conducted a series of experiments on children with ADHD to know how and if they benefit from immediate rewards in the same way as they do when giving the medicine Ritalin (Groom et al., 2009). Ritalin is a behavior modification medication prescribed to children and adults with ADHD to control their behavior and tone down the hyper-activeness a little.

During the study, researchers aimed to examine how rewarding children for good behavior impacted their brain's functioning. The children that participated were asked to play a computer video game devised by the researchers. Their brain's functioning was monitored via electroencephalogram (EEG). The biggest challenge in the game was to catch aliens of a certain color. The results proved that receiving immediate rewards did improve their performance in almost the same manner as did the Ritalin –although to a lesser degree. But when the researchers amplified the rewards as well as the punishments in the game – the children's brains showed signs of complete normalcy.

Hence, they were able to deduce that incorporating reward systems in the lives of children with attention and hyperactivity disorder can result in performance improvement as well as behavior modification. This is hopeful for parents who want to avoid medication, as it means that our children won't have to rely only on traditional medication like Ritalin and engage in alternative programs to stabilize their behavior in the longer run. This possibility is indeed a rewarding one and can help parents as well as teachers all around the world to guide children with ADHD like other 'normal' children.

5 Ways to Make Your Child With ADHD Special

Now that we know that medication and praise can have the same impact on behavior and help improve it, how can we incorporate reward systems in their daily lives to enhance productivity and build focus? The first step is to eliminate problem behaviors. Meaning, we need to know which behaviors we need to reward and which ones to eliminate. Yes, you have to reward them for things that they aren't doing as well, such as not yelling or shouting their answers in the class and holding up their hands patiently. When we classify positive and negative behaviors in this manner, we will be able to improve interactions in a more suitable manner.

Introduce a Token Economy System

What is a token economy system? If we look at its literal definition, it goes something like this: a token economy is a form of behavior modification where the goal is to increase desirable behavior and limit or decrease undesirable ones (Morin, 2019). The children receive tokens for every positive action and behavior. They collect these and then exchange them for something of higher privilege. This also encourages them to learn patience as they delay the final dose of gratification throughout the day. To start with this, you can simply use coins or sheets of paper in different colors, cut into circles like a badge. You can also substitute it for stickers in the shape of a star. Next, you have to create a list of chores or tasks that you want them to perform throughout the day, like helping fold the laundry, taking a bath, organizing their room, putting their toys back, completing their homework, etc. Once they complete those actions, you give them a circle or place a star in front of the completed task. Now comes the step where you set up the rewards. They can range from simple things like getting an hour of free time to things like getting ice-cream after dinner. The more tokens they collect, the bigger the reward.

Praise the Effort, Not the Output

Praise, whether it comes in the form of a tangible or intangible reward, can build their self-esteem. As their parent, it is your job to appreciate them for their effort, regardless of whatever the outcome is. If you know that they put all their heart into something, it doesn't matter if they win or not. What matters is their concentration, focus, and effort to try to win. That, in itself, is something to boast about.

Be Specific With Praises

Be elaborative and specific so that they know what they are being praised for specifically. For example, if you notice that they help you set the dinner table without being asked, let them know that you appreciate them by specifically pointing out that action. Instead of saying, "Thank you, I appreciate it," say something like, "I am so glad you helped me with setting the table. I am very grateful. You are such a good kid." The latter seems to offer more recognition for a particular action. Chances are, they will start doing it more often, just for the sake of being praised and recognized.

Offer Immediate Feedback

Unlike most kids, children with ADHD need constant motivation and supervision. One of the most effective ways to help them stay focused is through immediate feedback. This means that if they are doing something, and that task involves several steps, you have to encourage them at each step and offer positive feedback on how well they are doing so that they stay attentive and motivated.

Frame Praises Positively

Saying something like, "Thank you for not shouting," or, "Thank you for staying put in the car," aim to make your praises more positive and uplifting. You can also say things like, "I am so proud of you for staying calm," or, "I feel so happy that you have behaved so well in the car." This will automatically point out the actions you are encouraging and praising and not the actions that you are trying to diminish.

Chapter 6: Vital Parenting Skill – Eliminate Distractions

T he very definition of distractibility means that an individual is unable to block out unimportant distractions, both mental and visual, and stay focused on the important matter at hand. Even for us, it can be hard to focus on things at times. Take a boring and slow day in the office, for instance. Nothing exciting comes up and you have been looking at spreadsheets all day. You will crave distractions if they aren't already present. Even the little crack in the wall will seem more interesting than doing the actual work. What you are doing is deliberately trying to distract yourself and avoid doing something important.

However, the only difference between you and a child with ADHD is that they don't have to deliberately distract themselves. Even the slightest of noises such as whispers in the classroom or a visual distraction like a bird sitting on a branch of a tree in the garden distracts them. They are unable to control their impulses and prevent themselves from being distracted and procrastinating. They will be distracted if their pet walks by or a cabinet in the kitchen is opened by you and have a hard time going back to doing what they were doing. Sometimes, distractions are so intense and serious that they forget about what they were doing beforehand. For example, you may have asked your kid to get a book from their bag from their room that is upstairs. They may have started the journey towards the stairs with a focused mind but ended up being distracted by the toy basket in their room. While you wait for them to get back, they may have already started on a puzzle.

Simply put, children with ADHD lack the filters other kids have to block out any distractions in the environment.

Why Distractions Are Your Biggest Enemy

A child with ADHD may not respond well when trying to listen or pay attention to something. They are more likely to start daydreaming, focus on other things of interest, look out the window or pay attention to noises like the chirping of the bird, the sound of the wind, and the movement of the leaves on a tree. When this happens, they are unable to stay in the moment. They are unable to pay attention to what is happening in the present or follow directions, lessons, or instructions. As we now know, ADHD isn't a disorder where the individual is unable to pay attention, it is about being unable to control attention. This is due to the low level of brain arousal which makes screening out of distractions in the external environment almost impossible. This means they can't be blamed or punished for being inattentive because it isn't their doing – it is how their brain functions.

When a child with ADHD becomes distracted, they require more time than others to finish a task or chore. They also need more convincing and encouragement than most kids to stay focused and not let their minds wander off. This causes delays. Similarly, if we evaluate their performance at school, they require more time to grasp new information and not miss out on some due to distractions. They need to make more efforts to learn, process, and retain information.

Strategies to Prevent the Distraction Trap

Have you ever noticed how your child can focus intently on a few things but not all? Like, if they are playing a video game on the computer or looking out of the car as you drive past restaurants, they can maintain focus and recall the scenes frame-by-frame when questioned. But when it comes to other activities like doing their homework, staying attentive in the classroom, or doing some other chore, they fail to achieve that level of focus and concentration. Ever wondered why that is?

Hyper-focusing is an experience where one can achieve intense bouts of focus and concentration, something common with people with ADHD. To be more specific, ADHD doesn't always mean that the child or adult has an attention deficit. Sometimes, it is the inability to regulate the attention span to the desired task (Flippin, 2007). Thus, during some mundane tasks, it is hard to stay focused unlike on others that are completely absorbing.

So how can you increase your chances of improving their focus and eliminating distractions? We have listed below some of the best strategies to choose from.

Maintain Eye Contact

It is very hard to keep your mind from straying when you suffer from a disorder like ADHD. This means conversations are a nightmare for some as they are easily distracted and lose track of what's being said, and hurt the feelings of the speaker. It can also lead to an argument. For example, you are in the middle of scolding your teenager with ADHD for being so careless about their hygiene and you notice that they are in another world, daydreaming about something else. Would that not make you madder than before? But it is rarely in their control. However, to keep matters from getting worse, encourage that they maintain eye contact with you, and you with them. This can help them stay in the moment and remain attentive.

Give Medication on Time

Medications are not only a necessity to improve behavior but also a life-saver when trying to build focus and concentration. Ensure that your child is taking their medication on time and regularly.

Introduce Active Learning

Active learning involves the usage of external tools, such as colored pencils, highlighters, stickers, and other artistic or creative things to encourage learning. For instance, if your child is doing math homework, you can make use of their marbles to help them get the right answers. Similarly, if there is something you want to highlight in their textbook or say, on a chores list, you can always underline it, write it using colored pencils or make it bold to be easily spottable. This will help build and maintain both focus and interest.

Let Them Catch a Breath

Short breaks during work can help too. It allows the child's brain to relax for a while and then get back to work while being in a more refreshed state. This also prevents things from becoming tedious and makes the workload manageable.

Break Up Tasks Into Shorter Sub-Tasks

Sometimes, a task seems uninteresting because it is too lengthy or time-consuming. However, if we strategically divide it into smaller sections and treat each section as an individual task, it will become more interesting and doable. Using this trick with your child with ADHD can also prove helpful when the goal is to eliminate distractions and improve focus. You can also add a ten-minute break time between each task to let their mind take a break and then get back to work. Besides, the act of ticking off each separate task will serve as motivation for the next one and keep your little one engaged and attentive. This will also minimize the overall amount of time spent on the task and improve efficiency.

Encourage Self-Monitoring

If the child is old enough to take care of themselves, it is best to teach them to self-monitor and identify the triggers that distract them. With some practice and time, they will be able to spot the triggers and become aware of them and what damage they cause. Thus, the minute they feel like drifting off, they will seek help or engage in self-talk to get back to work.

Supervise

If they are unable to self-monitor, you can supervise and help them stay focused. You can always start by giving them a distraction-free space in the house. If that isn't possible, you can sit with them while they take on some activity or try to do their homework to keep their mind from wandering off. You can repeatedly talk them into getting back to their work. Over time, the strict supervision can turn into frequent check-ins where you leave them on their own, with perhaps a designated time, to finish a task and check up on them often to see if they are still focused or not.

Chapter 7: Vital Parenting Skill – Set Reasonable Consequences

W e all have been told from time to time that failure is the best teacher. How many times have we allowed them to fall or get hurt so that they would learn the lesson? There have been instances when knowing the solution to their problems, we have taken a step back and let them figure it out on their own. We have seen them making a bad decision or a poor choice and yet not done anything to stop it. But letting them make poor decisions should also come with a price. If you are letting them fail, you have to let them deal with the consequences too. You can't shield them from consequences all the time. Because like failure, natural consequences are another important lesson they need to learn.

Consequences allow us to face our failure head on. It allows us to know the extent of our decision and how harmful or unsafe it can be for us. The difference with natural consequences is that it isn't a sort of a punishment you set up for them but rather a natural penalty that they have to pay. It is like if you eat too much junk food, you will have digestive problems. If you watch too much TV, your head starts to ache. If you jog on a hilly trek, your legs will hurt. All these are natural consequences of the actions we choose to do. As a parent, you don't instill them in your child. You just get out of the way and let them face the ramifications of their mistakes.

Why Natural Consequences Are Essential?

Sometimes, when parents are too overprotective of their children, they try to shield them from all natural consequences. It does say a lot about the intensity with which you love them, but this act does them more harm than good. When children remain clung to their parents, they become deprived of the opportunity to bounce back from failure. They never learn how to recover from their mistakes or learn how to regulate negative behaviors when things go wrong. Both of these skills are essential to learning, especially when they are growing up. You can't expect them to learn how to have a respectable conversation with someone if you do most of the talking for them. You can't expect them to learn to handle their fights or stand up for themselves if you keep getting involved. You can't expect them to follow the rules you have set for them if they don't know why they need to follow them, and what will happen if they don't.

They should be trained to own up to their mistakes from early on. If they act out or don't listen, let them face the consequence. If they persist on not wearing the jacket to school during a rough winter, let them manage on their own without the jacket once. Let them sense the regret when they feel like they would freeze without one. Another reason natural consequences must be enforced is that they prepare them for adulthood. When kids with ADHD experience the fruits of their actions, they are more likely to do better. It is only possible if they can link their actions with consequences.

Natural consequences also allow children with ADHD to build problem-solving skills. When they face the consequences of their actions and behaviors and don't like them, they look for ways to improve the result.

Next, it also helps parents avoid power struggles. You don't come in the way of your child and allow them to do things their way on their terms and conditions. They have no one to blame if they fail in their cause, because it was their idea. There are no arguments to be had or accusations to be made, because no one forced them to make the choice.

The reason we are stating all this is that children with ADHD need to be reminded of this from time to time. As parents, it is on us to teach them about why consequences can be bad for them and why they should try to limit negative behaviors. They should know that if they lie, people will stop trusting their word and if they speak ill of others behind their backs, no one would want to be their friend. If they create chaos everywhere they go, they will be labeled as troublesome and disobedient.

Another crucial thing you need to teach them is to be able to differentiate between positive and negative consequences. Where negative consequences are mostly reactive, positive consequences are proactive. Positive consequences encourage children to repeat good behaviors while negative consequences remind them of the behaviors they need to change. As their mentor, you have to encourage and reward positive behaviors with positive consequences like privileges, tangible prizes and gifts, and appreciation and recognition. You also have to use negative consequences sometimes like time-outs to improve behavior.

How to Discourage Bad Behavior and Mischief

When trying to limit mischief and improve negative behaviors, consequences can come in many forms. As stated above, they can be both positive and negative. But how do you use them to reinforce positive behaviors? Let's take a look!

Be Consistent

The first key thing to note is that when it comes to setting reasonable consequences, you have to ensure their enforcement. You can't just scare them off and let them get off the hook with a warning. You have to put into practice the scheduled consequences so that negative behaviors aren't repeated.

Don't Discipline in Front of Others

Sometimes, parents fail to judge their audience and start to yell or punish bad behavior right in front of others. Little do they know, children have self-esteem too. Disciplining a child with ADHD in front of a crowd can lead to poor self-esteem and low self-worth. They may start to see themselves as a failure and give up on themselves. Although it will limit bad behavior, it will also take away their confidence. Thus, this is not recommended at all.

Use Time-Ins

For many years, we have been told that to improve behavior or limit disobedience, you have to give your child a time-out where they feel the guilt and shame they have caused. However, recent studies are only proving this strategy as less effective. Time-ins, on the other hand, have been proven more effective to prevent bad behavior. Time-ins allow the child and parent to bond and reflect over the mistakes they made and talk about the consequences they may have to face. For instance, instead of telling your son to go to his room because he performed poorly on a test won't do much good as opposed to sitting him down and talking about the reasons and consequences they may have to face if they don't do well the next time.

Adjust Your Expectations

You can't change all the things that your child does. You will have to pick your battles and choose agendas worth fighting. You will have to ignore some minor issues and work on other more important things like disrespecting others, lying, or stealing.

Chapter 8: Vital Parenting Skill – Ignore Mild Misbehavior

C hildren with ADHD, unlike most kids, exhibit attention-seeking behavior. They want to be noticed. They want to be attended to. It doesn't matter to them if good or bad behavior gets the job done. However, when we give them attention when they do something wrong and not when they do something right, they start to assume that negative behavior is the way to go. They begin to depict more bad behavior which can make the mums and dads go mad.

Thus, this next parenting skill is more of an art where you deliberately ignore misbehavior in the hopes that they will give it up on their own.

Choosing to ignore certain behaviors doesn't mean you pay no attention to their distress or anger. If they genuinely seem in pain or emotionally-troubled, you need to be there for them. Ignoring mild misbehavior means that you ignore the way they are behaving, not how they are feeling. Attention, in itself, is a big positive reinforcement, even if it comes out of negative action. But when you choose to not give it to them purposely, they look for other ways to get it. Thus, it is important that good behavior gets attention every time it is noticeable to encourage it.

Ignoring mild misbehavior also discourages it from being repeated and prevents power struggles. Ever had a moment where your child dropped to the floor in a busy grocery store because they wanted something? Well, it is their way of getting attention. But yelling and shouting only makes it worse, doesn't it? It is because when we do that, we unknowingly give them the attention they seek. To save ourselves from further embarrassment, we let them have what they want, which in a way, reinforces that behavior. When you choose to ignore the temper tantrum and pretend that it isn't effective, they try other means to get to you. This is a silent yet a strategic way of letting them know that being obnoxious won't get them the desired results.

Why Do You Need to Keep Your Cool?

Another thing that happens frequently with many parents raising a child with ADHD is that they lose their patience after some time. They resort to yelling, shouting, and setting harsh punishments in hope that it will prevent misbehavior. Sadly, it doesn't work that way. Remaining calm and keeping your cool, on the other hand, does!

It is researchers at Ohio State University who believe so. The study offered biological evidence that positive parenting - parenting without punishments or using care and compassion to deal with misbehavior – may help children with ADHD master their behaviors and emotions (Bell et al., 2017). The study included both children with developmental disorders and their parents. Theodore Beauchaine, the leading author of the study was surprised to report that the psychological impact of praises and compliments instead of shouting and criticizing were almost instant.

The responses of the participants were monitored and evaluated during a special intervention program. The intervention program offered small group sessions for children and parents. The parents learned how to respond to their children's behaviors and the children were taught some strategies for anger management, emotion regulation, and emotionally aware and appropriate social behaviors. The researchers assigned renowned therapists to work with ninety-nine children aged four to six with ADHD. Two-thirds of the children were boys. Beauchaine believed that often these children had strained relationships with their peers, teachers, and parents. Thus, during the sessions, parents were taught better disciplining strategies. They were reminded of how they can sometimes overreact and get physical while trying to discipline their kids with ADHD. He suggested that it was common for parents to slip into negative behaviors when they felt frustrated and tired by the actions of their child.

He proposed that when parents were introduced to the concept of positive parenting, they instantly knew what it entailed. They knew that praises, smiling, flexibility, hugging, focusing on rewards and privileges, setting achievable goals and expectations can help discipline them in a less threatening and adverse way.

As weeks passed by and parents learned of effective problem-solving techniques, positive parenting responses, and adaptive emotional regulation, the children also began to depict improvement in their behavior. Additionally, following the intervention, it was also notable that the heart rates of the children with ADHD slowed down a little and their breathing became calmer. All of this happened in just two months when the researchers predicted that the behavioral changes will start to show well after one year. To further prove that the behavioral improvements were the result of the intervention program, he divided families into two groups. One group received 20 weeks' worth of sessions whereas the other received only 10 sessions. The behavioral changes in the first group were more evident and long-lasting than the ones depicted by the children of parents in the second group. In his concluding remarks, Beauchaine proposed that the earlier parents of children with ADHD started taking therapy and practicing positive parenting, the better the results will be.

How to Improve Misbehavior Without Yelling or Shouting

Parenting kids with ADHD is a challenge for many parents. It is a test of their patience and good judgment to the point where they end up making bad decisions while disciplining misbehavior. Yelling and shouting don't always work but choosing compassionate approaches surely does. Below are some friendly approaches to discipline misbehavior without losing your mind.

Keep it Short

When disciplining your child, be concise. Many parenting experts believe that the best way to discipline children with ADHD is to use fewer words. The more direct you are with your commands and orders, the more effective they will be. Be very clear about what is expected of them so that they can hear and remember it.

Don't Bully Into Submission

When we yell at our kids, we generate fear. This is no less than a form of bullying where they begin to behave out of fear not out of their own will. Thus, you have to show them that you care and look them in the eye when telling them how valuable they are and how grateful and proud you will be when they behave well. You can achieve a lot more when you talk to them, not at them.

Choose an Appropriate Time to Have a Talk

Every child wants to feel valued and respected. They want to feel validated and important. Thus, when they do something you don't like or agree with, ignore it instead of yelling at them at the moment. Choose another time to bring it up and talk about it in a calm and composed manner.

Be Proactive When Discussing Negative Consequences

Another great approach to handle misbehavior is to make them aware of the consequences that await them if they break the rules. When setting consequences, you can use strategies like time-outs or taking away privileges to discipline them and learn from their mistakes. If any other consequences put them off, communicate them beforehand to prevent misbehavior before it even begins.

Set Punishments for Misbehavior

Appropriate punishments are another approachable way as long as they aren't too harsh or demeaning. For instance, suppose the child has spilled some juice on the kitchen tiles. An appropriate punishment would be to ask them to clean the mess instead of belittling them for their poor handling of the glass and being hyperactive.

Chapter 9: Vital Parenting Skill – Give Positive Attention

P arenting a child with attention or hyperactivity disorder can be both challenging and exhausting. The children are always brimming with energy and want to be attended constantly. This can tire out even the most patient and tolerating parent. But in recent times, positive attention is considered one of the greatest parenting skills and thought of as a good investment.

But what does it mean to give your child positive attention?

The core idea behind positive attention is to praise positive behaviors and actions instead of reacting to negative behaviors. It is very common for parents to get annoyed, and sometimes lose their patience when their child does something they aren't supposed to. However, when the same child does something good and expects praise, parents often fall short. After all, why should they be rewarded for something they are supposed to do? Positive attention requires a change in approach to the way we interact with our children. It teaches us not only to be patient and kind but also to ignore behaviors that are not-so-good and praise the ones that are.

Positive attention can be further explained in several forms. It can come in the form of a hug, a pat on the back, smile, compassion, and empathy and praises, and recognition. It can also come in the form of quality time spent with the child where they feel like they are the center of attention and feel validated.

Positive Attention and Its Benefits for Children With ADHD

Having a positive and healthy relationship with your child is important for many reasons – discipline being one of them. When a healthy relationship is established between you and the child, they strive to do better under your mentorship.

Would you not be more motivated to work under someone that respects you and shows you appreciation too? Or would you be okay working under someone that never appreciates you or shows you any respect?

Parents who spend quality time with their children and offer praise and appreciation wholeheartedly raise compassionate and confident children. When children with ADHD feel respected and encouraged to do better, it serves as a motivating factor. Daily doses of affection and positive praise can reduce behavioral problems. It can also strengthen the bond between you and your child. Moreover, they will stop trying to seek attention by acting out, crying, or shouting. They will also avoid repeating the same mistakes over and over again. They will also keep to themselves and not poke their noses in others matters.

Tips for Daily Doses of Positive Attention

When quality time is valued and efforts are made to make communication more prevalent, the child also starts to look forward to spending time with you. This is especially important if your child is already a teenager and started to spend more time in their room, immersed in their phones than with you or their siblings. Additionally, they will be more driven to follow the rules and expectations as well as listen to what you have to say. So how can we encourage communication with daily doses of positive attention? Let's take a look!

Be Positive With Your Praise

There are times when you unintentionally call out bad behavior in a demeaning and insulting tone. It just happens out of habit. When dealing with children with ADHD, we have to improve on the way we comment on behaviors – both positive and negative. As we now know that the very goal of positive attention is to praise positivity and ignore negativity, the first thing you need to do is mold your sentences in a way that they come off as positive, even when trying to prevent misbehavior. For example, instead of saying, "Why did you bring your dirty shoes inside," say something like, "Oh, I see you have mistakenly brought your shoes inside with you" – the same thing but in a positive manner.

Resist the Urge to Correct

Again, as parents, we want to save our children from harm and pain. So we are quick to spot something wrong and try to correct them. Don't do that. Encourage them to imagine things differently. If they want to paint an apple purple, let them. If they want to give cows a pair of wings, hell yes! It will make them feel more confident in their abilities and you can always choose another time to correct them subtly.

Abolish Distractions When Interacting

When spending time with them and appreciating their efforts, do it whole-heartedly while being present in the moment. This means that you have to put down your phones, switch off the TV, and listen to them. Distractions can undermine their self-worth. They may not feel as important and validated when they feel you aren't 100% interested in what they have to say or do. Besides, distractions will also prevent them from completing things.

Give Them Undivided Attention Daily

Ideally, you should give them at least 15 to 20 minutes of undivided attention every day. You can do things together and sit down with them in their free time and have a real one-on-one conversation about their school, peers, and aspirations. It's simple math. When you listen to them, they will listen to you.

Make Interactions More Meaningful

This means choosing activities they are interested in. You must introduce to them games and activities that boost their attention and require them to stay focused. If confused, let them pick what they want to do for the time being and just get along with them.

Conclusion

R aising a child with ADHD can be mentally-draining. They need more attention, extra time, and extreme patience. Indeed, they aren't deliberately trying to be difficult but it makes it difficult for parents to deal with them, especially when they have little knowledge of how to.

Hopefully, this book will be a good start to learn of some great parenting skills in case your child has been recently diagnosed with the disorder. However, there is one thing that it didn't cover. The one thing that, perhaps, is the most important of all: Self-care!

No one can prepare you for the battle you are heading into but you can't win unless you are prepared for it. You have to take care of yourself first to be able to take care of your child. Chances are, they are going to be needing every last bit of energy. This requires that you are mentally and physically prepared for it. You have to get rid of all the negative self-talk about how it must have been your fault. You also have to stop worrying about how you are going to raise them or whether or not you are able to do enough.

Next comes, taking care of your health and wellbeing. You will need to find ways to manage your stress and anger. You will have to learn ways to identify the triggers that build frustration and find healthy ways to vent it out. A big part of this starts with the right diet and foods that alleviate stress levels and release happiness-inducing chemicals.

Remember, you are your child's first role model. You need to lead by example. If you take care of yourself, they will learn to take care of themselves too. If you cope with stress and impatience in healthy ways, they will do the same. On the other hand, if they always find you running out of patience or overtired, you will be setting the wrong example to follow and risk losing sight of support and structure you want them to have in their lives.

So treat yourself well first, and then tend to your child with ADHD.

References

Attention-Deficit/Hyperactivity Disorder (ADHD).
(2017). Cleveland Clinic.
https://my.clevelandclinic.org/health/diseas
es/4784-attention-deficithyperactivity-
disorder-adhd

Bell, Z., Shader, T., Webster-Stratton, C., Reid, M. J.,
& Beauchaine, T. P. (2017). Improvements in
Negative Parenting Mediate Changes in
Children's Autonomic Responding Following
a Preschool Intervention for ADHD. Clinical
Psychological Science, 6(1), 134–144.
https://doi.org/10.1177/2167702617727559

Celebrity Spotlight: How Michael Phelps' ADHD
Helped Him Make Olympic History. (n.d.).
Understood.
https://www.understood.org/en/learning-
thinking-differences/personal-
stories/famous-people/celebrity-spotlight-
how-michael-phelps-adhd-helped-him-make-
olympic-history

Common Challenges of Parenting a Child With ADHD, Dyslexia or Learning Differences. (n.d.). Brain Balance. Retrieved June 8, 2020, from https://blog.brainbalancecenters.com/2015/10/common-challenges-of-parenting-a-child-with-adhd-dyslexia-or-learning-differences

Flippin, R. (2007, October 6). Hyperfocus: The ADHD Phenomenon of Intense Fixation. ADDitude. https://www.additudemag.com/understanding-adhd-hyperfocus/

Groom, M. J., Scerif, G., Liddle, P. F., Batty, M. J., Liddle, E. B., Roberts, K. L., Cahill, J. D., Liotti, M., & Hollis, C. (2009). Effects of Motivation and Medication on Electrophysiological Markers of Response Inhibition in Children with Attention-Deficit/Hyperactivity Disorder. Biological Psychiatry, 67(7), 624–631. https://doi.org/10.1016/j.biopsych.2009.09.029

LaMagna, M. (2018, May 6). Richard Branson says this one thing helped him become a better entrepreneur. MarketWatch. https://www.marketwatch.com/story/overcoming-childhood-taunts-richard-branson-says-this-early-challenge-helped-him-succeed-in-business-2018-05-04

Law, E. C., Sideridis, G. D., Prock, L. A., & Sheridan, M. A. (2014). Attention-Deficit/Hyperactivity Disorder in Young Children: Predictors of Diagnostic Stability. PEDIATRICS, 133(4), 659–667. https://doi.org/10.1542/peds.2013-3433

Low, K. (2019a, June 17). How Parents Can Make an Easier Life for Their Child With ADHD. Verywell Mind. https://www.verywellmind.com/understanding-children-with-adhd-20686

Low, K. (2019b, August 13). Children With ADHD Need Structure in Their Lives to Stay Focused. Verywell Mind. https://www.verywellmind.com/why-is-structure-important-for-kids-with-adhd-20747#:~:text=The%20symptoms%20of%20ADHD%20lead

Low, K. (2020, January 7). How to Set up a Reward System for Improving Your Child's ADHD Behavior. Verywell Mind. https://www.verywellmind.com/behavior-management-for-adhd-20867

Miller, G. (2017, November 16). Calm Parents Help Calm Kids With ADHD. WebMD. https://www.webmd.com/add-adhd/news/20171116/calm-parents-help-calm-kids-with-adhd#1

Morin, A. (2019a, February 13). How to Create a
Token Economy System That Will Motivate
Your Child. Verywell Family.
https://www.verywellfamily.com/create-a-
token-economy-system-to-improve-child-
behavior-1094888

Morin, A. (2019b, June 24). Why Ignoring Is the Best
Way to Deal With Certain Behavior Problems.
Verywell Family.
https://www.verywellfamily.com/is-it-really-
ok-to-ignore-mild-misbehaviors-
1094791#:~:text=When%20you%20ignore%
20your%20child

Morin, A. (2019c, September 12). How to Make
Natural Consequences an Effective Discipline
Tool. Verywell Family.
https://www.verywellfamily.com/natural-
consequences-as-a-discipline-strategy-
1094849

Sturiale, J. (2015, October 14). Stop Yelling At Your
Kids. WebMD.
https://www.webmd.com/parenting/features
/stop-yelling-at-your-kids#1

Understanding ADHD: Information for Parents.
(2019, September 25). HealthyChildren.Org.
https://www.healthychildren.org/English/he
alth-
issues/conditions/adhd/Pages/Understandin
g-ADHD.aspx

Vann, M. R. (2013, September 19). Create a Daily
    Routine for Children With ADHD | Everyday
    Health. Everyday Health.
    https://www.everydayhealth.com/add-
    adhd/create-a-daily-routine-for-children-
    with-adhd.aspx

Wymbs, B. T., Pelham, W. E., Molina, B. S. G.,
    Gnagy, E. M., Wilson, T. K., & Greenhouse, J.
    B. (2008). Rate and predictors of divorce
    among parents of youths with ADHD. Journal
    of Consulting and Clinical Psychology, 76(5),
    735–744. https://doi.org/10.1037/a0012719

Book Description

Does your child misbehave every chance they get? Are they always arguing and questioning your orders and requests? Do they deliberately throw tantrums to get the things they want? Is your first instinct always to yell, scream, or tell them no?

If so, then you need to change the way you parent!

Many parents think that they have it all figured out when it comes to parenting. They think that using punishments and other verbal abuses gets things done. They know how to fight back during arguments and conflicts, and assume they get their way. However, this isn't the best model of parenting. Your child shouldn't obey you out of fear. They should because they know it is the right thing to do. Positive disciplining can help teach them this difference.

In this book, we review what positive discipline is and how we can put its techniques into practice. We see how it can help parents improve communication and make interactions with their kids more fulfilling and meaningful. We look at seven vital parenting skills needed to facilitate parents to start with positive parenting.

- These include the following:

- Identifying the reasons behind misbehavior and how to prevent it.

- How being empathetic can help both parents and children.

- Why offering choices can go a long way when preventing misbehavior.

- Creating a YES environment to enhance confidence and self-esteem.

- Redirections and how they work towards improving child behavior.

- How treating mistakes as lessons can serve as a great opportunity to teach about resilience.

- How being consistent and clear about expectations can prevent misbehavior from the get-go.

Aimed to be a simple yet interesting read, this brief guide offers you everything you need to get started with the principles of positive discipline.

7 Vital Parenting Skills for Improving Child Behavior and Positive Discipline

Proven Positive Parenting Tips for Family Communication without Yelling or Negativity

Frank Dixon

been derived from various sources. Please consult a licensed professional before attempting any techniques outlined in this book.

By reading this document, the reader agrees that under no circumstances is the author responsible for any losses, direct or indirect, that are incurred as a result of the use of the information contained within this document, including, but not limited to, errors, omissions, or inaccuracies.

Introduction

Parenting—a skill that comes highly underrated. Think about it, isn't it odd that you get paid to go to work, drain your energy, get those juices flowing in your brain to concoct a great business plan, strategy, or perhaps birth a new idea that will change the lives of many; you get credited for it in the form of a promotion, an upgrade on your car or house, or receive bonuses big enough to plan another trip with the spouse and the kids, and yet, when it comes to parenting—the most important job in the world—we fall short on our praises.

We see a kid throwing a tantrum in the grocery store and we instantly blame the mom or dad for bad parenting. But do you know the backstory? Do you know how embarrassed they are to not be able to control their children's behavior? Do you know how terribly they want to discipline their children, but know that it would only worsen the tantrum?

Heck, you must have had a day like this too? A day where nothing seems to go according to the plan. The kid has been cranky since the morning, acting up, whining over little things. They are being pushy and testing your limits. To make them feel a little better, you think about taking a trip to the grocery store together, hoping it will lighten their mood and make them happy. And then it happens... They have their eyes set on something unhealthy or way too expensive or unnecessary and the next minute they are rubbing their toes, pulling out their hair, and crying at the top of their lungs.

And this is just a normal day in the life of parents. Imagine how difficult it must be to deal with them when they get sick and resist taking the medications? Or days when they won't get ready for school and want to skip it by faking a stomach ache.

So our question is this: why is there no prize, bonus or recognition? Isn't this the most important job?

Since modern-day parenting is becoming more and more challenging, and children are becoming harder to handle, there has emerged a new concept that suggests modeling good behavior using positive praise instead of all the yelling and shouting we normally do.

Positive Discipline.

Positive disciplining techniques are proven more effective than traditional parenting techniques in many ways. They promise improved behavior, a strengthened bond, and a calm and composed parent that isn't stressed about what the next day will bring.

Therefore, in this next book in the series, we plan to prep the parents with seven vital parenting skills needed to implement positive disciplining techniques and raise kids that are not only disciplined but also happier, confident, and empathetic.

Without wasting any more time, let's dive right into it.

Chapter 1: What is Positive Discipline?

"How to discipline my child" is one of the most widely searched terms on Google. It shows how desperate we all are to look for ways to discipline them. But if you ever notice, none of the websites, at least the most reliable ones, ever suggest punishments and negative reinforcements to instill discipline. Traditionally, we all thought it was a sure-fire way to teach manners, but new research suggests the opposite. Punishments do more than just physical or emotional damage. They affect the brain. Kids that are brought up in families where punishments and abuse have been considered a norm for disciplining children have raised mentally unstable, aggressive, and antisocial adults (Durrant & Ensom, 2012; Ohene et al., 2006; Smith, 2006).

So how do we discipline them if punishments are out? Well, you aren't the only parent grappling with that thought. Children of today are sensitive. They struggle with competition as well as social anxiety both online and offline. Despite knowing that, we are all guilty of screaming and yelling on our children.

That leaves us with only one thing—a new approach!

Enter positive discipline.

Understanding Positive Disciplining

The concept of positive discipline is based on a model first introduced by Alfred Adler and Rudolf Dreikurs. Dr. Adler, in 1920, introduced this unique idea of parenting in the United States. He believed that when children are treated respectfully, they behaved well. He also pointed out that leniency doesn't mean allowing them to do whatever they wanted to, and thus drew a clear line between spoiling them and respecting their wishes. Dreikurs and Adler wanted parents to adopt a kind and compassionate approach to teaching.

Later, based on the same principles, Jane Nelson, who was the director of the project Adlerian Counseling Concepts for Encouraging Parents and Teachers (ACCEPT), a federally-funded project that received excellent feedback in its developmental phase, self-published a book in 1981. It was called "Positive Discipline." Later, in 1987, it was published by Ballantine.

Research from recent studies confirms that children are hardwired from birth to connect with others. They have been doing it before birth—in the womb too. They want to have a sense of belonging, want to be pampered, and looked after and play a key role in shaping the community. Children that are able to connect with their parents, peers, and educators from an early age exhibit fewer behavioral problems.

Positive Discipline focuses on developing a strong and deep relationship between the parent and the child that is based on mutual respect and communication. It focuses on teaching parents to teach their children not just the *what* of things, but also the *why*. Positive disciplining uses approaches such as kindness, empathy, compassion, and respect. There are five important criteria for positive discipline:

- The first is being kind yet firm at the same time. This means that you have to guide your child towards the right behavior but also be firm and definitive.

- The second is promoting a sense of significance and belonging. This involves helping them with opportunities that allow them to connect with you and the family.

- The third is looking for effective solutions in the long run. The goal shouldn't only be to prevent misbehavior in the present, but to eliminate the bad habit altogether. This requires that we offer children solutions that are positive and acceptable to exhibit instead.

- The fourth is teaching valuable life and social skills. We must encourage our children to respect others, show concern for them, be accountable, problem-solve, corporate, and contribute at home and in the community.

- And finally, introduce kids to their own skills and talents so that they know how to use them in constructive ways.

The Perks of Disciplining Children Using Positive Parenting

When we allow kids to become active participants in their behavioral development, it teaches them independence and builds their self-esteem. This improves communication in the house as everyone feels like they're part of a team, equals. There is also the establishment of trust between the parent and child that further strengthens their bond in the future, especially when they enter adolescence.

Multiple studies prove the benefits of positive parenting and disciplining. According to one, positive discipline reduces the instances of childhood depression (Dallaire et al., 2006). The study focused on how different traditional parenting styles led to an increase in mental health issues in children when they became adults, and how positive discipline proved promising. It also talked about how being a disciplinarian led to increased stress levels in parents, and how they unintentionally pass it on to their children.

Some additional benefits of positive parenting and why parents of today should stick to it are discussed below.

Promotes Happiness and Boosts Self-Esteem

When the focus is on positive action and the child feels valued and cared for, it can lead to greater levels of happiness. When they feel included and important, their self-esteem also improves. When the focus is on encouragement of good behavior as opposed to discouraging the bad, the child develops a positive outlook towards life. They start to view mistakes as opportunities, and lacking and imperfections as normal and acceptable. They are more willing to try new things as there is no fear of punishments (Weintraub, 1998).

And as for the parents, this approach can reduce stress and promote happiness. There are fewer clashes over who gets to have the final say in things as both the parent and the child are aware of the expectations that have been set. Also, when there are fewer conflicts, parents can finally experience some peace of mind and prevent themselves from becoming overwhelmed by negative thoughts.

Eliminates Power Struggles and Negative Behavior

Sometimes, children try to get away with negative behavior using techniques like crying or whining. However, when you try to discipline them positively, you have to remember to set limits for them. At the same time, you have to focus on positive behavior instead of the negative, and offer positive alternatives. When children know of these ways, they are less likely to disobey you, and gradually, their bad behavior diminishes. It also leads to fewer arguments and fights between you and your child, suggests Natasha Becker, the self-published bestseller author and mother (Becker, 2019).

Makes for Effective Communication

Effective communication is one of the most essential components of positive disciplining. It is the very goal of this parenting approach. It allows us to communicate with our child in a positive and action-oriented way instead of yelling or punishing them for negative behaviors. Being positive encourages children to come forward and share their feelings because they know that they will be listened to and not judged or insulted. They know they won't be talked down and screamed at for having opinions. When children feel encouraged in this way, it develops a trusting relationship between the parent and the child (Building Trust through Communication with Teens, 2013).

Chapter 2: The Seven Vital Parenting Skills for Improving Child Behavior

A ll kids are unique in their way. Some are shy and introverted, while others can bring the whole house down with their energy and spirit. Some are empathetic and kind while others value power more than the love of others. Some want to be accepted by others while some don't like it when praised. Some want to explore the whole world while others enjoy living in their little bubble. Some are big with temper tantrums and stress out their parents while others are calm and subtle with their demands. Some are dreamers who see things imaginatively while others like to follow their peers and forebearers. Some are procrastinators and have things done last minute while others like to stick to their notes and play by the rules. Some want to be independent and crave more freedom while others like to be pampered all the time. Some want to have their way in everything and want more control over decisions related to them, while others want to have things decided for them.

Children, with their different personalities and types, make the world a better place to live. Their smiles, their laughter, happiness, and success are what we live for. We want to see them happy and accomplished. We want them to have the things we never had and want to be protective of them. We want them to have meaningful relationships growing up, friends they can always count on, and role models in the form of their teachers, coaches, and mentors. We want them to dream big and follow their passions with confidence. We want them to have successful careers, good finances, and peace of mind.

It all begins with good social skills and your parenting style. Social skills include skills like communication, listening, empathy, problem-solving, accountability, and positivity. It is our role to teach them how to hold proper conversations, behave well and be presentable, regulate their emotions in healthy ways, be accepting of others, be responsible and own up to their mistakes.

However, we can only teach these lessons if we adopt the right parenting style to begin with. If our children feel that we are too strict or too overprotective, they start to feel suffocated. They begin craving more privacy and independence and stop being transparent with us. On the other hand, if we are too carefree, they think that we couldn't care less about them and feel neglected.

Our parenting approach has to be positive and compassionate. We have to deal with them and their problems with a progressive and open mind. We have to lay the right foundations to let them soar high and aim for the skies using good social skills.

Positive discipline or positive parenting has shown promising results in the upbringing of today's children. They want more freedom, and this approach to parenting supports that. They want to do things their way but still have some rules to follow; positive discipline offers this. They want to feel valued and validated, and positive parenting offers that too. They want someone to pat them on their backs for a job well done, and voila, it offers that too. If we go back to chapter one and review the five important factors we discussed, this modern-day approach to parenting seems like the perfect package to improve communication, strengthen family bonds, and improve child behavior.

All that said, adopting positive parenting as the ultimate approach requires a set of skills. This is where our seven vital parenting skills come in. They are aimed at facilitating this approach to parenting simply and strategically. Before we get started with them in detail, let's unveil what they are and what they represent briefly in this chapter.

Vital Parenting Skill #1: Find Out the Reasons for Misbehavior

Misbehavior doesn't happen out of habit. There is usually an unmet need or desire which compels children to act negatively. The first parenting goal or skill is to identify that trigger or cause and then use it to prevent misbehavior from happening.

Vital Parenting Skill #2: Don't be Mean—Be Empathetic Instead

All parents must be empathetic towards their kids as it allows them to form closer bonds and improve family relations. Since the goal is just that, it can be a great skill to nurture.

Vital Parenting Skill #3: Offer Them Choices

Let kids have choices because when they do, they feel included and valued. Under this parenting skill, we shall look at how having choices empowers children, and minimizes negative behaviors.

Vital Parenting Skill #4: Stop Saying No

Most parents don't know about the negative influence the word "no" has on their kids. When their needs are repeatedly declined with a flat no, they lose confidence and develop poor self-worth. Thus, as parents, we have to create a YES environment for them to feel confident and motivated to take on new challenges, build resilience, and become self-reliant.

Vital Parenting Skill #5: Redirect, Redirect, Redirect

Redirection or distraction involves strategically moving the child from a negative or unsafe situation to a safer and more positive one. This parenting skill enables parents to prevent misbehavior from escalating, as well as lower the chances of a conflict or argument.

Vital Parenting Skill #6: Treat Every Mistake as a Learning Opportunity

Mistakes are nothing but disguised opportunities. We need to teach our kids to start viewing them as lessons and stay motivated instead of giving up or feeling shame and guilt. We need to prepare them for the worst and encourage mistake-prone attempts because it means they are at least trying.

Vital Parenting Skill# 7: Be Consistent with Expectations

The final parenting skill that all parents must possess or nurture in themselves is clarity. Children need structure and clarity in their lives. If we expect certain behavior from our children, we need to let them know of it from the start. We have to lay down the right foundations so that they don't get confused, forget instructions, or end up making mistakes.

Chapter 3: Parenting Skill #1 Find Out the Reasons for Misbehavior

Whenever children act out or misbehave, they are trying to tell us how they are feeling. It is often a sign that something isn't right with them and they are trying to seek our attention. They have been doing so since birth. Remember the time when they were little and short of words? How did they communicate? They cried, stomped their feet on the ground, clapped their hands, and screamed.

Thus, when the goal of parenting is to improve behavior, the most logical thing to do first is to determine the reasons for the misbehavior.

Have you ever taken medication without a proper diagnosis? To treat and prevent misbehavior, the first thing you need to do is figure out why they are acting the way they are, only then moving on to the preventive measures.

Why do They do What They Do?

When figuring out which disciplining strategy would work best for your child, find out what is causing them to act out of their character. Some of the most common reasons include:

Trying to Get Your Attention

Sometimes, we fail to realize how little time we have for our children. We stay busy at work all day and then come home to get busy cleaning, cooking, and then preparing things for the next day; we forget our children need us too. Spending time with our children, playing games with them, supervising their homework, and conversing with them is hardly ever on our to-do list. When children notice this, they start doing things that would get your attention. Naturally, we are quick to respond to negative things. For example, we may fail to praise them on cleaning up a table but we will surely point out their messy eating manners. Thus, children learn that negative behaviors are the way to get your attention and they resort to them.

Testing Your Limits

Children also try to test your limits and patience. When they are told to refrain from something, it piques their curiosity. They want to know if you are serious about the consequences you talked about or if you just bluffed. They want to know what will happen if they break the rules and whether you are consistent with agreed punishments or not. They test you to know if there is a possibility that you bluffed and thcy can get away with things.

Lacking Social Skills

Sometimes, children also misbehave when they lack social skills. For instance, your child may have a hard time sharing their toys with other kids or waiting for their turn because they don't know how to play collaboratively. Thus, they would try to hit another child and snatch the toy from their hands instead of waiting or their turn.

Being Unable to Control Emotions

When children don't know what to do about the big and unwanted feelings they are going through (such as sadness, failure, anger, disappointment, or even excitement) they act out to seek attention from their parents or others to guide them through. We must introduce healthy ways of coping with negative feelings from the start so that they don't feel overwhelmed.

Having Unmet Needs

Children, when young, don't know how to be direct with their needs and demands. In households where parents are disciplinarians, children often shy away from discussing their needs and hesitate in telling their parents about them directly. For example, if they are still hungry, after eating dinner, they might act out but not come clean about their needs to eat more. If they are tired but don't want to go to bed, they might act out because, although their body wants to rest, they don't. An unmet need can be another reason why they misbehave.

Wanting Freedom

Children also misbehave when they want to feel included in decisions about their lives. They may want to pick out a dress for themselves and have the final say. They may want to be asked what they would like for dinner rather than just given something to eat. They might want the freedom to decide things for themselves, and when they feel their parents are trying to take that away from them, they disobey. They want to do things themselves, even if they aren't yet capable of them. Ever noticed how they want to wear makeup or drink from a full-size cup because they think they are all grown up? When we stop them from doing so, disobedience follows.

Preventing Misbehavior from the Get-Go

Once you have determined what causes all that anger and frustration to come out as chaos, your goal is to identify the triggers and act before they induce bad behavior. For instance, if you know that your child will have a hard time sharing his toys with other kids, be proactive, and don't give the other children toys that your child most loves playing with. Let your child have them to themselves so that a fight can be prevented. Prevention is one of the best techniques for discipline. Arguments and tantrums don't just start right away. They gradually build their tempo. You have to prevent it before it happens. It may seem difficult at first, but it is an investment you will be glad you made.

Here are a few ideas to get you started.

Have clear Rules

When children know how to behave and what is expected of them, they are more likely to act that way. If you are taking them outside and you expect them to not run away on the streets, let them know that it is forbidden before they leave the door. Be very clear and direct so that they fully understand the rules.

Let Them Know of the Consequences

Similar to the first point, you also want them to know about the aftermath of behaving badly. They should know what awaits them if they act out. Once clear rules have been set, they must know of the consequences if they don't abide by the rules. They will be less likely to test your limits or challenge you by deliberately breaking them.

Offer Structure and Routines

A structure or set routine about the day's tasks can also prevent misbehavior. Create a chart of every day chores, include how they will spend their free time so that they follow it. Be consistent with the schedule and don't allow too many changes, as children will see those changes as opportunity. Routines, if provided correctly, can soon turn into habits. For example, if they know they need to brush their teeth before getting into bed every night, they will start to do it out of habit after a week or two.

Teach Delayed Gratification

Delayed gratification or impulse control allows children to wait to have a bigger reward in the end. We all know of the marshmallow test (Mischel et al., 1972). Children who are taught to control their impulses and not give in to their temptations are more likely to show control over their emotions too (Morin, 2019). This will prevent many power struggles and temper tantrums.

Appreciate Good Behavior

We all love to be praised and recognized for our work. We want the applause, the pat on the back and being told that someone is proud of us. Well, kids want that too. Most of their childhood revolves around getting your approval and appreciation. They want to impress you. They want to be appreciated for their effort. Doing so, not only gives them a sense of accomplishment, boosts their confidence and self-esteem but also increases the likelihood of repetition of that behavior. Therefore, whenever you catch them doing something good, be appreciative.

Knowing why they misbehave and how to prevent it before it happens, is a great strategy to deal with misbehavior in children altogether. If we put the strategies to work, we are bound to notice a difference in the way they behave—hopefully, in a positive manner.

Chapter 4: Parenting Skill #2: Don't be Mean—Be Empathetic Instead

E mpathy makes us feel more connected and understood. We all want support from our loved ones. We want them to understand what we are going through, to listen to us with a calm mind and open heart, and not to judge us for our choices and decisions. Children are born empathetic, however, if they don't show compassion as they grow older, a lot of the blame can be put on the lack of opportunities provided by the parents, or the absence of a role model. Some may even say that ever-increasing competition and exposure to violence, crime, and peer pressure, has led to our children to become unsympathetic towards others. They see it as a sign of weakness, and so are quick to judge those who open up to others and want to be heard.

But what if we told you that teaching your child to be empathetic is one of the greatest gifts you can give them?

Empathy allows us to be able to hear someone, feel their pain, experience what it is like to be in their shoes, and see them for who they are—not for their actions. Empathy keeps us from judging others, while lending them our support and ear.

The Power of Empathy

But that still doesn't answer the question: why do our kids need empathy?

When we teach our children about empathy, we help them enrich the relationships they share with us and others. That leads to amazing things happening. Teaching empathy allows them to form deeper connections with everyone and offers valuable insights into the experiences of others. Experiencing what the other person is experiencing helps them step out of reactivity and form better responses.

When a child is empathetic, they are also better at regulating their own emotions. It promotes the art of reasoning, and rational thinking too. It also helps them deal with the everyday stresses they face, and view the world with a more positive outlook. Research proves that compassionate people are better at handling stress and unexpected circumstances than their non-empathetic friends. Empathetic people are also happier and less anxious (Henry et al., 1996). It also makes people more social and interactive. For many kids, this means the formation of new and strong friendships. Being compassionate is also a likable trait: children who have it are more attractive than others. Empathy may not make them the *most* popular kid in their class, but they surely will be someone everyone would like to hang out with.

How to be More Compassionate

The goal is not only to teach compassion and empathy but to model it so that it rubs off our children too. When they see us being compassionate towards them and, importantly, others, they start to see us as role models. They get inspired and wish to be more like us. Why? Because everyone likes people who are compassionate and kind. It is something that requires effort and patience and not everyone has it. So it becomes a valuable trait to have.

When the question is how we can be more compassionate and empathetic towards our children to improve family relationships and communication, here are a few tips that help.

Be Kind to Them

How would you want to be treated if you go up to someone to share your feelings? You would expect them to listen to you with an open mind, not pass judgment, not try to fix things for you, nor say things that seem disrespectful or insulting. Our children want the same. Therefore, whenever your child comes up to you after they have done something wrong, don't turn them down by yelling or humiliating them. Would you have liked it if someone did the same to you? Treat others how you would want to be treated.

See Things from Their Perspective

If your children come up to you for something, it means they want to be heard and guided. This isn't the time to scold or ground them. You need to take their feelings into account and try to understand why they did what they did. When children don't know how to deal with big emotions, say jealousy, envy, or pain, they experiment with things to find relief. So if your child tore his favorite shirt into pieces because everyone at school laughed at him for wearing it, don't scold them for it. Try to be supportive and see things from their perspective. Let them know that you understand how they must have felt and that you understand why they did what they did. Sometimes, they only need that.

Ask, Don't Presume

We all give away some non-verbal cues to let the other person know how we are feeling. When we are angry, we have a disgruntled look on our faces, when we are sad, our eyes water, when we are in pain, we make sounds like "ouch," or "oh." These are all non-verbal cues that children also give to let others know that they are struggling. Sometimes we misinterpret these cues. It is always wise to be on the safe side and be sure of what your child is going through and what they need. Let them explain things themselves instead of assuming things on your own and making things worse.

Validate Their Feelings

When we empathize with children, we normalize the emotions they feel. We may have our own opinions, and may not agree with the way they figure things out; letting them go with their plans and not intervening takes courage. That is what we want to teach our children too. As a parent, you have to know that even when they are overreacting or taking a wrong turn, you encourage them to go forward with it. Their feelings are important and if they feel strongly about something, you have to support them.

Don't Judge

A reaction is a natural response to an action. If we are being yelled at or receiving some harsh words, we are bound to react. However, when we choose to respond with empathy and not let our emotions take over, we let our children know that reactions don't always have to come first. We show them that patience and thinking rationally are more important. This is only possible when you stop for a minute, and keep from judging your child for an outburst or tantrum. You allow them to vent their frustration without reacting in the same manner, choosing instead to respond with compassion.

Introduce "I" Statements

Statements that begin with "you" feel defensive and harsh. Statements that begin with "I" seem less harmful and direct. I statements can start a conversation without starting the blame game.

For instance, you may want to burst out at them with statements like, "You are too careless. You never pay attention to anything I say." However, when you substitute something like this, "I feel disrespected when you act carelessly, ignoring the things I tell you to do," you leave some room for a decent conversation to happen, as this approach is less threatening. There is a better chance that the child will be willing to hear more about what you have to say instead of shutting you out emotionally because they feel disrespected or humiliated.

Don't Try to Fix Things

As a parent, we understand that you don't want to see your child get hurt or make decisions that are going to end in pain and suffering. However, one of the most crucial rules of being empathetic is to not try to fix things. Going into let-me-fix-this-for-you mode may seem right, but it doesn't always mean your child will be happy. Sometimes, they just need someone to vent their problems too. They just want to feel lighter and better. Only offer help or advice if they ask for it specifically.

Be an Active Listener

Being empathetic requires active listening. Active listening means that you give the speaker your undivided attention, full concentration, and read their mind. It involves paying attention to not just their spoken words but also their gestures, body movements, tone, and facial expressions. You have to listen not just to what they are saying but also to what they aren't saying. When we listen actively to our children, we make them feel truly heard. It makes the speaker feel respected and shows that they are valued.

Practices that allow us to develop and show empathy are of great value. We must, as parents, teach these to our kids too. Since they are known to be great imitators and look up to us, we are the best chance at helping them develop compassion for others and respect for themselves. So let's do it right and raise them as compassionate, kind, and well-behaved kids.

Chapter 5: Parenting Skill #3: Offer Them Choices

To make good and sound decisions, we need both practice and failure. We need to know what we did wrong the first time to be able to avoid it in the future. More practice also sharpens our minds and gets us thinking of new, more efficient ways to do things. It is a necessary skill to have. Another way to make better decisions is with choices. When we have more than one thing to choose from, it urges us to think sensibly and pick the one with greater benefits. Sometimes, those benefits come in the form of reduced time, less effort, fewer steps, and greater profits. Choices help us differentiate between the good and the bad and also between rewards and consequences. If we want our children to make better decisions and learn to problem-solve themselves, we have to give them several options to choose from.

In this chapter, we look at how offering kids with choices helps build their confidence and self-worth as they not only feel valued but also validated. In the first part, we talk about a particular connection between choices and behavior—if there is any; and in the second part, discuss scenarios where giving choices to our children makes them better at decision-making and improves their behavior.

How Having Choices can Minimize Misbehavior

Being a parent with a busy schedule, having a pre-planned routine offers peace of mind. With a plan in the process, we make decisions for our children and expect to see them follow through. However, this isn't always in their best interest as it limits their ability to think freely and become self-reliant. We want them to grow up confident and handle their affairs themselves. That includes making as many as a hundred decisions per day or more. When decisions are made for them instead of with them, they feel less empowered. Conversely, having choices can go a long way. You can always start with simpler choices like what they would like to do, take a bath or a nap, eat a fruit or a veggie, do their homework before playtime or after it, etc.

The goal is to let them think rationally and choose wisely after pondering over the pros and cons of each choice. There are multiple benefits to giving them choices.

Prevents Temper Tantrums

What are most of the temper tantrums about? They are about gaining more control over their lives and activities. Your kid isn't deliberately trying to be hard, they just want a sense of control. When was the last power struggle you had with your kid? Was it over applying peanut butter before jam on a peanut butter and jam sandwich or was it because you poured their milk for them when they wanted to do it themselves? Most tantrums happen over stupid events, but the reasons they happen aren't stupid. Children need a bigger say in the matter that concerns them. When offered choices, they feel more in control and special. They feel that their decision matters, and that changes the whole game. If you are trying to minimize outbursts, giving options is a good start.

Enhances Problem-Solving Skills

Not all decisions taken by your child will have a fruitful or rewarding outcome. Some of their choices might even make them suffer, such as choosing to eat out instead of having something healthy, which can lead to digestive problems. However, since they made that choice, they have to deal with the consequences too. This type of parenting not only teaches them about responsibility but also encourages them to find solutions once things have gone haywire. This means that it can force them to change their current state and seek means that will bring relief and happiness. This is where problem-solving comes in. The next time they are given the same options to choose from, they are going to choose the one with a positive reward. Meaning, they may choose to eat healthily.

Builds Their Confidence

When allowed to make decisions for themselves, children feel confident. When they decide something and it ends well, they feel proud of themselves and elevated. To encourage the habit, start with simple choices to get their morale high, then let them have a say in bigger matters, for example, as to how they would like to spend their free time, or what they would like to wear or eat.

Cultivates a Sense of Worth

One of the most neglected areas of parenting is making your kids feel valued. In reality, kids are more perceptive and creative than adults. Thus, it is wrong to assume that they won't make good choices for themselves. When we offer them choices, we are telling them that we acknowledge their wisdom and knowledge. This can improve their self-worth, and they will be less likely to misbehave as doing so would mean losing the opportunity to have a choice.

Teaches Accountability

When children make their own decisions, they have no one to blame but themselves when things go wrong. This teaches them about accountability and how to own up to their blunders, and face the consequences of their actions. Additionally, offering them choices teaches them to act responsibly: they need to control their impulses and think logically in order to make choices that don't have bad consequences. This also boosts their cognitive development.

Smart Ways to Give Your Kids Choices

Depending on your parenting style, there are various ways to offer your kids choices. The earlier we encourage them to make sensible decisions based on smart choices, the sooner they will learn to be independent. Before you know it, they will have no trouble relying on their sound judgment.

Here's how you can make them ready for the world out there and promote confidence and rational thinking.

Let Them Choose Which One

This is one of the smartest ways to get them to do things. You simply have to ask them to pick one of two or more choices and let them have the final say. When given the choice between things like reading or doing math, cleaning the windows or helping set the table, putting the dishes in the dishwasher or folding the laundry, etc., whichever choice they pick, they will at least have to do one of the two things.

Give Them the Option to Choose Their Clothes

Kids, when growing up, want to play by their own rules. They are seeking a new identity for themselves. Dressing a certain way is usually one of the many things that allow them to express themselves as unique individuals (Rasicot, 2019). If they are nerdy and shy, they may not want to dress up like their peers. Let them choose as long as it isn't too provocative, statement-making, or questionable. As long as they look decent and well-dressed, don't try to force your opinions on them. This isn't the battle you need to pick, as it will go on forever. Let them decide how they wish to portray themselves.

Give Them the Choice to Decide When They Want to do Something

Again, being too opinionated or strict with the rules can promote misbehavior. Since the goal is to minimize it, ask them if they would like to do something right now or at a later time. For example, you can ask them if they would like to change into their nightdress now or after five minutes. If you notice carefully, it still implies that the action has to be taken. It just leaves them with the choice to decide when they want to do it. Chances are, they are going to pick later, but that should work for you too, as long as they stick to their promise.

Give Them Choices Between Foods

Their health is a prime concern. You want to feed them with the best, but that isn't always possible. However, with choices, you can let them have their way as well as feed them something nutritious and healthy. Choices between different types of foods, like between different vegetables or breakfast items, can also minimize tantrums. You don't have to cook them exactly what they want, rather, ask them to choose between the two things you are ready to prepare. For instance, if there is rice and soup available for dinner, you can ask them to pick one. Or you can ask them to choose between a buttered or toasted bread, a bowl of salad or beans, etc.

Let Them Choose an Activity

Let them have a say in what they want to do with their free time. Of course, as a parent, you would want them to do something productive or imagination-building, but let them decide what they want to do. You can always suggest things like painting or reading, playing basketball or making a puzzle. You can even direct their choices by being more specific, like asking whether they would like to play a monopoly or another board game. If they are younger, you can ask them to decide if they would like to walk to the park or ride in the stroller. When they feel more in control, they act out less.

Chapter 6: Parenting Skill #4: Stop Saying No

G o back to when you were a kid. Can you recall the times you were told no? How did that make you feel? Did it not feel disheartening and demotivating? Now think about how your child must feel when you do the same? The word "no" is mostly the first-word children pick up when they start speaking. It isn't because it is simple and has only one syllable. It is because it is one of the most repeated words they hear. Some evidence suggests that a one-year-old hears the word "no" at least 400 times per day (Aria, 2008). Hearing no can be stressful for both the parent and the child. When parents say no to their children, they know they are discouraging them from things they are interested in or want to do. When children hear the word no, it affects their confidence and self-esteem. They feel devalued and unimportant. They also feel neglected, and start to believe that their parents aren't interested in them.

Thus to reduce stress, strengthen the bond between a parent and a child, a positive environment is essential. A positive environment is one where the child hears less of the word no and more of the word yes.

Children are born with an inquisitive and curious nature. They want to discover new things, gain more experience, and safely explore their surroundings. When we repeatedly put them down by saying "no," we unintentionally kill their natural curiosity. We take away their confidence and make them feel worthless. As they grow older, they become more independent and want to push limits. However, when parents bind them with the burden of the word "no," they may feel suffocated. They may also begin to see their parents as their enemies and become distant.

The Importance of Creating a YES Environment

Just to be clear, a Yes environment doesn't mean that we never use the word no in front of our children. We still have to for safety and health reasons. However, what's unique about a Yes environment is that we don't limit or neglect exploration. We promote it. We use the term, Yes to address behavioral concerns. We use it to model good behavior and to fortify communication and interaction. We don't want children to hide things from us or keep secrets. We don't let them go behind our backs and do things we wouldn't approve of. We want them to be more open with us and see us as their mentor and friend. This is only possible if we provide them with opportunities that promote happiness and confidence in them, not diminish it. When we say yes to a child, not only do we boost their confidence, but we also empower them to be more comfortable expressing themselves. Ask yourself this: if you keep saying no to your child repeatedly, do you think they will continue to come up to you, continue to inquire? Saying yes also shows our appreciation for the ideas that take birth in their heads. When we allow them to do the things they want to do, we show them that we are interested in their interests and happy in their happiness.

A Yes environment also prevents misbehavior as we willingly allow the child to have what they want. Thus power struggles and temper tantrums are minimized. But it all seems rather theoretical. Is it practical, and can we break the habit of saying no?

Cultivating a YES Environment— The How-to

There are many ways to create a Yes environment. However, the biggest challenge isn't creating a Yes environment, it's turning a toxic and strict environment of No into Yes. The reason many parents find it difficult is because we are so used to the term no. In many cases, it comes out as a natural response. That is the habit we need to kill as we know how damaging the word no can be to their self-respect and confidence. To get you on the right track, here are a few examples and strategies to create a more positive and encouraging environment for your children.

Give Your No A Valid Reason

Children are inquisitive. They want to know the science behind things. They want to know the *whys*. Therefore, at times, when they misbehave, like pull your hair or hit you, instead of just screaming "no," tell them why you are saying it. Tell them that pulling your hair or hitting you causes pain. Tell them that you feel hurt when they do it and see if they stop doing it or not. This is a more positive and calm way to handle things without going into a full power-struggle mode. It also tells them that you aren't shouting at them, but objecting to the behavior they depicted. It can also build empathy in them as they wouldn't want to intentionally hurt you.

Let Them Be Kids

They are going to be chaotic. They will run to your dresser to apply your makeup, get in kitchen cabinets to take out the pots and pans, open the fridge to find themselves something to eat or drink, etc. How many times are you going to stop them? Besides, you can't always be running after them, saving them from trouble. You have to give them independence and control. You have to empower them to be able to initiate things on their own. When you continuously reject their ideas and choices, and scream at them for things that count as a mere exploration on their part, you undermine their confidence and self-worth. A yes environment doesn't have to be this toxic. To create one, be proactive. If they have the habit of sneaking into the cabinets, place things that aren't costly or are of no interest. For instance, there is less chance that a child would be interested in playing with rags and mops. If they are after your makeup, put stuff that you don't use or wouldn't mind getting broken or misused. That way, you won't have to say no to them and be able to create a more inspiring and positive environment.

Saying Yes can Increase Happiness

The habit of saying "no" is too common and natural that sometimes we say no without even giving a child's request any thought. How many times did you say no to playing hide and seek because you just didn't have the strength to? How many times did you say no to a fun activity because you were worried about the potential mess it would lead to? How many times did you say no when your child wanted to go to the park but you didn't want to? We bet a lot of times!

However, if you want to create a Yes environment, know that you will have to put their demands first. As the goal is to minimize bad behavior using positive disciplining, let them do the things they want to as long as they are within the limits set by you. Why? It is because you are not only going to make them happy but also feel happy yourself. Chances are you will have more fun in the park than you expected if you give in to their request to go there. Not to mention, giving in to their little wishes can strengthen the bond between you two.

Save your Noes

The word "no" must have effectiveness and significance. When you say it too often or over everything, it loses that importance. It should be used sparingly and only for rather serious things. This will teach them to respect a no, and they will become more obedient when it is used. When we save the word for important occasions, it keeps it meaningful like a full and final order. There is no room for argument left after a sparsely used no.

Get Organized and Smart

Creating a Yes environment will become impossible if there are more than 100 different toys to choose from. Go Marie Kondo and limit the choices they have. Keep in mind that the more items there are, the bigger the tantrum and outburst will be when they are told to clean up after playing. Worst still, you may have to clean up afterward in case the child feels sleepy or has moved on to another activity. From the start, let them have a few things to play with instead of saying yes to taking out every last toy from the toy basket.

The more interested we are in the things they do and the more willing we are to cultivate a favorable and encouraging environment for them, the more they will behave. If we look at the strategies mentioned above, they should help you get started and offer them an environment that prevents the need for misbehavior altogether.

Chapter 7: Parenting Skill #5: Redirect, Redirect, Redirect

R edirection or distraction are great disciplining techniques intended to modify a child's bad behavior and prevent it from happening again. Redirection is the opposite of punishment. It involves relocation or engagement in another activity—something more healthy, safe, and positive. Redirection prevents the outburst of negative emotions and saves the parents from having to say "no" repeatedly to their children. We already talked about the dangers of saying the word "no" in the last chapter, which is why we need to focus more on how to distract them to safety without causing a scene. Psychologists like J. Burton Banks believes strongly in the redirection approaches. In one of his books coauthored by two others, he suggests that redirection can help children modify their behaviors from being inappropriate to appropriate (Esther Yoder Strahan et al., 2010).

How do Diversions Work?

Diversions, distractions or redirection works simply. We all know that children have a short attention span when they are young. They are also quick to become angry and frustrated which usually ends with a temper tantrum or an outburst of crying. Using their short attention span, we remove them from the activity they are engaged in and onto another without them fussing. For example, if they have mistakenly taken up a knife in their hands and are running around the house pointing it at everyone, there are two ways to handle it. Either you run after them, take it from them and scold them for being careless, or you distract them with something as equally interesting as the knife and hope that they give up the knife on their own in the pursuit of the other thing. For instance, you can take up a spoon, show it off a little, talk about how it is better and more useful than the knife, and make them want to give up the knife for the spoon.

There are many benefits of redirection. For example, it can ease physical pain. With our brain's limited ability to focus, it is hard for us to take note of all the things happening around us at once. We need to be wise about what we choose to focus on and why. As limiting as this sounds, we can use it to our advantage. We can use it to distract ourselves from pain and discomfort. The same thing applies to kids. If they have just fallen flat on their face and you know they are about to cry any second, use those few seconds to distract them from the pain and sudden shock to something more pleasant and rewarding. Similarly, you can use the same technique when you take them to the doctor for vaccination shots, and turn their negative experience into a positive one by distracting them to focus on something other than the needle piercing their skin.

But most importantly, for younger children, it can prevent misbehavior from escalating. The minute we see our kids getting out of control or becoming aggressive or frustrated, we know what's about to come next. By pulling their attention elsewhere, we can nip the outburst right in the bud before it even begins. It can help parents avoid situations that soon become out of their control and lead to embarrassment, such as when they are in a grocery store and their kids and want something they can't have. Diversions, in such a case, can be considered a preventive measure.

Another benefit of distractions is that it can also prevent children from engaging in dangerous behavior. Ask yourself this, have you never caught them trying to do something that can result in injury? Maybe they tried to get onto the stool by themselves, tried to dig their hands in the cookie jar over the shelf, went near a socket with a fork in their hands, or decided to act like an adult and take the stairs by themselves when they have just started walking. We don't need much imagination to think about how they could have ended up with injuries and trauma. In those cases, where your instinct is to plain-out say "no" or scare them into not trying such things on their own, distractions can be a life-saver.

Strategies to Redirect Negative Behaviors

How do we go about diverting their attention to something else? Is it as simple as relocating them from the place or taking whatever they have their hands and giving them something else? Yes, and no.

As simple as it sounds, you have to be rather strategic with it. If they are on to it and realize what you are up to, all hell will break loose. So what are these strategies that will help you redirect negative or unsafe behaviors? Take a look!

Make Requests Less Threatening

There should be a way of saying things. Your statements about negative behavior shouldn't be harsh or too direct or else children may become defensive. They need to be reminded of the negative behavior subtly. For example, if they are running into the house, don't yell at them to stop running. Instead, tell them that they can hurt themselves if they keep running so fast indoors.

Offer Substitutions

If you notice a fight is about to break out between your child and their friend because they want the same toy, act fast. Offer them an equally interesting substitution and try to convince them of why it is better than the other toy. Remember the example where we talked about a child running with a knife in their hands? When you try to offer them a spoon, you have to convince them that it is better than the knife so that they decide to give it up on their own without you needing to snatch it from them. When situations are handled strategically like this, it prevents misbehavior from happening.

Relocate Them

We have mentioned relocation several times in the chapter as it seems to be a fool-proof strategy for redirection, but it doesn't always guarantee the desired outcomes—unless you are tactical about it. For example, imagine you take your child to the park. Unlike other kids that are taking the stairs to climb the slide, your child is repeatedly trying to come up with the slide and block other children's way. There are two things you can do here. You can either explain to them the right way to go or you can redirect them into going to another swing or area of the playground. The first method, although effective, doesn't always stop the negative behavior. The second, however, does because the child relocates themselves willingly without throwing a tantrum.

Chapter 8: Parenting Skill #6: Treat Every Mistake as a Learning Opportunity

I f your child's first thought after they have done something wrong is "Mom's gonna kill me," instead of, "I need to call mom," you aren't parenting right. Children shouldn't have to hide or be in fear of being caught and punished by their parents. They should see parents as mentors and coaches who don't scold them for mistakes, but help them view challenges as lessons.

It has become a norm that we try to keep our children away from all things we think are harmful for them. Although sensible and rather proactive, it sometimes limits their potential and development of skills. When they are repeatedly inhibited from something, they start fearing it. They avoid making mistakes but it also stops them from learning and experiencing different outcomes and emotions.

As parents, we have to prepare them for the unknown. We have to let them make mistakes so that they learn how to avoid making them in the future, and when they inevitably do, they know how to deal with the consequences and regulate their emotions.

The Upside of Letting Children Make Mistakes

It is scary, from a parent's perspective, to allow children to make mistakes. However, if we continue to shield them from the realities of life, they will never learn to stand tall and high in front of challenges. They will always seek shelter behind their parents' backs which isn't the best way to live. Children must be taught to become resilient from an early age. They must be taught to acknowledge their mistakes, accept them and look for ways to get past them. They should know how cruel the world can be, but at the same time, not fear it. They shouldn't panic at the thought of failing, and shouldn't give up without trying. Some of the most important benefits of making mistakes are below.

Children Learn about Resilience

Resilience is the ability to recover from a setback. This is only possible when there is a failure or setback to begin with. As we all know, it is only when we go through some trauma that we are able to know how it feels. Children need to experience the same thing to build resilience. Besides, when they make a mistake, it allows them to look for the reasons why things went sideways. When they think instead of give up, they are also less prone to throw temper tantrums or blame others. Instead, they look for ways to spring back into action.

Becoming resilient also helps them take on new initiatives with confidence. This enables them to experience new things.

Children Learn About Responsibility

When children make mistakes, they are able to see the consequences of their action in reality. This helps them take up the responsibility for their mistakes and encourages them to become more vigilant and smart the next time. For instance, if a child fails in an exam because they didn't study well, they will act more responsibly the next time because the consequences of failing aren't fruitful. Having developed this sense of responsibility is a sign of maturity. If they aren't responsible, it means that they are careless, lazy, and give excuses for when they fail instead of working to prevent them from happening again.

Children Learn About Decision-Making Skills

When we let children make mistakes, it also gets them thinking of the decisions they made that led to the failure. They start thinking about what they could have done differently and what they will do differently the next time. They also learn about how important good decision-making is and what impact it can have on the outcome. As they keep on making mistakes and reviewing the things they did wrong, their decision-making skills improve. This allows them to gain wisdom from their failures and mistakes, and to improve their behavior. This is classic positive disciplining in action because we no longer hold our children back or dictate the steps that lead to guaranteed success. We let them figure it out on their own and take the back seat. When this happens, parents can gradually pull themselves back from the equation and trust their child's ability to manage things without parental supervision. When kids sense that, they feel more independent and self-reliant.

How to Encourage Children to Learn from their Mistakes

Now that we have allowed them to be kids, have fun, taste wins and failures, how do we encourage them to get over their failures and learn from their mistakes? How can we teach them to not lose heart or their will to keep going when they have committed a blunder? How can we teach them to see failures as opportunities to grow?

Below are a few strategies to help them learn from their blunders and build resilience to move past them.

Don't Rescue Them

Every parent's first instinct is to run to their children and prevent them from making a mistake. If the mistakes have already been made, the instinct is to make amends. For instance, if they spilled their juice on the floor, we instantly run towards them to remove them from the place, get a towel and start cleaning it. It is hard to leave them on their own, relying on their undeveloped judgment. When we allow them to deal with the natural consequences, we are preparing them to deal with the fall-outs in future.

Let Them Try

Let them have some time to do things their way. They may take some time to figure out how to tie their shoes or how to use a fork, but let them. Don't try to overtake and do things for them. Encourage them to try once before offering help. This will jump-start the process of learning. Soon they will feel fearless when trying new things and taking on new challenges. Letting them sense independence, and later, victory or failure, makes them feel more confident and self-sufficient.

Be a Good Example

Another smart way to encourage trying new experiences and not fearing making mistakes is to be an example they can relate with. Talk about your mistakes in the past, the consequences you had to face and how you overcame them. Emphasize how they taught you valuable lessons that helped you succeed. They are likely to listen to your stories and take note because they trust you the most. They will comprehend that even you, an adult, can make mistakes and move past them.

Praise Them when They Admit Mistakes

This is one of the most important and hardest things for a child—acknowledging that they had been wrong and blaming themselves. When they come to you and accept that they had been wrong about something, use that moment not to yell at them, but praise them for having the confidence to come clean about it. This will not only prevent secrecy when they grow older but also make them less afraid of making mistakes in the future. When we sympathize with our kids over their mistakes, they feel valued and cared for.

Look For Teachable Moments

There will be times when you catch them making a mistake. For example, you notice they aren't doing the calculations right, or putting their food plate on the edge of the table. Instead of pointing it out harshly in a disrespecting tone, use that moment to teach them the right way to do things. This has to happen in a polite and subtle manner where they don't feel scolded or disciplined.

Chapter 9: Parenting Skill #7: Be Consistent with Expectations

S etting limits can be rather challenging for parents. But what if we told you that there is a way where you wouldn't need to? Would you be interested? The majority of parents would agree that the word "no" has been the most frequently used word with their kids. They have told them "no" repeatedly, and in most cases, it hasn't helped improve behavioral problems. But the reason these behavioral issues arise is that children don't know what is expected of them. For instance, how would they know to respect their elders when you haven't told them to? However, if you had told them about it and made your expectations clear from day one, there would have been less conflict.

Some parents make rules as they go along. It works fine for older kids but young kids need structure. They need to know what is expected of them *before* (Postal, 2011). The purpose is, of course, to limit misbehavior and help parents set healthy boundaries and limits without being nagged at or questioned. Clear expectations set the foundations right. They assist in building a child's patience, resourcefulness, self-discipline, problem-solving skill, and responsibility.

Why Communicating Clear Expectations is a Necessity

If only our children came with a clear instruction manual or user-friendly guide on how to parent them, wouldn't that have made life much easier? The manual would have had a checklist of the duties parents would have to do to raise a well-manned, disciplined, and happy child.

Since there isn't one, we have to find other means to ensure that we raise them to become successful, happy, and resilient.

It all starts with how we want to raise them and what we expect from them in return. Having clear expectations from the beginning helps navigate the road to success. Since they have a short attention span, they often forget instructions or fail to hear them in the first place. This happens more so when we don't set the right expectations. Children misbehave when they don't know how to behave otherwise. A lack of expectations not only undermines their performance but also affects the result. It also hampers with their engagement and focus. Unclear expectations can lead to confusion and pave the way for arguments and conflicts. It can also cause children to get frustrated when scolded for something they weren't taught about before.

How to Set Clear Expectations

We now know that children do well when they know what is expected of them. It offers them the structure they need to do things right. When it comes to setting expectations to promote good behavior, the first and most important step is to give instructions. You also have to keep them short and direct so that there is no room left for the confusion. Furthermore, a lot of times, we give more than one instruction at the same time, overwhelming them.

Picture this: you just came back from outside and you tell your kid the following: Hang your coat on the coat hanger and take off your shoes before coming inside. Then go to your room to change and then brush your teeth before getting into bed. It may seem simple and direct to you, but for a child with limited vocabulary and a short attention span, you have just given them a list of things they need to do in a particular order. Chances are, they might forget a few, or get the order wrong. So, whose fault is it?

Here are other ways to set good expectations.

Make Expectations Realistic

Of course, as parents, we want our children to attempt challenges with confidence and progress forward. However, goals that are far from their reach can become a hurdle. Taking on too big a task may even trigger misbehavior. Your goal should be to encourage them to try new things and take initiatives. The best way to do so is by letting them focus on small, realistic, and achievable milestones. If the expectations are big or lengthy, you can always break them down into several goals. That way, your child will have a few accomplishments to celebrate along the way and feel more empowered and motivated.

Provide Structure

When things follow a set routine and structure, it creates rhythm in the room. Everyone knows what is expected of them and thus, peace becomes a real thing. Putting routines for children allows them to develop good habits when they follow them. For example, if they know what comes next, like play-time after completing homework, then dinner and then bedtime routine, they will be less likely to act out and argue. This prevents negative behaviors from taking over, all thanks to clear expectations.

Review and Reward

Rewards play a key role in the management of child behavior. We are all tempted to give our best when we are excited about the result. It also prevents procrastination and gets things done promptly. But before the rewards comes a review of the progress. The only way kids are going to follow through with the set expectations is if they are being held accountable to them. This requires that we keep a check on them at all times to ensure they are adhering to the rules properly. Reviewing progress can also help parents identify any shortcomings and help their children accordingly. Therefore, when setting expectations, don't leave things to your child entirely, offer support and counseling from time to time to know they are alright and progressing well.

Make Chore Charts

Chore charts are simple and effective. They are the best way to outline the behaviors and actions you want your child to exhibit. Many smart parents use chore charts to pre-plan the activities for the day so that things get done in an orderly and less fussy manner. Your chore chart can include things like cleaning their room, setting their bag, putting out the dress for school, brushing teeth before going to bed, putting dirty clothes in the laundry basket, etc. This also lays out a clear plan for them to follow.

So we now know how crucial a role setting expectations plays in the raising of disciplined and self-reliant kids. We also know that giving them a heads-up will only make things easier for us, so why not start to pre-plan?

Conclusion

The day we become parents, so many things change. For starters, our mindset changes altogether. Before their birth, we were most concerned about their wellbeing and health; and then when they were born, we became more concerned about their needs; and then gradually, when they started crawling and running, we became worried about their safety. When they became teenagers, we became worried about their emotional needs. We have been worried for so many years and all for nothing. Had we chosen the right parenting style from the start, we would have had less burden to carry. If we had chosen to take up positive disciplining, we would have easily avoided conflicts, prevented arguments from escalating, and worried less about their mental and emotional needs. Had we chosen to apply the principles of positive parenting, we would have avoided most of the misbehavior from becoming a habit and stressing us out.

Parenting is hard—true. But we make it harder by doing the wrong things. We don't set healthy boundaries from the beginning which makes them bold enough to demand things rather than ask for them. We don't appreciate or validate their opinions enough which leads to poor self-esteem and poor confidence. We don't focus on developing habits like empathy, resilience, and kindness, which makes them aggressive and unable to regulate their emotions.

Thus, a part of the fault is ours. If they misbehave, we have allowed them to. If they don't listen to us, maybe it is because we aren't telling them the things they would be interested in hearing. If they disobey and act out, maybe we are not focusing on their true needs.

But before you go into guilt-mode, there is still time. Habits like empathy, honesty, resilience, and transparency can be taught at every age. We just need to equip ourselves with the right techniques and resources. As you may have noted, we highlighted various strategies to adopt this modern-day and effective parenting style. We gave you the means to deploy these techniques and prepare your children for the outside world. We laid out the methods to help strengthen the bond and improve family communication.

We hope this brief guide has helped you get started on the right foot and change the way you parent. Discipline doesn't have to mean punishment. You can use the 7 vital parenting skills instead to teach them discipline and model good behavior.

References

Aria, B. (2008, January 14). How to Say No (Without Saying No). Redbook. https://www.redbookmag.com/life/mom-kids/advice/a2560/how-to-say-no/#:~:text=The%20average%20toddler%20hears%20the

Becker, N. (2019). Positive Discipline□: 2 in 1: how to handle conflicts, eliminate tantrums, and raise confident children. Natasha Becker.

Benefits of Positive Parenting. (2019, January 21). Royal St. George's College. https://www.rsgc.on.ca/news-detail?pk=998751&fromId=248258

Brehse, T. (2016, August 31). The Importance of Setting Clear Expectations for Your Team. Ignite Spot. http://blog.ignitespot.com/the-importance-of-setting-clear-expectations-for-your-team

Brill, A. (2012, July 9). Creating a Yes Environment. Positive Parenting Connection. https://www.positiveparentingconnection.net/creating-a-yes-environment/

Building Trust through Communication with Teens. (2013, July 24). Secureteen.Com. https://www.secureteen.com/parenting-style/building-trust-through-communication-with-teens/

Caroll, A. (2019, September 5). 4 Powerful Benefits of Letting Your Child Make Mistakes. Simply Family Magazine. https://simplyfamilymagazine.com/4-powerful-benefits-of-letting-your-child-make-mistakes

Couttouw, S. (2017, May 16). Why Children Need Empathy. I Heart Connection. http://iheartconnection.com/children-need-empathy/#:~:text=Empathy%20helps%20a%20child%20regulate

Dallaire, D. H., Pineda, A. Q., Cole, D. A., Ciesla, J. A., Jacquez, F., LaGrange, B., & Bruce, A. E. (2006). Relation of Positive and Negative Parenting to Children's Depressive Symptoms. Journal of Clinical Child & Adolescent Psychology, 35(2), 313–322. https://doi.org/10.1207/s15374424jccp3502_15

Durr, J. (2012, December 29). How to Set Clear Expectations for Kids. Meaningful Mama. https://meaningfulmama.com/day-362-make-expectations-clear.html

Durrant, J., & Ensom, R. (2012). Physical punishment of children: lessons from 20 years of research. Canadian Medical Association Journal, 184(12), 1373–1377. https://doi.org/10.1503/cmaj.101314

Esther Yoder Strahan, Dixon, W. E., & J Burton Banks. (2010). Parenting with reason☐: evidence-based approaches to parenting dilemmas. Wiley.

Farnham, K. (2018, December 5). Strategies Used to Redirect Child Behavior. Hello Motherhood. https://www.hellomotherhood.com/strategies-used-to-redirect-child-behavior-5750989.html

Henry, C. S., Sager, D. W., & Plunkett, S. W. (1996). Adolescents' Perceptions of Family System Characteristics, Parent-Adolescent Dyadic Behaviors, Adolescent Qualities, and Adolescent Empathy. Family Relations, 45(3), 283. https://doi.org/10.2307/585500

Learning from Mistakes: The Upside. (n.d.). The Center for Parenting Education. Retrieved June 14, 2020, from https://centerforparentingeducation.org/library-of-articles/self-esteem/learn-from-mistakes/

Learning from Mistakes: Why We Need to Let
      Children Fail. (2019). Bright Horizons.
      https://www.brighthorizons.com/family-
      resources/the-importance-of-mistakes-
      helping-children-learn-from-failure

Mischel, W., Ebbesen, E. B., & Raskoff Zeiss, A.
      (1972). Cognitive and attentional mechanisms
      in delay of gratification. Journal of
      Personality and Social Psychology, 21(2),
      204–218. https://doi.org/10.1037/h0032198

Morin, Amanda. (n.d.). 9 Ways to Show Empathy
      When Your Child Is Struggling. Understood.
      Retrieved June 15, 2020, from
      https://www.understood.org/en/learning-
      thinking-differences/understanding-childs-
      challenges/talking-with-your-child/9-ways-
      to-show-empathy-when-your-child-is-
      struggling

Morin, A. (2019, August 15). 10 Fun Ways to Help
      Your Child Gain Better Impulse Control.
      Verywell Family.
      https://www.verywellfamily.com/ways-to-
      teach-children-impulse-control-1095035

Morin, Amy. (2019a, June 28). How Can Parents
      Prevent Behavior Problems in Their
      Children? Verywell Family.
      https://www.verywellfamily.com/ways-
      prevent-behavior-problems-before-start-
      1094761

Morin, Amy. (2019b, September 12). 10 Surprising Reasons Why Kids Misbehave (And How to Respond). Verywell Family. https://www.verywellfamily.com/surprising-reasons-why-kids-misbehave-1094946

Nelson, J. (2018, November 21). About Positive Discipline. Positive Discipline. https://www.positivediscipline.com/about-positive-discipline

Ohene, S.-A., Ireland, M., McNeely, C., & Borowsky, I. W. (2006). Parental Expectations, Physical Punishment, and Violence Among Adolescents Who Score Positive on a Psychosocial Screening Test in Primary Care. PEDIATRICS, 117(2), 441–447. https://doi.org/10.1542/peds.2005-0421

Postal, K. (2011, November 11). How Structure Improves Your Child's Brain. Psychology Today. https://www.psychologytoday.com/us/blog/think-better/201111/how-structure-improves-your-childs-brain

Rasicot, J. (2019, March 19). Why Do Teen Girls Dress the Way They Do? Bethesda Magazine. https://bethesdamagazine.com/bethesda-magazine/november-december-2008/why-do-teen-girls-dress-the-way-they-do-2/

Shealer, K. (2016, December 2). 4 tips for cultivating a "yes environment." APtly Said. https://attachmentparenting.org/blog/2016/12/02/4-tips-for-cultivating-a-yes-environment/

Smith, A. B. (2006). The State of Research on the Effects of Physical Punishment. Social Policy Journal of New Zealand, 27.

Stasney, S. (2019, May 31). 10 Smart Ways to Give Your Child Choices and The Benefits. This-n-That Parenting. https://www.thisnthatparenting.com/10-smart-ways-to-give-your-child-choices-and-the-benefits/

Ticktin, D. A. (2018, November 7). Foster creativity. Motherly. https://www.mother.ly/child/benefits-of-giving-child-choices/foster-creativity

Weingarten, K. (2014, December 8). 8 Positive Discipline Techniques Every Parent Should Know. A Fine Parent. https://afineparent.com/be-positive/positive-discipline-techniques.html

Weintraub, S. (1998). The hidden intelligence□: innovation through intuition. Butterworth-Heinemann.

Why Do Children Misbehave? (Better Kid Care).
    (n.d.). Better Kid Care (Penn State
    Extension). Retrieved June 15, 2020, from
    https://extension.psu.edu/programs/betterki
    dcare/parents-families/families-count/why-
    do-children-misbehave

Book Description

Does he act mean, rebellious, and undisciplined? Are you getting one-word replies back from him? Do you wish you were closer to him, like old times?

Teenage boys have minds of their own. They also have mood swings; one day he'll be talkative and helpful, and the next he'll be gloomy, secretive, and shallow.

With so many hormonal changes happening inside them, they are as confused as you are. Parents have it a little rough, because they've been used to looking after their boy... and then suddenly, he doesn't need them anymore. Without proper knowledge on how to raise this almost-stranger living in your house, who's been eating like a monster and staying locked in his room all day, it can be hard to know how to raise them into being responsible, empathetic, respectful, and disciplined adults.

In this brief, groundbreaking guide, Frank Dixon discusses the seven parental skills he finds most effective in raising, understanding, and communicating with teenage boys. With his profound knowledge and expertise in the area, he offers readers a glimpse into his methodologies in facilitating parents' raising of confident and intelligent boys.

Readers will find that his seven vital parenting skills are backed by science, and that they make a remarkable difference in the lives of both parents and teenagers.

With both wit and passion, Frank spills the beans on what works and what doesn't while guiding parents on how to learn each skill, and later apply it to their own boys.

Trust Frank, and you will not regret it!

7 Vital Skills for Parenting Teen Boys and Communicating with Your Teenage Son

Proven Positive Parenting Tips for Raising Teenage Boys and Preparing Your Teenager for Manhood

Frank Dixon

Introduction

One-word replies, grumbles, grunts, back-talking, lack of discipline, and no respect... wait, is this the diary of a teen boy's parents?

Raising boys is a different ball game, and here's why: unlike girls, boys' mood swings happen rather quickly. One minute they're chilling in the living room, and the next, they're locked in their bedroom. They are inexplicably messier, and they often sleep like logs, eat like the Hulk, and are always in a hurry.

But you're there too, to ensure that they smoothly navigate their way into adulthood. We may not always understand our sons' needs, or what's going in their heads, but that shouldn't stop us from preparing ourselves to understand them better. We must arm ourselves with the right tools to be responsible and admirable parents, so that they follow in our footsteps and not be led astray.

Parents of teenage boys often feel that they don't have the power to steer their child's life in the right direction. The best strategy to combat this is to anticipate the problems before they arise. For starters, we know that as boys reach their teen years, they will go through the many hormonal and bodily changes of puberty. They will be excitable and act a little reckless too at times, but it won't be their fault; their raging hormones compel them to try things they wouldn't otherwise. Thus, parents must keep a vigilant eye on them to ensure they don't get mixed with the wrong crowd, or indulge in self-harming or other dangerous activities.

We have been teenagers once, too; perhaps this is one of the greatest gifts we can offer. We know what it's like to feel so full of energy all the time. We went through the same experiences, and thus, we need to remind them repeatedly that we get it. It is very uncommon for boys to open up with their parents; therefore, we must offer support and a keen ear to lend when they do decide to.

In this guide, we take on the challenge of understanding a teenage boy's mind, and help parents to raise them as confident adults who will enter manhood with improved self-esteem, a disciplined mind, and a self-reliant attitude. We shall look at seven vital parenting techniques and skills that will aid parents in facing the challenges of connecting with their boys.

So, let's dive right in and begin with a basic understanding of what to expect in terms of your boy's cognitive and physical growth as they enter their teen years, and how to brace yourself for the challenges coming ahead.

Chapter 1: Let's Get into the Budding Man's Mind

D uring adolescence, children continue to grow physically, emotionally, and cognitively. Some of the most prominent and differentiable features in the young boy as they make their way towards adulthood are increases in their size, weight, and height. As they hit puberty, their sexual organs become fully functional, their voices become deeper, and they go through many outbursts of hunger and sleep. Like girls, they also want to become more independent and forge their own identities. But since so much is happening at once, it can be stressful for them–especially if they are early bloomers. When no one in their social circle is going through the same changes, it can make them freak out a little about theirs.

But hitting puberty isn't all bad. It's also the time when teenagers learn about responsibility and power. Although most teenagers are stereotyped for their reckless behavior, like trying new drugs, getting drunk, or engaging in unprotected sex, they still are beginning to make sense of the importance of good friendships, career choices, following their passions, etc. They'll start to think about their future, and whether or not they are doing enough to land a decent college or internship.

We shall discuss this, as well as how parents can help teenagers with their moodiness and surliness, but before we do that, let's discuss the many physical, social and cognitive changes they go through.

Physical Changes Teen Boys Go Through

Puberty in boys doesn't always mark the age of adolescence. Some late bloomers hit puberty well after sixteen, or even eighteen. However, the changes that take place in their mind and especially physicality begin to show up a few years after they've entered the teenage years. You can't be certain when puberty is coming, but some of the most noticeable physical changes include:

- **Body hair:** The appearance of body hair, especially pubic hair, is most commonly among the first signs. Hair will usually grow darker and coarser with time and continue to spread around the thighs, underarms, legs, and chest.

- **Enlargement of Genitals:** As they get older, their genitals (such as the scrotum and testes) will start to grow in size.

- **Increase in Body Size**: Adolescent boys will start to build muscle and gain weight. They may feel clumsy at times, as their legs, hands, and arms will grow faster than the rest of their physique.

- **Swelling of the Chest**: Some teenagers also experience swelling around the nipple region. This is due to hormonal changes, and is only a temporary condition.

- **Facial Hair:** Facial hair, especially on the chin, neck, and upper lip, will start to grow in length.

- **Oily Skin:** Although breakouts aren't as common in boys as in girls, some still develop open pores. Due to excessive sweating, their skin could also become oily and cause acne to break out.

- **Deeper Voice**: When boys hit puberty, their voices may get deeper. This is also a temporary condition, and they eventually will find their normal range and pitch.

Cognitive Changes Teen Boys Go Through

Did you know that our brains reach their largest size when we are adolescents?

For boys, the brain becomes its biggest at age fourteen; for girls, this happens around the age of eleven. However, this doesn't indicate or confirm in any way that girls are smarter than boys. There are many other changes we can expect to notice in the brain as boys turn into teenagers:

- **Flexibility in the Brain:** Although the brain reaches its biggest size, it still has lots of elasticity for taking in, processing, and storing new information. This also means that it has the potential to adapt, change, and respond to its environment accordingly.

- **Brain Continues to Mature:** Though the brain may stop growing in size after boys turn fourteen, it doesn't mean that it has matured completely. It is still developing, and does so for some eight to ten years from then.

- **The Prefrontal Area Remains Underdeveloped:** The front part of the brain is called the prefrontal cortex, and it takes the longest to mature. In some, it isn't mature until adulthood. This is important to note because this region of the brain is responsible for logical and rational thinking. Its main job is to plan, prioritize, and control impulses. Thus, teenagers often engage in risky behaviors, as they aren't able to assess the depth of their decisions.

- **The Brain Becomes Stressed:** The brain of a teenager becomes more vulnerable to stress than before. This is true for both girls and boys. Pressure from peers, parents, and online influences are all key factors in contributing to the amount of stress teenagers undergo.

- **Developing Mental Illnesses:** The ongoing changes in your boy's body, mind, and emotions can lead to the development of mental health problems. The more stress a teenager feels, the more anxious or depressed they get.

- **Needing More Sleep:** The quantity of melatonin in the body is higher in teenagers, which makes them want to sleep more. It must also be noted that the production of melatonin starts later in the night in most teenagers, which is why they have the habit of staying up late and then sleeping in late. On the whole, you can expect them to require more sleep.

Social Changes Teen Boys Go Through

Emotional or social changes in boys are often a neglected area. Parents assume that all teenagers misbehave, aren't disciplined, or crave more freedom, when in reality, the situation is often a lot more nuanced. Some of the most common social changes you can expect your boy to go through include:

- **A Need to Show Off:** Teenage boys often like to pretend they're tougher than they really are, and be show-offs. They may tell lies and boast about their sexual experiences or their fitness levels.

- **Giving in to Peer Pressure:** Teenage boys are also quick to give in to peer pressure. This can be linked to their need to act cool, so that others don't find them uninteresting. They will go as far as attempting risky behaviors, like smoking or doing drugs, just because their friends are doing them too.

- **Increase in Aggression and/or Tension:** Increased peer pressure also leads to increased tension and aggression. Boys are more expressive when it comes to exhibiting negative behaviors. They will mostly spend time in their room or hooked to their phones and video games. This can build up tension with others close to them, and also cause mood swings.

- **Need for Independence and/or Power:** Boys will also seek more control over their decisions, from what they wear to what they do in their free time. They may need ground rules about such things, which can sometimes give rise to conflicts.

Teenage Boys and Body Image Issues

Although teen boys aren't as anxious about their appearance as most girls, they still are often dissatisfied with their weight, height, and appearance (Hargreaves & Tiggemann, 2005). When they see their favorite celebrities on TV or follow them on social media, they want to be like them. They want to have the same haircut, the same clothes, tattoos, and even similar hobbies and interests. They internalize societal ideals that they see in TV shows, movies, and sports, and then struggle with low self-esteem.

Men, in general, have always been expected to look ripped, macho, or strong. They have repeatedly been depicted in that manner in pop culture, which informs them that this is what they must look like in order to be desirable. After internalizing these depictions, young boys start to assume that this is what girls like, and then feel dissatisfied and insecure with the way they look. Many boys take up exercise to build body mass, and some even take steroids to improve their physical appearance and sexual performance. According to one study, 38% of teen boys have admitted to using protein supplements to boost muscle mass, and out of those, 6% have admitted to experimenting with dangerous steroids (Eisenberg et al., 2012).

As he moves through puberty and toward adulthood, your teenage boy will begin to observe, and actively partake in, these new changes in his body, mind, and environment. As a parent or guardian, it's important to be cognizant of these changes as well.

Chapter 2: The 7 Vital Parenting Skills to Understanding Teen Boys

S ocietal constructs often don't let young boys and men express themselves and seek the emotional support they need from their peers, educators, and parents. We have long denied them a listening ear because we think they can deal with their problems on their own. What we fail to see is that they are still too naïve and young to understand the different changes they are going through, and thus need someone to make it all easier.

Thanks to this stoic culture, it has become even harder for parents to approach their teenage son to discuss the various topics they need clarification on. For instance, it is harder to talk to them about drug use, substance abuse, intimacy, and relationships because the gaps between parents and their teenagers have widened. Whenever we do try, sometimes the words fall short, and sometimes we feel too ashamed or embarrassed to keep trying.

But like girls, boys need to be encouraged to open up and be themselves. They need to know that they don't have to conform to the standards that society has set for them, and that they can be as expressive and compassionate as they want to be without being beholden to the "typical man" image in their minds.

What they need is an understanding parent that is willing to share some of the load they carry on their backs, and offer them the support they desperately crave. They want to be understood, heard, validated, looked after, and cared for. Is that too much to ask?

In this chapter, we shall discuss the seven vital parenting skills that will allow parents to be more supportive and present in the lives of their teenage boys. They may look like different creatures with their body hair, increased build, and weird choice of clothing, but they're still your boys! These essential skills will not only help you develop a stronger and meaningful bond with them, but also make room for improved communication and family relations between you and him. The more he feels looked after and supported, the higher the chance that he won't turn to unhealthy or risky behaviors (Neppl et al., 2015).

Let's take a look at these seven skills, now:

Vital Parenting Skill #1: Institute Responsibility

Your son needs to grow up to be responsible. He needs to learn how to own up to his shortcomings, accept his blunders, and make amends. He must be taught to contribute to domestic chores. When parents teach young boys about responsibility, they allow them to taste what power and control feel like, which then prepares them to handle the uncertainties that adulthood brings.

Vital Parenting Skill #2: Provide Structure

Structure and routine make us accountable, too. They allow us to make the most of available hours, with the biggest long-term rewards. Having set expectations and routines can make young adults feel more confident in their capabilities. It also prevents procrastination, and allows your teenager to get things done efficiently.

Vital Parenting Skill #3: Break Stereotypes

Parents must teach their boys about privilege, and to recognize their place in society. They should teach them about the expression of emotions, and encourage them to deal with them in healthy ways. They must be taught to not feel any awkwardness in doing things that the society labels as feminine, and to treat all genders equally and with respect.

Vital Parenting Skill #4: Show Interest

Showing interest in the lives of your teenager allows you to feel more connected with them. It opens doors for healthy and consistent communication to take place, and strengthens the bond between the child and the parent. By showing interest in his activities, passions, and dreams, parents tell their children that they love, value, and care for them.

Vital Parenting Skill #5: Discipline Strategically

Discipline doesn't always mean punishment. It shouldn't involve humiliation and shaming; it has to be more tactical. Teenagers are known to be rebellious, and have a short temper. They are likely to misbehave, or disobey orders when they aren't in the mood for them. This doesn't mean that parents can use verbal or physical abuse to knock some sense into them. Disciplining strategically involves hacks that improve behavior without punishments. It challenges parents to use positive parenting techniques to modify behavior, instead of using abuse or fear.

Vital Parenting Skill #6: Give Privacy

Too much prying into your boy's life can backfire big time. If the goal is to build channels of communication, teenagers must be allowed to have some privacy. Parents who think that prying in their children's lives will make their children open up to them are mistaken. If anything, they will start to hide things and become more secretive than before. They may also start to lie. Thus, we must look at not only the importance of distance and privacy, but also at how parents can maintain a healthy distance from their teenager.

Vital Parenting Skill # Use Restitution

Restitution requires that a person must be held accountable for the mistakes he made and make amends, or face the consequences of his actions. Teaching your child about restitution and how it works will make him more responsible. No one likes to have to face the consequences of their actions. When your boy knows that he will be held accountable for all of his deeds and have to pay for his mistakes, he will be less likely to misbehave.

Let's learn how each of these seven vital parenting skills can be put into practice, and further help us understand our boys and improve communication with them.

Chapter 3: Vital Parenting Skill #1 - Institute Responsibility

I n many cultures, men hold the responsibility of arranging the finances for the house. When it comes to house chores, very little is expected of them. Women, on the other hand, have always been portrayed as homemakers. They have to ensure that the kids are fed, dressed, and disciplined. They also have to perform all the domestic duties, like cooking and cleaning.

But, the world is changing. Both partners have to contribute financially, as well as domestically, in the upbringing of a family. Are you doing your part to raise a responsible adult?

You may expect your teenage son to behave like an adult already. But, he is still going through a very beautiful yet confusing transition. His growth is affected, his emotions are becoming stronger, and his anxiety is on the rise too. You may assume that he will figure things out on his own, but believe it or not, he needs your guidance now more than ever.

Teaching responsibility to a budding man is important. You can make them pick up the habit early on by assigning them little chores to carry out. You can praise their contribution to make them feel proud of their effort, and inspire them to be more willing and motivated to contribute further. Responsibility leads to maturity and improved self-worth. It allows the child to feel like they are capable and in control when they do tasks themselves.

Ideally, your boy should now be responsible for looking after his hygiene, homework, room, and cleaning. As soon as he starts to show interest in performing these without supervision or assistance from you, you can decide what more he can assist with in the matters of the house. Sooner or later, he will have to live on his own, which is why you shouldn't feel any shame when asking him for tasks like setting the table, folding the laundry, or doing the dishes.

Why Teach Them about Responsibility?

Parenting is like coaching. We are responsible for coaching our children to do everything. They learn everything from us, such as our eating, sleeping, walking, and talking habits. We shield them against all harm and want to pamper them unconditionally. If it were up to us, we would have never wanted them to grow up! But since they do anyway, they need to know how to manage things for themselves. You can't keep tying their laces for them, or ask them to get in the bathtub every day. You need to teach them to fend for themselves, learn to cook, know basic etiquette, work towards the attainment of their goals, and follow their passions without any fear. In short, they need to be held accountable for the actions and behaviors they exhibit without having to rely on you forever.

Teaching your child about responsibility is crucial for many reasons, one of which being that it promotes a healthy and smart lifestyle. Being responsible requires teenagers to make the most of their valuable time by investing it in activities with long-term benefits. This means they will be occupied with essential tasks, rather than spending all their time watching TV, sleeping all day, or being hooked to their phones. If they know how to cook, they are less likely to indulge in junk food. If they know how to clean, they won't spend their day in a dirty room. If they are aware of the importance of personal hygiene, they will keep themselves clean.

Your boy will also learn about staying away from trouble, or how to get away from it if trouble finds him. Taking responsibility for one's misdeeds is another aspect of learning to own your mistakes and make amends. That also shows how responsible you are as a parent. If you teach him about responsibility, he will feel more capable of taking care of his troubles. You have to take a step back and let him handle things on his own first. If he needs your support or assistance, he will ask for it eventually.

Lastly, in a competitive world like ours, he needs to learn how to take jabs from people. He needs to learn how to take constructive feedback and criticism from others. Teaching your child about responsibility will prepare him to deal with such people and instances without feeling shy or like a failure. It will teach him about resilience, and how he needs to stay in control of his emotions when things don't go the way he planned.

Teaching Responsibility – The How-To

You love your teenager – it's a fact. Your love for him goes beyond expectations. You want to see him happy, but that shouldn't make you want to lose focus on being a parent. Keep in mind that he may be a boy today, but tomorrow, he'll be an adult who has to face the world on his own. He has to form relationships, meet new people, and be expected to be civil and responsible. The question is, are you raising someone like that?

It isn't a secret that parents pamper and shelter their children. The more we do for them, the less they learn about the importance of responsibility. Then, we become the same parents to nag when they aren't unable to keep up with our expectations. But blaming them won't solve the problem. We need to make them see what responsibility looks like, and what happens when they don't become responsible.

Allow Him Choices

He may not feel up for a chore that has been assigned to him. When this happens, parents need to modify their strategy. Offering him choices is a great start. When you offer choices to your teen, you bind them into having to do at least one of the two chores, while still giving him the freedom to choose. You leave it unto him to decide which one he wants to do.

Include Him in Decision-Making

If you are about to make a decision that concerns him or affects him in some way, let him have a say. If his opinion sounds genuine and sensible, go with it. This is another way to teach your son what responsibility looks like. He chose to put forward that suggestion, and since everyone is going with it, he is now responsible for the outcomes it brings. If things go right, don't forget to praise him. If they don't, let him show accountability and make amends.

Make a List of Chores

When parents choose to pre-plan who does what, it prevents both confusion and procrastination. It also makes one accountable, as they will be held answerable if they fail to do them. To upgrade the list of chores, add in a few positive and negative consequences so that your son is aware of what he gets and loses if he fails to do the chores.

Have Clear Expectations

Clear and concise expectations are also important in preventing misbehavior. If your boy doesn't know what is expected of him, how do you think he will live up to your expectations? Having expectations set and communicated are two different things, with the latter being more important. Once your teen knows what is expected, it will serve as motivation and drive him to work for it. But you have to ensure that the expectations are reasonable and achievable, as unrealistic expectations only lead to frustration and anxiety.

Set Consequences

Consequences reinforce responsibility. They develop the connection between a choice and a result. If a teen makes a certain choice, he has to face the outcomes too. Having consequences, both negative and positive, can help teenagers to ponder the choices they make. It also teaches them to make sensible choices in the future.

To begin, use the SANE acronym.

- Set small consequences

- Avoid punishing yourself for the poor choices of your teen

- Never abuse your teen with a consequence

- Effective consequences are better when consistent

With these tips, your teenage boy will be acting responsibly in no time!

Chapter 4: Vital Parenting Skill #2 - Provide Structure

T eenagers can be out of control. They may want more freedom, complain about everything, request more privacy, and demand to have a say in family matters. Freedom always comes with a price. To be able to afford independence, they need to first learn about responsibility and commitment. They need to know what it means to own up to their mistakes, accept their weaknesses, and work on their strengths. They need the vision to follow their dreams, a roadmap entailing the steps along the way, and an undivided focus to strive for the best.

However, all of this requires discipline. Any teenager lacking basic social skills will have a difficult time in his adult life. Discipline and social skills are what make us well-mannered and self-reliant. They make us ready to face the world, as well as the challenges that come with adulthood. To hone their sense of discipline, teenagers need sharp focus and a 100% commitment to stay true to their course without ever losing sight of their goals.

When boys reach adolescence, they start to explore activities that pique their interest. This doesn't necessarily mean that their time is spent on things that matter. For example, your boy may become addicted to video games, which aren't the best use of his spare time. As a parent, your goal should be to teach him how to make sensible choices. This starts with structure.

Why Teenage Boys Need Structure

Routine and structure allow teenagers to be more responsible while teaching them about self-discipline and control. Teens, especially young boys, often struggle with structure in their lives. A good sense of structure can allow them to regulate themselves better for the sake of improvement. Improvement is only possible when one is self-disciplined. Discipline, along with structure, also encourages teenagers to better manage their emotions.

Structure also helps young boys learn about time management. As school gets tougher and expectations increase, teens are likely to be overwhelmed by the many activities that fill their day. Most of the time, they are left with very little time on their hands to spend doing the things they love. Thus, we must teach them how to make the most of their time and spend it on things that enhance their talents and skills rather than on things that add no value. For example, remind them that they only have 24 hours in a day to spend. It encourages them to think rationally and choose between several options. When boys have routines and structure, they can better devote their time to several important activities.

Structure also prevents procrastination, which is another thing many parents worry about. Teenagers are master procrastinators, as they often have no problem delaying things like homework and chores to a later date. Though you shouldn't worry as long as your teen completes his tasks, the thing that you should worry about is their effort.

It is no secret that when we fully commit to something and give ourselves as much time as we need to work on it, our progress and accomplishment show. When we have more time to think, we can get creative and not just do something for the sake of doing it. Teenagers need to be creative, too. They should be encouraged to give their best shot at everything. Having structure in life can help with that.

Having a consistent routine every day can prevent anxiety and depression. We are our most anxious when we feel scared, excited, or short on time. Although many believe that having a complex schedule is what makes one feel anxious, the opposite is true.

Have you ever wondered that whenever we are recommended to start something new like a diet, we are told that we need to bring more structure in our lives? If we see a therapist, they tell us to re-engage in life and start with regular activities to prevent internal anxiety and depression. With expectations running high and peer pressure getting to them, our teenagers are angry, irritated, and depressed. They feel that they need to constantly prove themselves to their parents, peers, mentors, and teachers. To prevent them from going down a dark path, we need to give them a roadmap to success. This is only possible when their days are structured, and they know what milestones to accomplish.

Getting Started with Routines and Structures

If having a structured lifestyle will give our teenagers an edge over the others, it makes sense to create one for them. However, there's no guarantee he will follow it; it highly depends on how the rules are communicated. Teens have a mind of their own. They want to act rebellious and play by their own rules. They will disobey for the sake of disobeying, or to see you get annoyed. But as stated before, if you communicate structure in the right manner, he will soon start doing things out of habit. To help you set the right foot forward, take a look below.

First, identify your routines:

- What routines do you want to begin with?

- What are the important activities you need to map out on paper?

- What should be the order of performing these activities?

- How many times a day should an activity occur, and at what times?

- What is the goal you need to accomplish from setting this routine?

Having answered these questions, you will feel more ready to have a detailed plan laid out in no time. Imagine that the goal is to manage time. How are you going to implement it? Would each task to be done have a designated amount of time? How will you make the most of the available hours? Will each task be repeated every day or between intervals?

Once you have created a chart, or listed the routines, the next step is to explain those routines to your boy. To do so, you have to ensure that he is aware of the end goal you have in mind for him (or that you've decided on, together). He must also know when the goals have to be completed. Remember that because teenagers are so occupied with their lives, they often forget what needs to be done. Thus, set reminders about what they need to do. Place the chart or list in a location where your child can view it easily.

And finally, if they are unwilling to adhere to the set routines and rules, you can motivate them by using positive reinforcement, like setting rewards for completing a task, or praising them for being responsible. You can ask your boy to get on board when deciding how to reward them. That way, he will be more driven to complete the task and follow the routine. If positive reinforcement doesn't work, you may choose to utilize negative consequences instead.

Chapter 5: Vital Parenting Skill #3 - Break Stereotypes

*"T*oughen up. Men don't cry."

Boys have been told this for years. Even when they are too young to know any better, we tell them to take their traumas "like a man," without even knowing the impact of what we are teaching them. To us, it comes so naturally. We expect our boys to toughen up, even when they are breaking down. We expect them to deal with their problems like grown men, even when they haven't gotten a clue about the next step.

We have, for many decades, given into the cultural stereotyping dictating that men should act tough, and women should be soft. The reason why we as parents need to set the record straight is because this affects the way we interact with our boys, and how they interact with others...as well as how they manage their feelings.

Before we move to break the stereotype, we need to understand what the stereotype is, and why it feels so natural to us. Society has told us that boys have to be strong and confident. They are knights in shining armor, winning wars and women. They have been painted in glory by famous artists, labeled as brave and valiant by poets, and depicted as handsome and charming in the media. This can lead to dehumanization, in that we see them as robots without hearts or an ounce of emotion. And the minute they try to be open and breathe a little, we mock their sensitivity and label it as "femininity."

This also enforces the idea that there are right and wrong feelings. Some feelings are okay for men to have, such as anger and aggression, whereas others like fear, sadness, and grief are too emotional and grounds for silencing. The more we tell them this repeatedly, the more they start to believe in these norms. They start to believe that being loud and pushy is ideal. They start to believe that they have to toughen up, mask their emotions, and act all cool, because the world won't have it any other way. They start to believe that they have to use sarcasm, stoicism, nonchalance, and irritability as their shields. They are then prevented from expressing themselves, or showing their vulnerable side.

This gives rise to a confused generation, where men's feelings and emotions go misunderstood and neglected. When basic needs like the freedom to express joy or grief are silenced, it can lead to several mental health conditions–depression being the most common. In short, boys are expected to appear in control at all times and mustn't appear emotional or weak. As a result, they often hide, downplay, and silence their sadness, fears, and vulnerability.

The Dangers and Damages of Stereotyping

In one study published in the *Child Development* journal, 1,500 children from sixty fifth and sixth grade classrooms across Germany participated in an experiment to show differences in reading levels among genders (Muntoni et al., 2020).. The goal was to provide proof that girls were better at reading than boys, which was a presumed stigma. During the first few sessions, researchers asked the students about how confident they were about their reading abilities, and if they felt motivated to improve their ability to read. The session administered a questionnaire regarding gender stereotyping and reading. After the students filled the questionnaire, their reading ability was tested.

About a year and a half later, the same students were again called in for a session and retested for their skills and reading levels. The boys who had believed in the reading stereotypes earlier showed less improvement than those who didn't believe in it. They also showed less motivation to read, as compared to those who believed that their reading skills and interests (or lack thereof) had nothing to do with the fact that they were boys. The study also reviewed the role of positive peer engagement, and how it benefited the girls in improving their ability to read. For many years, it was believed that boys were supposed to be good at sports and math, and the girls were supposed to be good at reading and art.

The stereotype that boys had weak reading skills created a self-fulfilling prophecy for poor performance and motivation among the boys. The lead researcher, Francesca Muntoni, concluded that stereotypes did affect the mindset of boys, and devalued their actual reading abilities. Less motivation to read resulted in poor performance.

The reason why we need to emphasize the negatives of stereotyping is because it has stopped parents from encouraging children to follow their passion, no matter what that is. We are so accustomed to teaching our boys their assigned gender roles, that it shocks us when they want to break from those roles. For example, in a 2018 analysis reviewing three different studies, it was found that both parents and educators play a crucial role in making their toddler boys act masculine and play with boy toys (Koenig, 2018).

Ditching Labels for Good

Now that we are aware of the dangers of stereotyping and how it can limit one's potential for greatness, we must create an environment for our boys that allows them to be who they want to be. Our only goal should be to encourage and motivate them to go after their passions and dreams, no matter how "feminine" the world defines them. It has to start with us. How do we go about encouraging this?

Accept ALL Emotions

In many homes, cultural stereotypes prevent boys from expressing their emotions healthily. They are told to stop crying because it makes them appear weak, and told to talk loudly because that is how men are "supposed to talk." They are also told to adhere to other socially-acceptable, traditional emotions. But when we raise them in this way, we tell them that it isn't normal to have feelings.

This mindset needs to be discouraged, and boys must be offered every chance to express themselves, especially when they feel their emotions are overpowering them. Don't tell them to wipe their tears in the car when they want to take another ride on the swing because "tears aren't manly." Don't tell them that they shouldn't be sad over their broken heart. Let them be themselves. Let them be humans.

Don't Assign Them Tasks Based on Stereotypes

Just because he is a boy doesn't mean that he will be good with machinery and bad with poetry. Don't assume that he will be better off with sports, and not in drama or arts. When it comes to household responsibilities, we often see men getting assigned certain tasks, such as mowing the lawn or climbing ladders for repairs and installations. We also see women being expected to do the laundry, set the table, or do the dishes. Unintentionally, we have been assigning them tasks based on stereotypes.

Make a conscious effort to avoid this; try creating a list of chores and expecting your teenage boy to pick whatever they like from it. Better yet, have a rotating schedule where he gets to do everything. Additionally, encourage him to do tasks that actively work against stereotypes, such as learning to cook, fold the laundry, and clean the house, because these skills come in handy regardless. Let work be work.

Reinforce Behaviors that Smash Stereotypes

Your teen may not be interested in doing "feminine" chores. He may suspect that if he does them, his peers will make fun of him. To counteract this, place them as a challenge in front of him. For instance, if he is younger, say something like, "I bet you can't fold the laundry or wash the dishes," or "Wearing those colorful socks was a good idea, as they go with your outfit". Or, try normalizing certain behaviors: a father or father figure may say something like, "I cry too sometimes," so your boy knows it's okay to do so himself.

Be Careful of the Words You Use Around Him

The words that we say send out a message about our expectations. When we tell girls that they look pretty, and tell boys how strong they are after they have taken a fall, we are telling them what we expect of their gender. Therefore, from the beginning, use gender-neutral words like "them" instead of "he" or "she". Moreover, when you are using specific terms, don't gender them. For example, instead of saying "fireman," say "firefighter," or "police officer" instead of "policeman."

Encouraging your teenage boy to break stereotypes will help him become a kinder, more socially conscious, and ultimately more empathetic adult–all of which are things that will help him succeed in later life.

Chapter 6: Vital Parenting Skill #4 - Show Interest

H umans are curious beings. As much as we like to inquire about things, we are also interested in the lives of the people around us. For instance, it's natural for a sibling to worry about the other and look after them. It is also natural for your grandma to want to feed you or your children with as much food as she can. It is also natural for educators to worry about the progress of their students. We are social animals, and for a reason. The human race can't survive without interacting with one another. Think about this for a second. How would the world look like if no one interacted with one another? How would it look if no one showed an interest in our lives?

Humans need to interact with, and care about, one another. They need to show interest in the lives of others, especially their partners and children, so that they feel connected and become one another's support system.

When parents exhibit genuine concern and curiosity about their child's dreams, passions, and future, the chances of establishing a strong relationship increases. When children know that their parents support their interests and are keen to know all that is happening in their lives, it makes them feel valued.

And as a parent, you don't have to make any extra effort to show affection and interest. You simply have to be present and willing to hear them out when they seek your assistance.

For boys, especially in their teens, this is a rather difficult process. They are less likely to come to you with their complaints and problems than girls are. They would often rather seek assistance and guidance from a peer or mentor instead.

Showing interest in your boy's life will allow you to know them better, and have more things to talk about. The reason it is a vital parenting skill is that it strengthens the bond and allows parents to be more involved in their boy's life.

One of the biggest challenges parents face is choosing what to talk about with their teenagers. Generally, teenagers show interest in various things such as:

- **Controversial Issues:** Questions like, why they can't drive before they are sixteen or can't drink before they are twenty-one.

- **Family-related Issues:** They want to have a say in decisions concerning the family, such as which place to visit during summers, or whether or not the family should move.

- **The Big "Why"s:** Questions about major forces, such as war, racism, spirituality and religion, etc.

- **Personal Interests:** What activities they like, or what passions they have.

- **Their Parents' Marriage:** They might be interested in knowing how you two met, when you got married, what mistakes you made as a newly-wed couple, etc.

- **Their Future:** They are interested in talking about their prospects, and also concerned at the same time about the uncertainties and weaknesses.

- **Current Events:** They are interested in the world around them and all that is happening in their community, in politics, the economy, and their health (and the health of those around them).

How Showing Interest Improves Communication

The benefits of showing interest in your boy's life are many. When you show interest in his life, he no longer feels alone or left out, and instead feels supported. It helps teenagers in general to unburden themselves and feel a little lighter. It allows them to be more expressive when they see that the person in front of them is interested and curious about what they have to say.

Moreover, when you give your son the chance to be involved, it will also boost his confidence and self-esteem. His teenage years are his years to make mistakes. Your son will make them too. How he copes with failure will determine the level of self-confidence he possesses. If he thinks he can own up to his mistakes on his own, then he is already en route to becoming an emotionally intelligent adult. But if he isn't, and struggles to deal with the overwhelming negative emotions and resorts to drugs or other forms of substance abuse, they will need someone to prevent them from it and instead turn to healthy ways of coping with them. This person can be you, given the relationship you have with him is strong. When he sees in you a mentor and confidant, it will boost his self-confidence too. He will feel more in control of his emotions, and it will also increase his sense of self-worth.

Finally, one of the scariest things for a parent is secrecy, or lack of transparency. When you don't know what they're up to or involved in, it will only increase your fears and lead to sleepless nights when he is out with his friends. Thus, to encourage honesty and transparency in the house, you need to make communications more effective. He shouldn't only see you as a parent figure but also as a friend. He shouldn't fear coming up to you to inquire about topics that bother him. When you show interest in the things he is interested in, it will give you the leverage to be in the know. You won't have to worry about him lying behind your back, or disobeying rules set by you or your partner.

How to Show You Are Interested in His Life

There are tons of ways you can let your boy see that you are interested in his life, and want to be more included and involved in it. For starters, your general attitude should depict this. Try using affection; being affectionate towards him doesn't mean you have to kiss him on the cheek every night before he goes to bed, but it does mean that you have to make him understand that you're just as invested in his goals and passions as he is. You can start to spend quality time together after school or get started on a fun project together to show him you are interested in his life. Other than that, you can also:

Love What They Love

You aren't as crazy about the musician he loves, or the athletes he admires, or the football team he wants to see play live one day. But you can always make the effort to show happiness and excitement in his excitement. By doing so, you tell him that he is important to you. Keep checks on the celebs, musicians, and other inspirational personalities he looks up to, and stays updated about their lives (and why your boy loves them so much). This will give you

345

ample opportunities to converse. You can even schedule to watch a match together, or go to a concert. You can also show an interest in the company he keeps, or the partner he's dating. That too is a great way to show concern as well as interest in his life.

Ask Concerning Questions

Inquire about his health –emotional, mental, and physical. Go past the generic. For instance, instead of asking about how he's feeling, ask him if anything made him particularly happy, sad, excited, or angry that day.

Ask questions about his school, his friends, or any other relationships he holds close. Show concern over small things, like what they would wear to the school dance or if they have eaten lunch or not. However, there is a fine line between a clingy and a concerned parent. You have to be the latter. You have to probe, but not too much, and the minute he shows irritation, stop.

Spend Some One on One Time Together

Be it on the way home from school, to the park, or simply on the couch in your living room, make time for him even when he doesn't seem interested. Let him see how invested you are. Similarly, when communicating, give him your undivided attention–which means putting your phone down and being all ears. Quality time is one of the greatest gifts we can give to our children and ourselves. After all, these are the memories that we are left with as they move onto the next phase of their lives.

Take Up On A New Project

It doesn't have to be anything as grand as building a treehouse together. You can also get on board with him on a school project, or put a puzzle together. Find things that you two can do together, specifically the ones he is interested in. For example, if he is into sports, you two can spend an evening playing the sport or watching a professional team play one. Similarly, if he loves to cook, you two can go and take a baking or cooking class together or spend the day baking some goodies together.

Make Eye Contact

Remember we talked about dropping everything and lending him a curious ear? Well, take it up a notch by making eye contact. Eye contact, when made with the speaker, makes a person feel truly heard and seen. This means that you have to listen and notice for any specific awkwardness, fear, signs of depression, or anger in their body movements or facial expressions too. You also have to look him in the eye to let him know that you are giving your undivided attention. Failing to look someone in the eye makes you appear distracted. If you are busy and wish to choose a better time to communicate, let him know subtly.

Chapter 7: Vital Parenting Skill #5 - Discipline Strategically

S o he messed up again, didn't he? Isn't this the third time in the week that he has done something stupid? Why does he not learn to do things the right way? The steps are so simple...

Sometimes, our children, especially boys, do things that make us want to deny that we know them altogether. But that is the moment where we need to encourage them to continue trying, instead of discouraging them or dooming them as a failure for life. Just because they did something unpleasant doesn't mean that your love for them has diminished. The right time to support them is when they mess up. Why? Because that is the time when they need it the most to continue moving forward. This is the time when they need someone to come up to them and tell them that they don't need to be ashamed of their mistakes, or feel guilty for trying. This is the time when we need to show compassion instead of denial. We don't need to be paranoid, but rather discipline with kindness and empathy.

But what is discipline? Is it not a synonym of punishment? If you thought so too, you aren't the only parent.

The majority of the parents when asked to discipline their children rely on punishments both simple and severe. With teenagers and their raging hormones, punishments usually come in the form of curfews, being grounded, or having their privileges taken away for a certain time.

But disciplining a teenager or a child, in general, doesn't involve punishments… at least not in its literal sense. The word "discipline" has a Latin origin, and translates to "to teach," whereas the word "punishment" also comes from Latin, and means "to cause pain."

As tempting as it seems to punish them, we never want to hurt or cause pain to our kids. We simply want them to learn from their mistakes. We should make it known to them that our goal isn't to punish, but rather "teach" a lesson so that they know better. The goal should be to discipline, so that they are aware of the natural consequences of their actions and can reflect upon the mistakes they made.

How Discipline Works

Discipline is about shaping behavior. Its goal is to show a teenager how you want them to navigate the world. It involves making your expectations clear, as well as laying out the steps they need to take. It allows them to find motivation and the drive to do the right things, as well as in the right manner, even when no one is watching. For example, they must tell the truth even when you aren't around, or not be tempted to steal when no one is watching. They must also show respect towards elders and be compassionate and kind towards children.

To make it work, sometimes parents need to instate consequences, which not only pose some fear but also serve as motivation. However, when disciplining, ensure that the child knows why they are receiving consequences. They should understand that their actions will eventually impact their life for better or for worse and thus, they should always act responsibly.

Focus on trying to teach a lesson without mocking them for their effort. There has to be a thin line between a concerned talk and a needless, shaming lecture. Punishments make children feel ashamed of themselves, and discourage them. They tell children that they are a failure and are therefore punished for it. However, when we try to discipline them using the right strategies, we are essentially telling them that though we aren't happy with the outcomes, we still want them to try again.

Disciplining Teenagers the Right Way

Since your child has grown beyond the years of time-outs, he will be happiest if sent to his bedroom as a punishment. So how do you make disciplining effective? Let's look at some strategies to help struggling parents come up with ideas that work.

Have Clear Rules

From the beginning, ensure that the rules are set and understood. Teenagers, especially young boys, like to push boundaries to see how their parents will react. If they get some leniency, they try to misuse it. To prevent that, having clear-cut rules and regulations in the house from the get-go is a smart strategy. You don't have to run after them to make them follow the rules, you simply have to address them and discuss the aftermath in a firm yet kind manner. Being kind will portray concern, and your boy will be less likely to disobey as a result. You can also have them design the rules. That way, they will feel included and validated. However, you must have the final say in what works and what doesn't so that they don't get away with too many privileges.

Be Consistent

Making rules isn't the only tool for disciplining. To make them effective, you have to be firm and consistent. Young boys and girls can be master manipulators and negotiators. If given the leverage, they will try to abuse the power and control they have. They are also quick to spot any parental weaknesses. Thus, be consistent about your disciplining strategies. You can't have one parent clean up after their mistakes; you both have to act like a solid team. If you say "no" to them for something and your spouse says "yes," who do you think he will go to the next time he wants something?

Stay Involved

To prevent misbehavior and misunderstanding, always know what your teenager is up to. This doesn't mean you spy on them, put a hidden camera in their room, or browse through their phone for anything fishy when they aren't in the room. This also doesn't mean that you eavesdrop on their conversations or befriend their best friend to know what is going on in their lives. You just need to show interest in their lives and the things that they do. For example, if you are friends with them on Facebook and you notice that they have shared a video about saving polar bears in Antarctica, you can have a grown-up conversation about it during dinner to let them know that you are interested. You can also lend a listening ear if you notice they are going through something, so that they know that the door for communication is always open. You can also plan activities to do together, or trips to go on to during summer break.

Being involved in your teenager's life gives you a heads-up of what they are doing and why. For instance, when you are interested, you may observe signs of distress and depression early on. Then, you can take them to a therapist if they aren't too keen on discussing their issues with you.

Praise

When parents catch their children doing something good and offer praise and appreciation, it makes them more likely to repeat the behavior. For example, if he has abided by the curfew time and home early, let him know that you appreciate it. Make it clear that you noticed this positive action and are happy about their decision. This tactic makes the reinforcement of the said behavior more likely to occur again, and also makes your teen feel valued and cared for.

Give Natural Consequences

Knowing the consequences of his actions can make your teen feel more responsible. For example, you can tell him that if he doesn't study, he won't pass with a good grade. Or, if he doesn't learn to drive responsibly, he won't be given a car of his own. Consequences, when tied to the choices he makes, can make your teen accountable for them.

Let Them Face the Consequences

If they still don't listen, or mock your rules and concerns, let them face the consequences of their actions. Natural consequences are sometimes the best teacher. Some stubborn kids learn things this way.

Chapter 8: Vital Parenting Skill #6 - Give Them Privacy

We have all come across the term "man cave." Although your boy is still not an adult yet, he needs his space and privacy more than ever now. He is going through many physical changes that he can't even talk to you about, or discuss with his peers openly. He is also dealing with a set of emotions he never felt too strongly such as jealousy, love, envy, anger, or anxiety. Unlike girls, he doesn't want to talk about things in detail or share his experiences. He needs to figure it out himself. Thus, the need for privacy.

Although we are socially-bound to crave interactions, sometimes we want to allow a certain amount of access to the people around us. Teens want the same. They want to be able to have the right to decide how much access someone has to their personal lives. According to Alan F. Westin, a professor Emeritus of Public Law and Government and a best-selling author, privacy is a claim made by an individual, a group of them, or by an institution to determine for themselves to what extent they want the information about them to be shared or communicated to others. This also applies to countries or sects that wish to stay remote and inaccessible to the main public. Think North Korea, or many rural tribes in South Africa.

We all have traits that compel us to widen our circles, soak in new information, and meet new people. Sometimes, a little peace of mind in the form of isolation isn't unheard of. This desire for privacy in teenagers is natural and critical, as it pushes them to develop an unobstructed zone for themselves. They feel safe in that space; they feel they aren't being judged or criticized, and can hear their thoughts and vent out their feelings without having to conform to established rules made by society.

Why Do Young Boys Need Privacy?

What does privacy mean to a teenager? Does it only mean that he will have his room locked the minute he comes home? Does it only mean that he will avoid taking calls in front of you, or spending time with you doing things together?

Privacy is more than that. It is an expression of independence and freedom. He doesn't want his parents or siblings sitting on his neck 24/7. He doesn't want them to be concerned about him like before. He doesn't want to have to tell his parents where he is, what he is doing, or who he is with. He wants to be able to have a friend over and not have parents roam around the hallways being inquisitive. He needs space where he can think independently, and not be bombarded or invaded by others. Privacy has more to do with eliminating the mental clutter in the head than in the room. Your son needs privacy and control to make decisions for himself. He wants to be able to wear what he wants, befriend whoever he wants, and do things in his style whenever he feels like. He doesn't need others dictating things to him.

This, to him, is the meaning of privacy.

How to Respect Their Need for Privacy

It can be hard to balance your desire to know what your son is up to with the need to not be too prying. Your reasons to keep a check on his activities are natural; after all, you have been doing so from the time he was born. However, he doesn't need you as often now as he did before, and that can be depressing.

So, how do you respect his need for privacy without losing your control and give him what he needs within set parameters? Let's take a look:

Don't Be Nosy

This is a given. You can't be nosy. Don't dig too much into his things or sneak into his room to look for something suspicious. Never eavesdrop onto his conversations, because that is a breach of trust. Furthermore, don't try to dictate who he should or shouldn't be friends with. This will annoy him, and in a deliberate attempt to get back at you, he might engage in bad company that can hurt him in the long run. Being nosy or too inquisitive is never acceptable because it takes away a child's liberty and freedom.

When you pry on him, you are essentially saying that he isn't smart enough on his own, or that he can't make sensible decisions. This can drive him away from you, which is the exact opposite of what you have been trying to do.

If you still can't control yourself to not be inquisitive, imagine how would you feel if someone did the same to you? Would you not feel judged and manipulated? Would you not feel trapped or imprisoned?

Your first step is to do your best not to be a nosy parent. Do not go digging around your teenager's belongings. Never try to listen in on conversations. And avoid trying to keep your kids away from friends or activities out of spite to try to keep them safe.

Don't Investigate – Probe Instead

Not all teenagers are talkative. They like to keep some things private. Probing is good, because it allows you to play it safe. It involves piquing his interest, but not too much. You want him to come to you. So you deliberately, but subtly, ask questions about things that concern you but stop the minute you sense that he is getting irritated or bothered. This technique of communication will allow you to give back the power to him and establish a good rapport with him in return. Asking, not demanding, is key.

Keep Your Hands Bound

Intruding isn't allowed either. If you keep looking for moments to sneak into their bedroom to look for some clue or to find something dangerous every time he leaves his room, you are being paranoid. Unless you are certain that there is some problem you need to take care of, like why are his grades falling or why does he seem sleepy all day, you have no business in sneaking into his room or checking his drawers or personal laptop. Also, make it a habit to knock before entering his room, as it shows that you respect his privacy and space and don't want to invade it unnecessarily.

Don't Try to Befriend His Friends

You may want to try to act like the cool parent and hang out with his buddies from school or neighborhood, or want to stay in the room with them when they all are hanging out, but don't. Even if you are close to your teenage son, you don't fit in. No matter how friendly you guys are at home, when he is with his friends, he is a completely different individual. It's okay to walk in on them a few times when they are in your house, but don't make it a habit to hang around for too long. His friends might not mind, but he might. Would you prefer that they hang out at some other place, instead? Therefore, don't give him any reason to want to choose another place or time.

Chapter 9: Vital Parenting Skill #7 - Introduce the Rule of Restitution

D o you ever feel that your son got away with less punishment than he should have gotten? Maybe not punishment in the literal sense, but you feel like you could have chosen a better way to instill discipline than by just taking away his phone for the weekend? Think about it: do things like these make a difference in his behavior? Does he give up the behavior that got him into trouble the first time? Or does he repeat it a week or month later?

If you feel the same way, then you aren't the only parent in this boat. Sometimes, we need to make consequences a little scarier or memorable to prevent negative behavior, as well as instill some discipline in our kids.

This is where restitution comes in. By definition, restitution is the method where we allow our children to face the consequences of their actions without intervention or any leniency from anyone, including parents. This means that if they don't study for their exams, they fail their tests. It means that if they are too lazy to wake up in the morning on time, they miss the school trip they had been looking forward to for weeks. It sounds harsh, but restitution is the best way to teach children how to respect others and exhibit well-mannered behavior.

The restitution method is one of the most effective disciplining strategies in classrooms. Often referred to as restorative justice, it holds children accountable for their misbehavior. If your son misbehaves, let him be schooled by a stranger for having poor manners instead of covering up for him. Also, make him apologize for being rude and disrespectful.

Putting Restitution to Practice

Have you tried using external rewards to encourage good behavior and discipline? Did you feel that every time you rewarded your teen for something good, they demanded more, and soon, you were taking in requests as if collecting tickets to the roller coaster ride?

And have you experimented with punishments too, only to end every argument with yelling, anger, or the door being slammed in your face? Even if our anger or rewards get our kids to behave for the time being, does it promise anything in the future? The most important question of all is whether or not we are facilitating our boys to become independent, self-disciplined, motivated, and responsible problem-solvers. If not, then what are we doing?

The reason restitution is different and an essential parenting tip is because it doesn't focus on rewards or punishments, but rather on understanding the depth of the actions. It focuses on the "why" of things, such as why do kids misbehave, what are their triggers, why they act angry and annoyed when asked a simple question, etc. Restitution allows teenagers to face the consequences of their actions in a logical way, where they understand that their actions cause certain outcomes.

Restitution gives your teenager a chance to make amends as well as make compromises. For example, if he punched a hole in the wall out of anger, he must pay for the patchwork from his lunch money or weekly pocket money. If he deliberately acts out and abuses someone verbally, he must earn their respect once again by doing whatever it takes after he has apologized. It may seem that restitution has more to do with shame and humiliation, but it isn't. No parent would ever want to shame their child. The purpose is simply to make him accountable for his actions, own up to them, and make amends wherever necessary.

How to Get Started with Restitution

The rules to put restitution into practice are varied. It doesn't involve making your child stand out in the yard holding a sign that says, "I was wrong." We have to differentiate between punishment and discipline. We need to use strategies that help improve behavior, not just eliminate bad behavior for the time being. Here's how you can get started with restitution techniques.

Let It Make Sense

Restitution has to make sense. You have to be strict about making them face the consequences, and not cover for them. If they have gotten themselves into trouble, they have to come up with ways to crawl out of it. Additionally, negative consequences should be directly linked to negative behavior.

Let Them Have a Say

Having a say in determining what the restitution should be for misbehavior is also a good start. Both you and your son should mutually decide on the consequences, and under what conditions they apply. When your child feels included this way, he will be less likely to disappoint you as you allowed him to engage. This shows a friendly exchange where he knows that he shouldn't make mistakes or hurt anyone, and what will happen if he does. Even if he commits fault, he will at least have the guts to acknowledge and accept it.

Walk the Talk

They look up to you for things. They learn behaviors from you, take up after your actions, and consider you a role model. However, if you aren't being the right role model, you are the reason for their lack of social skills and disobedience. They need to see you owning up to your mistakes, so that they feel no shame in doing it too. They need to see you making amends so that they become responsible for their actions too. Model what you preach.

Set Up Other Consequences

If the misbehavior and disobedience continue after they have made amends, it is acceptable for you to combine restitution with other consequences, too. Sometimes, restitution fails to model the correct behavior, and thus, we need to remind the child what more could happen to them if they continue to misbehave.

Conclusion

B elieve it or not, raising a well-mannered, decent, and compassionate teenager isn't hard. It's just that parents have heard so much about how difficult it is, they always feel a little under-prepped. This brief guide provides you with the right tools and strategies you need to get started. The secret is to start early; train him from an early age so that when he grows up, he doesn't feel entitled or privileged to certain perks. Additionally, being a little strict, consistent, and firm about the rules and regulations is also another great strategy to put to practice.

When parents are consistent and firm about their rules, there are fewer chances of misbehavior and arrogance from the teen's end, which are the two most common challenges parents face. Another important thing, as previously discussed, is breaking the stereotypes. We need to remind him that they are no greater than the opposite gender. We need to tell them that they both should be treated equally. You tell them that doing chores that the world classifies as "feminine" isn't a real thing, and that young boys shouldn't feel any shame in doing them.

We must make them responsible, kind, and compassionate. We must prepare them for the next phase of manhood, as such social skills are highly valued in the professional world. We must teach them about the importance of routines and rules, and why they must adhere to them.

If you recall, we also discussed why we need to use restitution. They need to know how to own up to their mistakes, accept them, and face the consequences of their actions.

Finally, teach discipline strategically. Boys tend to misbehave, and punishments only make them more obstinate. Thus, you have to discipline them in a strategic manner where they don't feel that they are being lectured or punished over something, but rather view it as an improvement strategy.

When raising young boys, make an effort to understand them, try to make communications more effective and deep, learn to respect their privacy, and don't pry too much. You want to raise them to be confident and mature adults, and that is only possible if they feel respected and self-reliant. They need to feel freedom. They need to experience what independence looks like.

Hopefully, this will be all that you need to raise a resilient, emotionally-intelligent, and compassionate young boy.

References

Bare, L. (2019, March 7). Why Do Teenage Boys
     Need Structure? Psychology Today.
     https://www.psychologytoday.com/us/blog/
     boys-will-be-boys/201903/why-do-teenage-
     boys-need-
     structure#:~:text=Teenagers%2C%20especia
     lly%20teenage%20boys%2C%20need

Chakravarty, C. (2014, December 19). 10 Handy Tips
     On How To Make Your Teenager
     Responsible. MomJunction.
     https://www.momjunction.com/articles/han
     dy-tips-make-teenager-
     responsible_00118480/

Eisenberg, M. E., Wall, M., & Neumark-Sztainer, D.
     (2012). Muscle-enhancing Behaviors Among
     Adolescent Girls and Boys. PEDIATRICS,
     130(6), 1019–1026.
     https://doi.org/10.1542/peds.2012-0095

Ginsburg, K., & Pontz, E. (2019, March 18). Having
     trouble disciplining your teen? This expert
     explains why. Parent Toolkit.
     https://www.parenttoolkit.com/general/new
     s/general-parenting/rethinking-discipline-
     for-teens

Hargreaves, D. A., & Tiggemann, M. (2005). Idealized media images and adolescent body image: "comparing" boys and girls. Body Image, 1(4), 351–361. https://doi.org/10.1016/j.bodyim.2004.10.00 2

Koenig, A. M. (2018). Comparing Prescriptive and Descriptive Gender Stereotypes About Children, Adults, and the Elderly. Frontiers in Psychology, 9. https://doi.org/10.3389/fpsyg.2018.01086

Lee, K. (2019, July 4). Most Effective Ways to Discipline a 6-Year-Old Child. Verywell Family. https://www.verywellfamily.com/discipline-strategies-for-school-age-kids-620099

Linetti, L. (2019, March 29). Why Is It Important To Teach Your Child Responsibility - Thrive Global. Thriveglobal.Com. https://thriveglobal.com/stories/why-is-it-important-to-teach-your-child-responsibility/

Morin, A. (2019, February 20). These Consequences Will Change Your Teen's Behavior. Verywell Family. https://www.verywellfamily.com/discipline-strategies-for-teens-1094840

Muntoni, F., Wagner, J., & Retelsdorf, J. (2020). Beware of Stereotypes: Are Classmates' Stereotypes Associated With Students' Reading Outcomes? Child Development. https://doi.org/10.1111/cdev.13359

Neppl, T. K., Dhalewadikar, J., & Lohman, B. J. (2015). Harsh Parenting, Deviant Peers, Adolescent Risky Behavior: Understanding the Meditational Effect of Attitudes and Intentions. Journal of Research on Adolescence, 26(3), 538–551. https://doi.org/10.1111/jora.12212

NIMH□» The Teen Brain: 7 Things to Know. (n.d.). National Institute of Mental Health. https://www.nimh.nih.gov/health/publications/the-teen-brain-7-things-to-know/index.shtml

Puberty: Adolescent Male. (n.d.). John Hopkins Medicine. https://www.hopkinsmedicine.org/health/wellness-and-prevention/puberty-adolescent-male

Quick Tips | Creating Structure | Essentials | Parenting Information | CDC. (2019, November 5). Centers for Disease Control and Prevention. https://www.cdc.gov/parents/essentials/structure/quicktips.html

Wilson, J. (2018, April 22). Your Roadmap + 10 Tips: How To Raise A Boy Right (and Keep Your Teen Boy Emotionally Healthy). Parent Remix. https://www.parentremix.com/blog/2018/4/22/how-to-raise-a-boy-right

Book Description

Who would have thought that the world would see such a day? With more fatalities and hospitalizations, COVID-19 has turned the world upside down for many. With schools being shut down, people working from home, public places closed and social distancing protocols in place, life isn't the same anymore.

How are we going to cope with the changing dynamics? What does the future ahead look like? How will parents make both ends meet? Will our children's education suffer?

All these are questions on the top of the mind of everyone. Some are worried about keeping their jobs while others mourn the death of a loved one.

Children have been hit by the pandemic too. They are missing out on some of the most important milestones in their lives and are pissed about it. So how can we, as their parents, help them handle the stress and uncertainty about things? How do we make them see the bright side of things and avoid going into depression fearing for their and their loved ones' lives?

In this unique and much-needed guide, Frank Dixon offers his readers an insight on how to help calm the anxiety many children and teenagers face today. With groundbreaking research, and scientific studies under scrutiny, he compiles seven essential methods to calm anxiety among kids and help them regulate negative emotions better. This is a guide for parents to help them find healthy ways to deal with this unexpected chain of events and continue to hope for the best amid these difficult times.

7 Effective Methods for Calming Kids Anxiety During the Covid-19 Pandemic

Easy Parenting Tips for Providing Your Kids Anxiety Relief and Preventing Teen Depression Caused by Coronavirus Isolation

Frank Dixon

professional advice. The content within this book has been derived from various sources. Please consult a licensed professional before attempting any techniques outlined in this book.

By reading this document, the reader agrees that under no circumstances is the author responsible for any losses, direct or indirect, that are incurred as a result of the use of the information contained within this document, including, but not limited to, errors, omissions, or inaccuracies.

Introduction

Who would have thought that we would see a day like this? A time when uncertainty walks the streets. A time when we would have to stay indoors for an unknown number of days, stuck with every other family member of the house. A time when all forms of movements would be restricted, and we need a solid reason to leave the house—all while wearing a mask and a pair of gloves. Yes, lockdowns can be scary. They are even scarier for our children who can't cope with the uncertainty. They are missing school, their friends, important milestones like prom and graduation, etc. They don't know when things will get back to normal or if they ever will.

As more and more countries restrict movement to reduce the number of COVID-19 cases, we are all left with nothing but to make some drastic changes to our lifestyles and routines.

The new reality where adults are bound to work from home and still worry about having a job at the end of this, and children missing social interactions and the casual hustle-bustle of the day, lack of physical contact from relatives, and spending public holidays and celebrations in the vicinity of our homes is strikingly unreal and depressing.

We are all living in constant fear of contracting the virus and what will happen if we don't make it. We are worried about our children, about our partners who have to go to the office a couple of days in the week and about the elders in the family who are the most susceptible to contracting it. Add to that, the effect all of this has on our and our children's mental and emotional health.

As parents, we have to watch out for our family. We have to ensure that we keep them safe. We have to abide by the safety measures set by the government and avoid unnecessary outings to risk bringing the virus back home with us. We have to work on our immune systems and prepare ourselves for countering any viruses and seasonal diseases such as common cold, flu, fever, and cough.

Most importantly, we have to gear up to offer our children—especially teenagers— the emotional support they need in a time of crisis like this and ensure that they don't become too anxious, worried or depressed about the pandemic.

In this guide, we shall talk about the methods and effective tools that parents can use to prevent anxiety in children and counter negativity. We shall look at ways of how to prevent depression from setting in when our kids practice social distancing from their friends and partners.

Chapter 1: Anxiety and Teen Depression during COVID-19

S ocial distancing, a requirement due to the pandemic, has been rather challenging for school-going folks. Not only are they missing out on a lot, but the lack of certainty about when things will be back to normal also adds to the mental stress and anxiety they experience. Children thrive on social interactions. Today's generation is mostly about connectivity and staying in touch with one another 24/7. Imagine taking that away from them? They are bound to act out, throw temper tantrums, exhibit frustration by picking fights over petty issues, and being distant and closed up emotionally.

Many children are mourning the loss of important milestones like their proms and graduations. Many had great opportunities to come up in terms of scholarships and internships at their favorite firms. All seems to have gone into a pending mode and the worst of it is no one can say for certain when all of this will come to an end. They are experiencing the social distancing blues and are finding this transition rather difficult and redefining.

The reason our children are facing the worst is that they are in the prime age of youth. This is supposedly the time when we create memories with friends that last a lifetime. It is the time when they fall in love for the first time, share some special moments with a beloved, have butterflies in their stomachs, support school teams during ball season and go through many things together.

This leaves parents rather confused as to how to make their time at home more fun, collaborative, and joyous. For if they don't, their children can easily go into depression or face quarantine fatigue. We are tasked with educating them, not just about the virus and its effects, but also about how they can keep their anxiety and stress managed. This will surely help them achieve a better state of mind and find some positivity in this otherwise gloomy situation.

How COVID-19 Is Affecting School-Going Kids

Researchers at the University of Bath, led by a clinical psychologist Maria Loades, explored how isolation and disease containment measures affected the mental health of both kids and teenagers. The study was published in the Journal of American Academy of Child and Adolescent Psychiatry. Following the current change of events, the researchers wanted to understand how abrupt changes in one's lifestyle and routine affected their mental health. Since many children and adolescents are suffering from loneliness caused by social distancing, it has led to many negative psychological effects such as post-traumatic distress (PTSD), confusion and anger, etc. In the review, Loades and her team of experts examined articles and studies from 1946 to 2020. Of the articles 83 met the inclusion criteria and 63 reported some form of isolation with a strong link to depression, anxiety, obsessive-compulsive disorder, trauma, and mental health concerns. The studies included approximately 51, 576 children with a mean age of 15.3 years. Of the studies articles, 43 were cross-sectional studies, 61 were observational, and 18 were longitudinal.

All the studies included some manipulation and biases, but longitudinal studies provided the most apt statistics and graphical measures. They were mostly based in Asian countries like China, Malaysia, Russia, Thailand, Iran, Korea, and India. They all implied that social distancing and loneliness increased the chances of developing depression over time. The majority of the participants in the studies self-reported feeling anxious and stressed out even five to nine years later. The duration of loneliness impacted how depressed or anxious the then adult was. It was also found that young adults were the most likely to feel the stress caused by prolonged isolation and loneliness. They were three times more likely to become depressed in the future due to social isolation. They reported seeking therapies and counseling to overcome anxiety and reduce the severity of the symptoms of depression.

If this remains the case, policymakers and public health officials will have to adhere to the rise in demand for therapists and social services for younger people because if this continues any longer, a generation of depressed and anxious people will be raised.

Another study also suggests that many children, as well as adults, will need clinical therapy to go back to living their normal lives as these many months are enough to form new habits and behaviors. Therefore, the normal we used to live in, won't seem normal at all and thus, many people will have a hard time adapting to the changes in the dynamics of how things work (Fegert et al., 2020).

Signs My Child Is Anxious

Teen anxiety and depression have been on the rise since the past decade. The advent of social media has led to bullying and encouraged teenagers to mock one another from behind screens. They are more exposed than ever to triggering marketing which compels them to believe in looking and feeling a certain way. When they don't, they feel less worthy. The National Institute of Mental Health estimates that an average of 32% of adolescents experience one or another form of anxiety, females more prone to it than males (Sorbring & Lansford, 2019). Now add to that picture the current crisis and you have depressed, anxious, and confused teenagers who don't know how to regulate their emotions and deal with the uncertainty of things. They feel powerless and out of control. Some are simply bored while others don't know what to make of their free time.

Some are coping with grief and loss while others feel lonely and left out.

As a parent, you must be able to spot the symptoms of anxiety in your child before it becomes a disorder. Some of the most common and earliest signs of anxiety in children include:

- Feelings of worry, irrationality, and fear

- Extreme irritability

- Mood swings

- Sleep disruption

- Restlessness

- Tense muscles

- Poor focus and concentration

- Hyper-vigilance

- Heart palpitations etc.

By being exposed to multiple, rather confusing messages about COVID-19 from the media and news channels, they are bound to feel anxious. Teens that experience anxiety may gravitate towards harmful coping behaviors such as substance abuse or self-harming actions but it is important to teach them about why these don't offer long-term comfort and peace. They may be worried about their friends and families getting sick or dying. They may be scared that there hasn't been any promising news about when the virus will end or when a vaccine will be available to kill the virus from the roots.

Chapter 2: The 7 Essential Methods for Preventing Anxiety and Depression in Kids

S ymptoms of anxiety may seep into teenagers as their feelings of isolation grow stronger. They have been bound at their homes and it can start to get boring. While they love spending time with you, they still miss being around their friends and video calls just don't cut it. There are always too many interruptions in the middle. Since they are no longer kids, they have also outgrown the phase where they enjoyed playing games with you. Besides, how many game nights can one have in a week? Even though Netflix, Amazon Prime, and Disney+ have taken up some of their free time, even streaming becomes boring after a few days when one can't decide which show is appropriate to watch with the whole family. You can sense their annoyance becoming more visible. But the situation isn't as grim as you think it is.

There is so much you can do to ease their tension and stress. There are tons of things you can do to spend quality time together with your teenager. Look at this time as a blessing in disguise rather than a burden. True, conflicts have increased and everyone seems to have a mood of their own but aim to make the most of this time to find things to connect and bond. Soon, your children will be headed for college or moving out and you will go back to thinking about the time you had with them and how beautiful it was.

Since you want them to be happy and comfortable instead of annoyed, bored, or frustrated, the first thing you need to do is alleviate their stress and anxiety. Even an ounce of stress in them can turn wonderful times stressful. No matter what you do, they won't feel the joy if they are anxious about their future and all that it holds.

Thus, to help parents get started on the right foot and connect with their adolescents better and eliminate all signs of anxiety and depression from them, we are going to recommend seven effective methods aka parenting tips to help them cope with their anxiety in a much more healthy, and capable way. Let's briefly review what they are here before going into the depth of each.

Stay Posted

Staying posted or updated about what's going on in the world through reliable and official channels is the first step to overcoming anxiety. A lot of times, misinformation can trigger anxiety. Wrong statistics, false news, manipulated information, and statistics can easily add to one's anxiety. Thus, help them find resources that offer confirmed and verified news. Tell them strictly not to believe in everything they hear or read about and teach them how to check for the reliability of the information first before sharing it with others.

Show Empathy

Showing empathy means letting them know that you acknowledge what they are going through. Having a strong support system in their lives is what they need the most, especially during the pandemic. They are worried about their friends, education, and dreams. They need someone to hear them out and let them know that things will be alright. Do we not feel a whole lot better when we know we have a strong support system? Let children feel the same support and validation.

Practice Mindfulness

A clear head, free from negative thoughts and feelings, is a space for creativity and positivity. Encourage your teens to practice mindfulness and become more aware of their surroundings and the present. Show them how they can pay gratitude for the blessings they have, even in such negative and scary times. Teach them to regulate their emotions better by using techniques like deep breathing to induce happiness and calmness in their bodies.

Provide Structure and Routines

Following the same structure and routine as before can also prevent anxiety and depression. If they wake up at the same time every day as they did for their school and then followed the same routine, they will have less free time to think about all that is going on around the world. Routines and structure provide predictability—the one thing your child needs the most right now. Having structure also helps kids to know what is expected of them.

Teach Coping Skills

Coping skills build resilience in children. They learn to move from things in healthy ways. It prevents them from gravitating towards negative behaviors and self-harming actions. Keeping the current state in mind, they are more anxious than ever. They are missing their friends and have too much free time on their hands. An empty mind is like a house for the devil. It is easier to allow negativity to set the house in the mind and become depressed. However, if children know how to overcome their grief, feelings of loneliness, and frustration, they are in a much better state to regulate their emotions and improve their behaviors.

Find Ways to Stay Connected

The teenage years are the time to develop new bonds, and connections. COVID-19 has taken that away from them. They can't meet their friends, hang out with them, go to the movies with them, or play games outside. They are struggling with the intense need to connect with their peers and miss school. But just because they can't physically meet their friends doesn't mean they can't meet them virtually. Also, if they promise to maintain social distancing, they can go on a walk with them or ride a bike with them too—of course, while practicing the safety measures. The reason staying connected is urged upon so much is because it keeps your child engaged and occupied. They shouldn't distance themselves emotionally from their friends as it may trigger anxiety, depression, and sadness.

Stay Active

Staying active allows children to take care of their bodies' physical as well as emotional needs. It prevents weight gain and worry caused by stress. It promises a stronger immune system and healthy stamina. According to WHO, we must all try to boost our immunity by eating the right foods, exercising, and sleeping for a good eight hours every night. Exercise is food for the body. When we sweat, we improve blood circulation. When we get those hands and feet moving, we improve our flexibility. When we meditate, we allow our mind to release all negative thoughts. Doesn't that sound like a good state to be in? Thus, encourage the same in your children too.

Chapter 3: Essential Parenting Skill #1—Stay Posted

T he World Health Organization lists COVID-19 related infodemic as dangerous as the pandemic itself. Information containing preventive measures that don't come verified, turning to Ayurveda or herbal cures to treat COVID-19 instead of recommended drugs and medications from medical experts, or not following the guidelines on how to maintain distance, wash hands, or cover your mouth with a mask because an article suggests so, can be destructive.

Not to mention, there are as many as a hundred different conspiracy theories put forward by people with no knowledge about what they are or their impact on the masses have also come to light. Some still believe that the virus is the government's intervention to control the population and gather information about them (Shih, 2020), China's revenge on us to ruin our economy (Beusekom, 2020), or personal interests such as that of the business magnate to insert a tracking chip into all of us via a vaccine to track our movements and manipulate our actions and behaviors (Goodman & Carmichael, 2020).

Such theories have done nothing but promote new types of xenophobia where people blame a certain country or race to have been responsible for the outbreak. China, which was hit worst during the start of 2020, has received the most hate followed by other East Asian countries for their inability to control the spread of the virus or for not warning the world about it earlier.

When memes, pictures, and videos promoting xenophobia are uploaded, liked, and shared, people fail to realize the severity of the situation we are currently in and start to mock the virus or the need to seek protection and go into isolation. Even today, there are hundreds and thousands of people who are against the use of masks to protect themselves and potentially others from becoming exposed to the virus because they don't think that the virus will get to them or that they are strong enough to fight it off. What they fail to realize is that it is no longer about them contracting the virus but rather about other people and demographics. For instance, from day 1, we were aware that people above the age of 50 are most vulnerable to the virus due to a weaker immune system, but there is very little that we have done to control its spread.

When we are exposed to fake or misleading information daily, it can also fuel confusion and a state of panic. I hope there isn't a need to remind people how stores were out of toilet paper in a matter of minutes after being restocked. The less informed we are, the more dangerous it is. But what is even more dangerous than that is being exposed to wrong information.

Thus the first parenting goal or skill is to limit the amount of misleading confusing information your child is exposed to. We need to keep a check on what they are watching online and what they are believing blindly.

Fake News and its Impact

According to a pilot study, believing fake news is bad for your heart and induces stress (Barlow, 2018). The study was led by a team of researchers at Manchester Metropolitan University. The researchers believe that people with low "information discernment (ID)" don't question the viability of the news or how reliable the source is. This causes them to exhibit unhealthy symptoms of mental stress.

The study consisted of 18, twenty-four-years-old males. They were asked questions about how they consumed information and news. The questions included topics like what were their favorite sites to view news, did they always turn to them for the latest updates, did they try to double-check the information they were consuming by going to another news portal, did they check for its reliability before sharing it with others online, and whether or not they opened the attached links and studies to see the facts for themselves. After the participants had answered the questions, they were connected to a Finometer—a device that measures cardiovascular reactivity. The device also measured their heartbeat, arterial blood flow, and tracked their eye movement. After they were connected to the Finometer, they were presented with six news stories to read based on a religious theme.

This was done to understand the difference between high and low information discerners. Did they read the whole story before believing a thing or did they just scroll through it mindlessly? As per the findings, the low ID group only concentrated on the first few paragraphs of the story whereas the high ID group scanned the whole news by giving special attention to the graphical information too.

Following that, the participants were asked to attempt an impossible-to-complete word search. This was to make them feel a little stressed. They were made to believe that by doing so, they were helping another participant win £100. The received information falsely revealed that the participant for whom they were trying to win had strong religious beliefs. Participants were asked about how they felt about the task and their physiological responses were captured.

The findings revealed that when participants that had low ID received false information about the other participants, their emotional and cardiovascular response was poor as compared to those with a high ID who seemed to have healthier responses.

Researchers also found that when participants with low ID were presented with false information in a stressful situation, they had a flawed 'threat' response. Their bodies produced more of the stress hormone cortisol which brought about unhelpful cardiac responses as well as caused erratic reading behavior. This type of stress, as per the researchers, can lead to psychological problems too and it was also evident in the research study. The participants with low ID lacked self-confidence and had a poor sense of self-worth. They were unable to make balanced, well-informed judgments, which is essential for our well-being. Principal investigator of the pilot study, Dr. Geoff Walton believes that people who are unable to make good judgments about the information they come across online, on TV or in the newspaper, experience a negative physical response, which indicates that fake or false news is bad for your health.

On the contrary, those that are good at making judgments about the information they come across on said channels of communication tend to have a more positive and healthier physical response to it. Given the amount of misleading and fake news we and our children are exposed to daily, it poses a rather concerning and worrying threat to our physical and mental health.

Infodemic—Get Your Facts Straight

One of the most important things at this date and time is to get your facts straight. Misleading information, as we now know, can increase anxiety and cause depression. Therefore, to promote health and wellness and prevent the onset of anxiety in children, it is best to stay true to the facts and only rely on authentic information coming straight from reliable resources, because believe it or not, the infodemic is a greater pandemic than COVID-19 itself today.

Here are some ways parents can save teenagers from giving into false and fake news and become more upset than they already are.

Turn To Authentic/Official Sources for Updates

The best way to counter misleading or fake news is to only turn to official portals for all COVID-19 related news. They may report things late or take time to update their website but only because they are bound to post things that have been verified from multiple sources. There is no room for errors or doubtful information on sites like the World Health Organization or Centre for Disease Control, or National Health Service if you are in the UK. Also, sites ending with ".gov", or ".edu" are the most reliable among others as they indicate that they are either government-owned websites or by academic institutions aimed at research and studies.

Don't Turn a Blind Eye

Everyone we talk or turn to seems to have figured it all out. They will tell you of herbal remedies, alternative medications, and therapies to 'cure'

COVID-19. But do you think that the things random people come up with can be trusted over the word of the officials, scientists, and medical experts who still aren't 100% sure about the basics of the virus, its extent, its mutation or how it's transmitted in communities? The point being, don't believe everything you hear or see. Be vigilant and rely only on news coming directly from the official channels and medical experts. They know more about the virus than anyone else. Let them be the only guide you trust and stay away from conspiracy theories like it was all planned and concocted in a lab somewhere in Wuhan, China. The only thing you need to worry about is how you are going to protect yourself and your family from the virus and play a key role in helping stop its spread.

Check Reliability

Many people circulate messages without checking for its reliability. How can you be certain that the information you are about to share or have just received is coming from the official channels and is verified news? Whenever you receive something shady or remotely worrisome, always check for its source and authenticity. Is the article coming from a professional expert? Is the article dated recently? Are the links provided active and real? Are the numbers on the studies real or manipulated to increase impact and share-ability?

Admit that Things Can Be Manipulated

It happens and it happens a lot. There is an exaggeration of numbers, untrue facts stated as true, and broken links attached. There are also misleading headlines or ones that are click baits. It is best to avoid clicking on them or looking up to them for reliable information.

Unplug

Sometimes, excess of anything becomes harmful too. The majority of the information about the pandemic is indeed available online, sometimes, too much of it can lead to anxiety. Isolation periods and lockdowns get longer within a day's notice which can lead to further anxiety. Moreover, the kids can get exposed to misleading or confusing information, which is why it may be in their best interest, and yours too, to unplug from time to time. Look for other activities and passions to spend your free time on. Bond together, have meaningful conversations, start a new project together, etc. The more engaged you remain, the less time you will have to tune into social media, and less will be the exposure.

Check Their Biases

We can be too quick to judge and move on. It is human tendency to quickly believe things they already support or know of and disregard information they don't like or support. For example, if you don't support a political figure, there are fewer chances that you will listen to anything they say or believe in it. Teenagers too, have a hard time being open to information they don't agree with. However, at a time like this, we have to adapt better. Our goal shouldn't be to focus on who is saying what but on rather what they are saying. If it makes sense and seems a rational, calculated, and reliable piece of information, it is best to keep your biases aside.

Chapter 4: Essential Parenting Skill #2—Show Empathy

L iving in seclusion for no one knows how long can lead to quarantine fatigue, a term used to describe exhaustion caused by the new restrictive lifestyle that we are forced to adapt to. In many cases, your teen might feel like hitting a wall, says Noelle Wittliff, a South Pasadena-based licensed marriage and family therapist. Having worked with families and teenagers, she understands the emotional turmoil children are going through thanks to the pandemic. She believes that children are craving to leave the house, go out, hang out with their friends, and connect with them like old times. The online connection, although it seems promising, just doesn't cut it.

Generally, this particular phase we call adolescence is marked by feelings of invincibility and impulsivity. If we recall the time when we were young and energetic and then try to make note of what our children are missing out on, we understand the reasons for their anxiety and depression. This is the time when children begin to separate from their parents and make friends out of choice. They seek companionship elsewhere and work on stabilizing bonds with their partners and peers. Since they have been confined to their homes with their parents, their need for social interaction and independence has been crushed.

They are sad because the prom has been canceled. They are sad that they won't make it to their graduation, they are sad because they miss their friends and teachers. The schools shut down so abruptly that many friends even didn't get a chance to say a proper farewell.

As a parent, the second most important thing you need right now is to show empathy. You need to tell them that you understand what they are going through and are sad that they have to face such uncertainty. Showing empathy involves not just consoling or trying to see things from their perspective but also listening and communicating in a way that they feel heard and validated.

Why Show Empathy?

For starters, showing empathy towards others is one of the greatest gifts to give others. It is an art that requires attention, care, and a strong need to strengthen the connection with the speaker. It takes guts to be able to put yourself in someone else's shoes. It takes guts to understand another person's point of view.

For you, it is a chance to get to know your teen better by building a bridge of communication. When you decide to show empathy, you tell them that your emotional needs will be taken care of. You tell them that you will support them every step of the way and help them cope with the new normal in healthy ways.

You are not only paving way for openness but also trying to become a friend with your child when you try to show empathy.

Another reason showing empathy is important is because sooner or later, your kids are going to move on and get busy in their own lives. They will be expected to form new bonds, meet new people, and have a job and a family. They need to know how to be supportive as well as express themselves better. They need not see the world from their eyes alone but also from others. When they see you showing empathy and notice how reassuring it feels, they are likely to take it on too. Empathy is one of the many essential social skills they need to develop as it will help them maintain healthy relationships in adulthood.

Secondly, empathy also builds resilience in children. When they feel appreciated, validated, and cared for, when they feel that their feelings and thoughts matter to someone, when they feel that their opinions hold value, it helps them build resilience. They feel gratitude for the things that they have instead of feeling sorry or getting stuck over one thing. Resilience is the ability to move on from failure or loss and learn to cope.

Finally, your teenager has lost most of their privileges and independence after the recent turn of events. They can't drive around, go to a gym or for a jog in the park, they can't meet their friends and go watch a movie. They are frustrated because they have to stay indoors and away from all the things they loved doing. Living indoors has also bound them to many household chores and they are back at being supervised 24/7 by their parents and siblings. This often makes them act out due to boredom and anger. Being understood, and heard can make a huge difference in toning down the level of frustration that's brewing inside them.

How to Be Empathetic Towards Children during these Tough Times

To get started with being empathetic is to know that whatever your child is going through is pretty normal as long as they don't depict any signs of extreme stress and anxiety. Showing empathy doesn't mean that you forget all the rules and structure you laid in practice. It simply means giving them the chance to feel a little better about their situation by helping them unburden and not let that frustration build up. It is about raising their self-esteem and self-worth by acknowledging their loss and sadness. There are multiple ways to do so and some have been highlighted below.

Connect with Others

In times like these, we often become focused on ourselves and forget about others and what they are going through. You may, unintentionally, be ignoring your children or assuming that they are alright but you need to reach out and keep a check on them. You have to find ways to connect with them and also with others in your community so that they do the same. To fight feelings of isolation, having someone's sincere company and presence can mean the world. Being a part of your child's life and engaging in helpful actions like donating things to charities, or supporting a social cause can increase their feelings of connectedness. Of course, you have to maintain social distancing but that shouldn't stop you from offering your moral support to others. The best time to get in touch with people you rarely talked to in the past, is now.

Be Compassionate

It is okay if there are days when your kids spend all the time in front of a TV or in their rooms with a locked door. Like you, they are also trying to make the best of the situation. Some days, you may feel like nagging or being harsh with them, but try not to. Instead, reach out to them with compassion. For all that we know, you two are stuck in this for longer than anticipated, so there is no point in trying to fight with your child over petty issues. Maybe the reason for the change in their behavior is because they are finding it hard to cope with the situation. Or perhaps they are too anxious and don't know how to manage the barricade of feelings. Show compassion. Don't try to be nagging all the time and let them have their space.

Stay Aware of Their Needs

Remember the time when you were a child or a budding adult, what were the things you needed the most? Now focus on how the pandemic has affected the life of your child. Try to visualize the things they are missing out on and how it might make them feel. They may need more than just your emotional support. Try to fill the voids by doing things together. Take up a project and work on it together. Show appreciation for the help they offer around the house. Help them with their homework.

Chapter 5: Vital Parenting Skill #3—Stick to Routine and Provide Structure

A s kids are confined to homes, there will be times when they will test your limits. They would want to go out, hang out with their friends. Since this isn't a possibility, they will try to manipulate you into other ways where they start to demand things from you simply because they are bored or don't know what to do in the ample amount of time they have. The first few weeks after the lockdown have passed and the things that interested them, in the beginning, don't anymore. They have watched all the interesting shows on Netflix, watched their favorite movies over and over again, and are done checking their phones every five minutes. What they need aren't more activities but rather a structure and routine.

Not long ago, they always seemed busy. They had school assignments to work on, limited TV time, short breaks for dinner. They never had any free time. How about restarting with the same routine again? Structure and routines allow them to follow the clock. They wake up at a certain time, go to bed at a fixed time, spend time working on their assignments at a certain time, etc. When bound by a consistent routine, they are less likely to act out or resort to negative behaviors like needless disagreements, secrecy, and deceit.

Routines, when put into practice, give them a list of all the things they are expected to do throughout the day.

Why Kids Need Structure

During a time as such creating a routine helps children, teenagers in particular, in several ways. Since they are the toughest to deal with, thanks to their moodiness and rebellious nature, having a routine provides them with some predictability and structure. They desperately need that as uncertainty about their future has them all worked up. A routine promotes reassurance. It promotes a sense of safety. It also gives the mind something to focus on and less time to think negatively.

Most teenagers are also impulsive by nature. They will act out harshly when they feel annoyed or frustrated. Structure not only keeps them engaged, but it also limits misbehavior. It gives them clear directions of what is expected of them and how they must do it. Take household chores for instance. If they have vague instructions about how to do them, they are going to be least motivated about them. This will lead to poor performance and guaranteed failure which will cause more frustration. They will most probably argue with the one who set the chore for them or act out.

Thirdly, the structure provides organization. Everything expected of them is consistent and planned out in advance. This leaves fewer chances of mistakes. Routines also prevent procrastination and improve efficiency. Everything gets done promptly and with effectiveness. The more elaborative the rules, the less anxiety your child will experience.

Establishing Routines for Teenagers

Now that we know of the importance of routine and how they promote wellness and mental health in children, below are some great ways to get started with routines. But before we do that, here's a helpful tip: Whenever deciding on a routine or structure, let your child have a say in it. It will make them feel like an important part of the rules and they will be more willing to adhere to them. Sit together and seek their input on how you can work out a plan that works best for you both. This will minimize acting out, temper tantrums, and arguments in the future.

Set Clear Expectations

Start with setting realistic and clear expectations. They should, at all times, know what is expected of them. Having clear goals and expectations increases the likelihood of their accomplishment. When children are unable to decipher what is expected of them, they feel confused and aren't able to give 100%

to anything. Thus, if you want them to follow a routine or structure, let them know the rules first.

Have Bedtime and Wake Up Routines

Since no one is going to school or the office anymore, it may seem tempting to sleep in till late. If your children's school isn't offering online classes and they are free for the whole semester, don't encourage the habit of sleeping in till late in the morning. Start the day early and go through the routines as if it were a regular school day. Don't allow them to stay in their jammies all day because then, it will become a habit. The same goes for bedtime routines. It is understandable to stretch the bedtime to an hour or two but not more than that, especially on weeknights. Having a routine will allow their physiological system to maintain a balance between rest periods and activity. It won't confuse the mind about when to go to sleep and when to wake up. It can also promote the onset of fatigue during odd hours of the day which can lead to hormonal imbalances.

Schedule Meal Times

The same applies to meal times. If they used to have their first meal of the day around 7:00 am, let that remain a staple. They may act annoyed but be strict about it. Eating at inappropriate times upsets the digestive system. Additionally, when food is offered at regular timings, there are fewer instances of feeling hungry. While at it, if you notice them eating at odd hours or feeling hungry all the time, teach them to differentiate between different types of hunger. Are they eating simply because they are bored or are they eating to feel less lonely?

Allow Breaks in Between

Realistically speaking, they are on a break currently. They deserve some time to cool off. They don't need to be disciplined all the time. Allow some free time during the day at regular intervals to uplift their mood and engage in things they are passionate about. It can mean playing their favorite video games, for some, it may be watching TV or listening to music. Having breaks in between will give their mind some rest and recharging time. Fun-breaks can also alleviate stress and anxiety.

Encourage Creative Outlets

Encourage them to pursue their hobbies and interests now that they have some free time on their hands. However, be sure to allow a certain time of the day to engage in them. Hobbies foster creativity and give children something to enjoy.

Chapter 6: Essential Parenting Skill #4—Practice Mindfulness

T eenagers are worried more than ever about their future and what it will look like. Their studies have come to an abrupt halt, they don't know what expectations companies will have from them and whether they will ever find a job of their choosing in such economically harsh times or not. Will they be able to get any summer jobs if the country continues to stay in a lockdown or be able to keep the one they have in case the stores don't reopen? These are genuine concerns that can keep them awake at night and cause severe anxiety.

But this worry is understandable. Nearly every generation ever since the existence of humanity, has gone through some economic recession period. It isn't the first time that people are being laid off. Some wars destabilized the entire continents, there were pandemics and the global recession that made our elders lose their job and sit at home. You can always encourage your children to read about it and learn how they coped with the ever-changing world and raised their value. Secondly, to reduce their anxiety, try using mindfulness techniques.

Being mindful requires a sane and present mind. When practicing mindfulness, one needs to focus on the present and stop worrying about the past or the future. When you can acknowledge and take in all that is happening around you, your mind becomes relaxed and calm. It is easy to focus on the things that aren't in our control, such as the pandemic, but it is more fruitful and peaceful to focus on the things that are in our control and be grateful for the blessings. When we feel focused, we are better able to steer in the right direction with rational thinking and manage our emotions.

Presently, most of the time our kids spent during commutes, at school and going out with friends isn't available. They have more free time today than they ever had before. The lack of activities and routines can lead the mind into thinking negatively. As parents, we need to make the most of that time, and practicing mindfulness seems like a good and beneficial option.

Being mindful takes time but once your children get the hang of it, they will begin to enjoy it. Their thoughts will become positive and intentional. They won't worry about what to do with their free time but rather, would already have many ideas to work upon as mindfulness boosts creativity and focus.

How Mindfulness Can Help Teenagers

Although life is complicated for teenagers generally, it won't be easy unless they do something about it. Remember the time when they were young and feared entering high school? Their concerns and excitement kept their mind occupied at all times. It seemed like a challenge back then. But now that they have made it and are in the second, third, fourth year, it doesn't seem as tough. This means that we are naturally capable of adjusting to a new normal. Right now they are worried about their future but two to three years down the line and they will be laughing about this among their college friends. But this isn't easy for everyone. For some, transitions are the hardest to make. This is where social skills come into play. This is the part where they need to learn some excellent and healthy coping skills to regulate their emotions better. But it all starts with a relaxed and eager mind which mindfulness can help achieve.

Some of the many benefits of mindfulness are:

- Reduced anxiety. When children can switch from thinking negative to positive, their anxiety levels are reduced too.

- Better quality of sleep. To get a good night's sleep, you need a clear and relaxed mind. Mindfulness techniques help students achieve just that!

- Improved emotional regulation. Children, and especially teenagers, can be highly emotional. The many bodily and hormonal transitions they are going through are enough to cause stress and anxiety. They were worried about how they look, if they will be socially acceptable or not, and whether somebody will like them or not. Introducing them to mindfulness and how it works can help them cope with negative emotions better. They can connect with their inner self better and not let it bully them into thinking that they aren't good enough.

- A focused mind. When children practice mindful techniques regularly, they improve their attention span too. They can focus on one thing for a longer period than before.

How to Practice Mindfulness–A Guide for Teenagers

Being mindful involves slowing down and focusing on the things in the present. It sounds simple but when one is stressed out or anxious, it can become rather challenging. But since the goal is to get started, no matter how big or small the effort, here are a few strategies to improve your focus and feel good about the present despite the current circumstances.

Stop Multitasking

There was a time not long ago when professionals urged us to multitask. They believed it helped finish tasks faster. But they failed to acknowledge one important thing—it butchers the quality of it. When we attempt to multi-task, we are unable to focus on a single task completed. Our brain isn't designed to do so. It is designed to single-task.

With so much time spent at home, teens are expected to help with the chores. But they don't want to put their phones down even for a minute either. Doing both can lead to more stress and anxiety as the brain becomes confused about the order of things, the specific demands of each, and becomes stressed. Thus, if you want to get all the chores done correctly and promptly, ask them to focus on just one thing at a time.

Use the STOP Strategy

The acronym STOP stands for the following

S - Stop whatever you are doing and take a moment to breathe

T - Take a deep breath and be aware of the action

O - Observe the many sensations, thoughts, and emotions you go through

P - Pause and be still for a few minutes to soak in positive energy from your surroundings before going about your day.

This is, by far, the easiest and most effective way to practice deep breathing and become more aware of the thoughts in your mind, and the sensations in your body.

Go for a Walk

Sounds rather conflicting to what we are told by public health officials, going for a walk in the park or the neighborhood is only dangerous if social distancing protocols aren't being followed. Going outside and breathing into the fresh air, hearing the chirping of the birds, watching the tree's branches sway with the wind, and the sun shining on your face can help you feel better and improve the functioning of your senses. The calmer you feel, the lesser the chatter in your mind.

Make Peace with Ambiguity

The virus isn't going anywhere anytime soon. Even if a vaccine is developed, it will take months of testing both on animals and later on humans to see if the drug is beneficial in the long run or not. After that, it will take months before everyone can afford one. That being said, you can't waste your time thinking about the things that aren't in your control. No one can say what will happen for certain in the future and what it will look like. Thus, there is no point in trying to get all worked up because of it. Your teenager shouldn't let this fear of the uncertainty get to them. If they can't change their current state, there is no point worrying about it. Instead, motivate them to acknowledge the uncertainty and make peace with it.

Show Gratitude

Amid the craziness, it can be hard to focus on the brighter side of things, but as their parent, you have to motivate them to. Focusing on the positive will keep their mind away from the negativity and the disappointment they face. Ask them to come up with three to five things they are grateful for in their lives every day. These can be as simple as good food on the table, good health, a roof over their heads, their family members and their safety, and friends they can count on. Acknowledgment of these will allow them to stay positive and not fall into depression or suffer from anxiety.

Chapter 7: Vital Parenting Skill #5–Find Ways to Stay Connected

T he need for practical distancing has put a pause on normal social activities like backyard barbecues, movie nights, date nights, sleepovers with friends, musical concerts and festivals, school functions and sports events, etc. While it is imperative that you maintain distance from others to flatten the curve, it doesn't mean cutting out on your friends and relatives in the literal sense. Social interactions must still be made, only virtually. Staying connected has become more important than ever as it promotes well-being and mental health when you have someone to talk to.

Social connections bring us closer to one another and make us feel an integral part of the community. Man has always been a social animal. His need for social interactions, to communicate, to express love and complain can't be denied. Every person we come across daily or on a routine basis plays some part in our lives–even the bus driver that comes to pick our children up every day or the garbage truck driver or the mailman. Each leaves behind some impression on our mind and mental health.

During these scary and uncertain times, we are all experiencing one or more forms of physical or cognitive symptoms of loneliness. We are confined in our homes with not much to do other than just eat, sleep, and watch TV. We desperately want to go out, hang out with our co-workers, friends, and relatives. News flash: teenagers feel the same.

They are bored and miss their friends. They are in that phase of their lives where they value their friends more than their siblings and parents because they can connect better with them. But since everything has been shut down, they feel stressed which is a scientifically proven aftermath of social isolation. The need for the physical touch even if it just means shaking hands, hugging each other, or patting each other's back is an ultimate stress-reducer. Teenagers, upon meeting one another during school hours mostly stayed in some form of physical touch. Physical touch floods our body with the bonding hormone, medically referred to as oxytocin. It is known to improve immune response and mental health. Since it is impossible to feel that way during the current pandemic, we have to let our children stay connected in some other ways.

How Does Social Connectedness Impact Our Health?

During these unique circumstances, you can't completely disconnect with everyone. We all have to come together virtually to support each other and look after each other.

Why?

Being isolated prevents us from expressing our feelings about both complaints and affection. It prevents us from venting out and thus, leads to unwanted stress. Children who are not encouraged to speak their minds have poor self-confidence and self-worth. They feel unvalued and unloved by their parents and others. When someone gifts us their attention and affection, it automatically reduces the stress hormones. When the body feels less stressed, the immune system is strengthened. Ongoing research also promises many other health benefits of staying connected. These include longer life, happier outlook towards life, improved cognitive skills and memory, and increased motivation to look after one's self.

Some studies stress the importance of friendships and their link with providing emotional support and intellectual stimulation in difficult times. With social distancing protocols in place, stress can easily find a way to creep up on us and leave us feeling depressed and annoyed.

How to Stay Socially Connected with Peers

Thanks to the internet, there are now tons of ways to stay in touch with friends and family virtually. Apps like Zoom, Hangouts, WhatsApp, and Facebook have made it easier to stay in touch with our loved ones and communicate with them whenever needed. Since this current generation is the master of apps and social media platforms, they haven't given up on their friends. They are constantly in touch with them virtually. As discussed above, staying connected is imperative. Here are some ways to further encourage social interactions without actually leaving the house.

Catch-up Virtually

Encourage teenagers to schedule video calls via several social networks to keep a check on one another. Being in touch allows them to feel connected as they are all going through the same challenges. This also goes for adults. They too should set up virtual hangouts with distant relatives, especially older ones to ensure their health is in prime condition and they aren't feeling left out.

Play Games

In their free time, your children can schedule games to be played together. There are thousands of free apps that allow participants to connect and play against one another or as a team. You can play Uno, Monopoly, chess, Scrabble, word puzzles, and similar board games that require more than one player. You can also play games as a family by organizing a game night.

Host Movie Nights

Thanks to Netflix Party, integration into the famous online entertainment service, it allows children to sync video playback with their friends. Every individual who is a part of the party can pause, play, rewind, or fast forward the movie from their screens so that everyone in the group views it at the same time. There is also a chat room they can use to share their thoughts about the movie or the show or simply talk with one another. The best thing about it is that only those in the group can send an invite which eliminates the chance of any stranger joining the chat room.

Write a Letter

This one is an old-school trick. Before WhatsApp or even text messaging, people used to write one another heartfelt letters to express their feelings and compassion. You can encourage your child to do the same and mail it to their pals. If writing a letter is too much, they can write an email instead and talk to their friends. The joy of finding that one email from a loved one is incomparable to a text that is received within seconds. The time they spend waiting for it to arrive is both pleasant and torturous.

Start an Activity Together

Although young boys may not be interested in this as much, teen girls can do stuff virtually-together. For example, they can all start a book club and read the same book throughout the week. They can later discuss the prose, characters, and story. If they are into fashion, they can sew masks or scarves for poor people and donate them to the homeless. They can also bake cookies for everyone in the neighborhood to spread some joy in these tough times.

Chapter 8: Essential Parenting Skill #6–Teach Coping Skills

When children are worried, stressed out, or anxious, it makes thinking rationally harder. They may fail to understand how to deal with the stress and resort to negative behaviors to feel better. The most common signs that your child is stressed or anxious include excessive clinginess, aggressiveness, emotional meltdowns, tearfulness, and regression among other behaviors. Some kids may often report headaches, dizziness, a racing heart, stomachaches, and poor sleep patterns.

As a parent, it is your job to take care of both their emotional and physical complaints. You have to teach them healthy and positive ways to express themselves as well as manage their anxiety. They need to address their feelings with a positive attitude and not give in to the overwhelming feelings. They need to know how to cope after a setback and move forward in their lives without clinging to the past. Easier said than done, it isn't easy for parents to connect with their children as they have grown into teenagers. They are rebellious and can counter your words and actions with even smarter comebacks. They may not understand why you need to sort things for them when they can do it themselves. But they can't and it's visible in the ways they are acting around the house. The first thing you need to do to connect with them is to offer them a safe space to be themselves. This means that they shouldn't feel the need to keep things bottled up inside and feel no shame in expressing their emotions. They need to know that expressing emotions doesn't make them weak.

Why Kids Need to Learn to Manage Stress and Anxiety

Stress is an uncomfortable feeling. But it is also a reality of life. Some stress is known healthy as it keeps us driven and motivated to change our current state. However, for kids who don't know how to manage anxiety, it can be detrimental to their health. It makes them uncomfortable and they do what they can to escape that. This escaping from a state of discomfort to comfort is what we call coping. How we cope with the various challenges we face in life is what determines whether we are stronger or weak.

The reason kids need to learn to manage stress is that it can make life difficult for them. They may report sleeplessness, depression, irritability, and anger. When we are stressed, our body releases cortisol which our immune system has to fight against. Now, had the situation been any different, we would have suggested that we let our immune system work things out. But we need it to fight against the more dangerous and potentially life-threatening virus. We can't have it doing overtime and making the body and all its organs face the consequences. Over time, stress can also lead to serious health issues such as high blood pressure, cardiovascular problems, and anxiety disorders. Thus, we need to eliminate the causes or prepare our children to fight against it.

In general, there are two approaches to counter bad feelings both, positive and negative. Negative coping strategies may seem tempting and offer short-term relief but they don't address the problem at the core. Meaning, you are soon going to find yourself in the same dark pit as before. If you get addicted, it can be harmful in the long run too. Thus, you don't want your kids to rely on quick fixes to overcome their anxiety and stress. Positive coping strategies, on the other hand, enhance emotional health, promote well-being, and build confidence in a child's strengths. They also help strengthen relationships and make kids more resilient. They may require more time to work and need more willingness and investment but the benefits are long-term and prosperous. Positive and healthy ways of coping are also preventive strategies as they not only offer relief from the existing anxiety but also reduces the chances of experiencing it later.

Our goal, as parents, should be to expose our kids to positive coping strategies.

Stress Management Strategies for Kids

Your role is a crucial one in developing healthy coping skills among children. Some of the most effective ways to get started are mentioned below.

Encourage Deep Breathing Exercises

Deep breathing helps relax our mind and body. It is the most innovative and effective way to tone down a panic attack and calm an anxious person. The best thing about this is how simple it is. Let your child experience calmness by taking a deep breath, holding it in, and then releasing it. Deep breathing activates our parasympathetic nervous system. In simpler terms, it reduces the feelings of fear and distress and allows the breather to feel a sense of calm. Teaching kids about using this strategy as the means to start their day can uplift their mood and make their minds more relaxed and creative. With COVID-19 ruining all their plans for the year, they can use this to alleviate their stress and manage their anxiety.

Give Their Feelings a Name

Before they start with the deep breathing technique, let them analyze the reasons for their stress and anxiety. They need to know what they are feeling exactly first. Many children are unable to distinguish between fear and anxiety or anger and frustration. Some think they are synonymous but as adults, we know that they aren't. Therefore, before aiming to control their emotional beast, they need to label the feelings they are going through.

Stop Worrying about Things They Can't Control

There is not much that you can control during the pandemic. Even if you are taking all the precautionary measures recommended by the public health officers, you can't be certain that everyone else is following them too. This means that as long as everyone doesn't abide by the rules and follow the instructions, our condition wouldn't change. This can lead to anger and frustration among teenagers who are waiting for the day to feel freedom again. Showing empathy and teaching them coping skills to combat situations out of their control is another important aspect. You need to shift their focus from the things they can't control to the ones they can and stop worrying about the former. Remind them that although they can't control or manipulate everyone's freedom of speech, they are accountable for their actions, words, and behaviors.

Offer Compassion and Validation

Children of all ages want to be heard. They want their concerns listened to with a compassionate and supportive heart. They want to feel validated and appreciated. They also need their parents to show empathy and validate their fears by acknowledging them. Let your kid know that they are not alone in this. Let them see that they have your moral, physical, and emotional support through thick and thin.

Empower Them

Ask for their input in things. Show them how they can help. Engage them in projects of their interest so that they don't feel left out. When we allow children to act like adults and empower them with some responsibility, they feel valued. Reassure them that their health is in their hands. Tell them that they need to protect themselves by practicing proper handwashing, wearing gloves when going out for a run, and wearing a mask. Teach them about the cough and sneezing etiquette and give them the responsibility to ensure that their presence doesn't become an inconvenience to anyone. They will be more willing to stick with the rules when they feel in control.

Chapter 9: Essential Parenting Skill #7–Stay Active

A s adults, we are fully aware of the many health benefits of staying active. As we cope with the new normal, every aspect of our lives has turned upside down. Businesses have closed down, social distancing measures have been put in place, homes have turned into office cubicles, classes are conducted online; we don't know what is next. With every business temporarily on hold, gyms and fitness centers are no exception. Try to recall the times when we would gladly skip leg day or purposely busy ourselves into work to avoid going to the gym. Well, look at us now—desperate to get out of the house, even if it means going to the gym. The good news, however, is that we are coming to this realization that we don't need gyms to stay healthy and in shape. We simply need a workout plan that keeps us in shape and gets rid of the excess fat.

But many of us are skipping workouts out of choice when this is the time we need to work out the most. According to public health officials, we have to work out to boost our immunity, build stamina, and give our muscles the flexibility they need to stay in shape. Too much muscle relaxation abruptly, especially for someone who worked out religiously can lead to poor muscle flexibility over time and make life rather painful.

Another important reason why we need to stay active and push our children to do the same is that when our bodies are constantly in stress or survival mode, it can trigger the fight or flight response. When the body of a child goes into the fight or flight mode, they either become too active or fidgety. Staying active keeps them maintaining sanity in the mind and prevents tension or frenetic energy.

Other than that, the more laidback and idle we allow our children to be, the more we are risking their chances of gaining weight. Add to that the poor dietary choices and high calorie foods, and we have the perfect recipe on "how to eat to get fat". Ever since the lockdown and pandemic warning, we have stocked up mostly on non-perishables which include frozen foods instead of fresh produce. We have also stocked up on ultra-produced, calorie-dense options instead of picking vegetables and fruits to boost immunity. Also, since we are spending all the time at home, we feel hungrier than ever and are always on the lookout for something to munch on. We have pushed our kids towards bad choices deliberately and then complain about why they feel so lazy and energy-less. Well, news flash, all that they have been eating recently is making them run on low energy yet consume more and more.

But that still doesn't answer as to why do we have to prioritize our fitness when we are already in a survival mode? The answer is simple: we have to!

We can't let our poor dietary choices and poor fitness regimes be the reason why first responders, doctors, and nurses have to work tirelessly and try to save us. It would be selfish not to take care of yourself and then burden them with our presence when our immune system fails to fight back the virus.

If we encourage our kids and motivate ourselves to take up healthy exercising, we may have a chance to beat the virus–even if we contract it. If we equip our body with the right foods that boost immunity and then maintain a healthy and active lifestyle, we may be able to save our families from the grief of losing a loved one.

The Perks of Staying Active

According to WHO, one must spend 150 minutes doing a moderate-intensity workout weekly or 75-minutes of high-intensity workout per week. The recommendations don't suggest the use of any weight-lifting or exercising equipment and can easily be achieved at home.

When data from a health study in Norway was examined consisting of the experiences of approximately 34,000 Norwegian adults following their lives for 11 years, it was revealed that the ones who had an active lifestyle and exercised regularly showed fewer signs of depression and anxiety (Storeng et al., 2018). This was one of the biggest studies and came to be known as the Health Study of

Nord-Trøndelag (HUNT study). The gathered data also looked at even small attempts to exercise and how it protected those individuals against depression. As per the findings, if only the participants had exercised for an hour per week, they would have prevented many symptoms of depression. In fact, 12% of the cases of depression—self-reported by the individuals—could have been prevented.

In another study's review published in the Journal of Sports and Health Science, working out for as little as 60 minutes per week while engaging in moderate to high-intensity workouts, can play a crucial role in boosting one's immunity (Nieman & Wentz, 2019). Additionally, the research also revealed that engaging in a moderate-intensity workout routine surprisingly reduced upper-respiratory infections too and decreased the incidence of fatality from pneumonia or influenza.

Apart from that, there are many other health benefits of exercising and opting for a healthy lifestyle. Knowing these will help you take up exercise yourself as well as convince your children to engage in some too.

Exercise reduces stress and anxiety. Exercise builds resilience. It releases mood-boosting chemicals that help one stay positive and ward off negativity. It makes us feel good about ourselves by releasing the feel-good chemical called dopamine which is the antibody for cortisol.

Exercise also helps us sleep better by improving the quality of sleep. WHO recommends sleeping at least eight hours every night to boost immunity. Additionally, it lowers the risk of cardiovascular diseases as well as lowers blood pressure, ultimately improving our cholesterol profile.

How to Encourage Teenagers to Stay Active

Staying active but indoors? That is something unheard of. Of course, a gym or a fitness center seems like the best place to work out and burn some calories but since it isn't an option currently, we have to make the most of what we have at home. You can always engage the kids to become more active by cutting down the amount of time they spend sitting and browsing Netflix. Not only are they tiring out their eyes, but they are also not doing their bodies any favors. Thus, the best way to ensure that they don't spend most of their days and nights binge-watching their favorite TV shows without moving an inch is to keep them busy with chores. This is what we call sneaking movement into normal routines. Here's how you are going to do it.

Start with dividing chores between yourself and your children. Some will get sweeping, some will be responsible for laundry and some for vacuuming. To guarantee implementation, you can set a certain hour of the day to set up a routine. Household chores like dusting, scrubbing, and cleaning allow children to incorporate some movement into their otherwise sedentary lifestyle and move their legs and muscles.

Other than that, if your kids remain glued to the TV screen all day, you can make it a rule to utilize the time for commercials to do a few squats, lunges, push-ups, or jumping jacks.

There are many other indoor activities that you can engage in together as a team. For example, you all can play your favorite songs, pump up the volume, and get dancing. Aerobics, Zumba, and dancing don't require any treadmills or elliptical machines. You just need some great music and your favorite people to accompany you on the floor and move your body. You don't have to coordinate your moves. You simply have to shake and move enough to get your heart racing.

If you want some calm and peace in the house, you can opt for Pilates or yoga too. Yoga has countless health benefits, a reduction in stress and anxiety being a prominent one (Sharma, 2013).

Take a Virtual Class

Many personal trainers have taken their businesses online by promoting online classes. There are many paid and free to subscribe to and join live exercise sessions with your fitness coaches. The reason it is ideal for you and your children is that it adds an accountability factor. When you have already paid the subscription fee or paid for the course, you are more likely to attend it. Some trainers are also featuring personal training sessions based on personal needs and preferences. Besides, since the overall goal is to find something better and uplifting to do during the pandemic, this will also provide your kids with the opportunity to interact with others in a fun and engaging way.

Go to YouTube for Free Videos

If you are not into the paid subscription thing, you can always ask your teenager to search for videos based on their personal preference. For instance, if your teenage daughter wants to learn belly dancing instead of opting for a high-intensity workout, you can help her come across many online free videos on YouTube or via mobile apps to learn. There isn't a doubt that portals like YouTube offer viewers millions of exercise-related videos to choose from, making it easier for everyone to find something they like.

Go Outside

Based on the guidelines provided by your local public health officials, you can also go out for a run or jog to the park as long as you follow the precautionary measures of maintaining social distancing and keeping yourself and others around you safe by wearing a mask and applying hand sanitizer from time to time. You can add riding bikes to your agenda and motivate your kids to join you. The less traffic on the roads also makes it safer for you and your child to enjoy some fresh air and clean views, all while you exercise. If you are too worried about leaving the house, you and your children can opt for activities like yard work, building a treehouse in the backyard, building a shelter for your pet, or growing fruits and vegetables in the garden. The more sunshine you get, the more vitamin D your body absorbs.

Conclusion

F or all we know right now, tougher times are coming. As soon as the pandemic ends, we will be faced with yet another and bigger problem (i.e. stabilizing the economy). The people who have lost jobs during the lockdown, the companies that have gone bankrupt or closed down due to lack of finances will need to restart from scratch again. The competition will only get tougher. Children will need to adapt to the changing demand and supply and make themselves valuable.

It all starts with the right social skills and flexibility. They do not need to be afraid anymore by the challenges that lay ahead; they know how not to give in to anxiety, and feel confident in their skills and talents. They must know how to communicate, behave, and respect others. They need to learn to listen and offer empathy. They must be open to collaboration.

The reason we are telling you this is because this, right now, is the time to train them and prepare them for professional life. Soon, they will head for college life and then into the professional world. They will need these essential skills to land themselves a good and promising job. Since they can no longer rely on their teachers and educators to work with them and train them for the upcoming future, you have to take up that role and ensure that they are their best selves. Use this time to teach them about the importance of time management, stress regulation strategies, and mindfulness so that when they step out of that door, they no longer feel anxiety creeping in. Instead, they must feel confident and ready for the world and all the challenges that lay ahead. Moreover, the busier they are, the more distracted they will be and the less time they will have to themselves to allow loneliness to set in.

References

Artley, A. (2020, April). Exercise During
 Coronavirus: Tips for Staying Active -
 HelpGuide.org. Help Guide.
 https://www.helpguide.org/articles/healthy-
 living/exercise-during-coronavirus.htm

Barlow, N. (2018, June 22). It's true-Fake news is
 bad for your health. About Manchester.
 https://aboutmanchester.co.uk/its-true-fake-
 news-is-bad-for-your-health/

Bentley, V. (2020, April 9). How mindfulness can
 help you cope during COVID-19.
 Intermountainhealthcare.Org.
 https://intermountainhealthcare.org/blogs/t
 opics/covid-19/2020/04/how-mindfulness-
 can-help-you-cope-during-covid-19/

Beusekom, M. V. (2020, May 12). Scientists: "Exactly
 zero" evidence COVID-19 came from a lab.
 CIDRAP.
 https://www.cidrap.umn.edu/news-
 perspective/2020/05/scientists-exactly-zero-
 evidence-covid-19-came-lab

BNI Treatment Centers. (2020, March 26). Isolation
 in Teens During Coronavirus. BNI Treatment
 Centers. https://bnitreatment.com/isolation-
 in-teens-during-coronavirus/

Boone, L. (2020, April 29). Teens are feeling lonely and anxious in isolation. Here's how parents can help. Los Angeles Times. https://www.latimes.com/lifestyle/story/2020-04-29/parenting-teens-coronavirus

Branstetter, M. R. (2020, April 7). COVID-19 Stress: Coping Skills for Parents and Children. Youth First. https://youthfirstinc.org/covid-19-stress-coping-skills-for-parents-and-children/

Building Blocks | Creating Structure | Essentials | Parenting Information | CDC. (2020, June 8). Www.Cdc.Gov. https://www.cdc.gov/parents/essentials/structure/building.html

Cherry, K. (2020, March 30). How to Practice Empathy During the COVID-19 Pandemic. Verywell Mind. https://www.verywellmind.com/how-to-practice-empathy-during-the-covid-19-pandemic-4800924

Coping with Coronavirus (COVID-19). (n.d.). Coping Skills for Kids. Retrieved July 3, 2020, from https://copingskillsforkids.com/coping-with-coronavirus

Exercise is Essential for Well-Being During COVID-19 Pandemic. (n.d.). Health Quest Patient Center. https://patients.healthquest.org/exercise-is-essential-for-well-being-during-covid-19-pandemic/

Fegert, J. M., Vitiello, B., Plener, P. L., & Clemens, V. (2020). Challenges and burden of the Coronavirus 2019 (COVID-19) pandemic for child and adolescent mental health: a narrative review to highlight clinical and research needs in the acute phase and the long return to normality. Child and Adolescent Psychiatry and Mental Health, 14(1). https://doi.org/10.1186/s13034-020-00329-3

Goodman, J., & Carmichael, F. (2020, May 30). The Bill Gates 'microchip' claim fact-checked. BBC News. https://www.bbc.com/news/52847648

Jacobson, R. (2020, March 23). How Mindfulness Can Help During COVID-19. Child Mind Institute; Child Mind Institute. https://childmind.org/article/how-mindfulness-can-help-during-covid-19/

Jones, J. K. (2018, December 2). The Benefits of
    Mindfulness Meditation for Teens. World of
    Psychology.
    https://psychcentral.com/blog/the-benefits-
    of-mindfulness-meditation-for-teens/

Kim, C. S. (2020, March 24). Establishing structure
    and routine for kids during COVID-19. CHOC
    Children's Blog.
    https://blog.chocchildrens.org/establishing-
    structure-and-routine-for-kids-during-covid-
    19/

Loades, M. E., Chatburn, E., Higson-Sweeney, N.,
    Reynolds, S., Shafran, R., Brigden, A., Linney,
    C., McManus, M. N., Borwick, C., & Crawley,
    E. (2020). Rapid Systematic Review: The
    Impact of Social Isolation and Loneliness on
    the Mental Health of Children and
    Adolescents in the Context of COVID-19.
    Journal of the American Academy of Child &
    Adolescent Psychiatry.
    https://doi.org/10.1016/j.jaac.2020.05.009

Nieman, D. C., & Wentz, L. M. (2019). The
    compelling link between physical activity and
    the body's defense system. Journal of Sport
    and Health Science, 8(3), 201–217.
    https://doi.org/10.1016/j.jshs.2018.09.009

Sharma, M. (2013). Yoga as an Alternative and
Complementary Approach for Stress
Management. Journal of Evidence-Based
Complementary & Alternative Medicine,
19(1), 59–67.
https://doi.org/10.1177/2156587213503344

Shih, G. (2020, March 5). Conspiracy theorists blame
U.S. for coronavirus. China is happy to
encourage them. Washington Post.
https://www.washingtonpost.com/world/asi
a_pacific/conspiracy-theorists-blame-the-us-
for-coronavirus-china-is-happy-to-
encourage-them/2020/03/05/50875458-
5dc8-11ea-ac50-18701e14e06d_story.html

Sorbring, E., & Lansford, J. E. (2019). School
systems, parent behavior, and academic
achievement□: an international perspective.
Springer.

Stein, N. (2020, March 25). COVID-19 and Exercise:
Staying Active while Socially Distancing. Lark
Health. https://www.lark.com/blog/covid-
19-and-exercise/

Storeng, S. H., Sund, E. R., & Krokstad, S. (2018). Factors associated with basic and instrumental activities of daily living in elderly participants of a population-based survey: the Nord-Trøndelag Health Study, Norway. BMJ Open, 8(3), e018942. https://doi.org/10.1136/bmjopen-2017-018942

Teens Need to Manage Stress. Parents Are Best-Positioned to Help. (2018, September 4). Center for Parent and Teen Communication. https://parentandteen.com/teaching-teens-coping-skills-one-of-the-7-cs-of-resilience/

Walter, K. (2020, June 2). COVID-19 Lockdown Having an Impact on Adolescent Mental Health. HCPLive®. https://www.mdmag.com/medical-news/covid-19-lockdown-adolescent-mental-health

Why Parents Must Have Empathy for Teens During the COVID-19 Pandemic. (2020, May 6). Center for Parent and Teen Communication. https://parentandteen.com/empathy-covid-19/

Book Description

Toddlerhood is the stage of immense growth. Little ones learn to crawl, walk, communicate, and understand orders and requests. The more effective their communication and social skills, the better their chances of learning things quickly. Social skills allow children to have more meaningful and rewarding interactions. What they need from their parents is some encouragement and inspiration to allow healthy habits and skills to set in.

In this exceptionally-researched and relatable guide, parents can find answers to questions that have been bothering them for quite some time. How to raise sensible and compassionate toddlers? How to develop social skills? How to boost their self-esteem and self-worth? How to raise them to become independent and resilient? Luckily, Franks answers them all with the help of his seven proven strategies to build quality social skills, raise self-confidence, and promote accelerated learning so that children can have a promising future ahead.

Here's a sneak peek of what parents can expect to find inside:

- Why empathy makes learning social skills easier

- How teaching basic manners can be life-changing for tots

- Why kids are playing parallel instead of collaboratively

- How expression is the key to building excellent social skills

- What role praise and appreciation plays

- Why it's imperative to fuel their passions and dreams

- How role-playing situations and emotions can help developing social skills

Getting started with the right strategies makes a huge difference in how children adapt and learn. The right foundation during these early stages of cognitive and emotional development can be a great help for parents to help them raise disciplined, well-mannered, and obedient kids with great social and emotional skills.

7 Proven Strategies for Parenting Toddlers that Excel, from Potty Training to Preschool

Positive Parenting Tips for Raising Toddlers with Exceptional Social Skills and Accelerated Learning Ability

Frank Dixon

been derived from various sources. Please consult a licensed professional before attempting any techniques outlined in this book.

By reading this document, the reader agrees that under no circumstances is the author responsible for any losses, direct or indirect, that are incurred as a result of the use of the information contained within this document, including, but not limited to, errors, omissions, or inaccuracies.

Introduction

Raising a toddler? What can be more fun than that?

Toddlerhood is a time of rapid development. It isn't just marked by the will to stand and walk but by much more that happens in their bodies and minds. It is a time for emotional, cognitive, and social development. Socialization and creating interactions are one of the many important aspects that mark these three to four years. Toddlers reach several milestones, and their ability to communicate and balance themselves on two feet are the two greatest and most pivotal ones to look for. With these in action, they are also introduced to several new emotions and feelings–many of which they don't comprehend yet.

As a parent, it is our ultimate goal to make things easier for our children. During toddlerhood, they are mostly dependent on us for all things from feeding to changing. They take up after our habits and mimic our style of walking, eating, sitting, or sleeping. They become inquisitive and want to poke their noses into things. They seek more freedom and independence.

We need to motivate social interactions from an early age. Toddlerhood seems to be the right age to start familiarizing yourself with the core concepts of the social skills you wish to develop in them. Social skills are a set of acceptable communication and interaction rules and strategies that help individuals form bonds with others and express themselves in both verbal and non-verbal ways. These include skills like communication, listening, coping, accountability, empathy, responsibility, and gratitude. These are the skills that allow humans, who are social creatures, to interact with one another without breaching the rules that make conversations uncomfortable.

The advantages of teaching good social and emotional skills to children go beyond the eloquent relationships that they will have with peers and relatives. Children with robust social skills experience less stress later in their lives, as per some ground-breaking studies. The earliest noticeable change, according to one study, was their reduced stress in daycare settings (Segrin & Flora, 2000). Where other kids cried and screamed, children with good social skills and empathy showed discipline and eagerness to help and be included.

Excellent social skills have also been linked to better performance in academics and a brighter future. According to a study published in the American Journal of Public Health in collaboration with the Penn State and Duke University, children that are emotionally and socially confident and disciplined in kindergarten have a better chance of succeeding in adulthood (Jones et al., 2015). It proposed a strong link between children with good social skills and college. It was revealed that children who knew more about sharing, cooperative, collaboration, and listening at the age of five had a better chance of going to college. They were also expected to have a full-time job at the age of 25.

Good social skills also help children pick things up faster. Since they are growing at a fast pace, you may be astonished to see how much they change every day in terms of their habits, speech, memory, and personality. The brain expands during the first two years which means that they are all set to take in more information, retain it, and process it. This is one reason why many parents stress teaching their children a foreign language as there is a much better chance that they will learn to speak and understand it at this age. Another reason to get started with social skills development early on is that this is also the time to promote accelerated learning. The more socially comfortable they are, the more expressive and open they will be. The more in control they feel about their actions and words, the more knowledge they will be able to pick up. This results in learning about new things easily and at a faster pace.

For instance, if we look at children, they don't usually have a sense of personal space. Teaching them how to communicate while respecting personal space, views, and boundaries makes them a more desirable candidate to form a bond with. On the other hand, children who don't know how to communicate or respect one another's uniqueness often have a difficult time making friends or finding people that stick with them through thick and thin.

Keeping all these crucial points in mind, we can't undermine the importance of good social skills. Therefore, in this book we shall talk about how parents can get started with teaching their toddlers how to develop excellent social skills using seven effective and proven strategies. We shall look at each in detail, determine how it helps children become more resourceful, and learn of several ways in which parents can implement those strategies to raise kids with exceptional social skills that promote accelerated learning.

Chapter 1: Understanding Social Skill Development in Toddlers

T oddlers are called toddlers because they are in that stage of development where they can't fully walk straight or are just learning to. It is derived from the word toddle which means to do the same. Toddlerhood begins when the child reaches the one-year mark. Scholars can disagree on when it ends as some suggest the developmental period ends when the child turns three, while others argue that it ends when the child reaches the four-year mark. Ideally, it ends when the child starts preschool, which isn't the same for every child. In some countries, children start school as early as three whereas in others, they don't go to school before the age of five, like in most states in the U.S.

From infancy, babies learn to form relationships with the people around them. They may not be the best judge of characters or features for that matter, but they do have strong hearing and smell senses. They can easily distinguish their mother's voice and smell when they are in their arms. Although crying is the only form of communication they know, they only nurture their skills as they grow older. As they reach toddlerhood, they are more expressive, understand several emotions like happiness, pain or sadness, and recognize people better. This makes interactions more meaningful. In this first chapter, we shall look at the various socio-emotional developmental milestones toddlers achieve to gain valuable insight into how they form relationships and learn about discipline. This will hopefully enable parents to devise the right strategies that work best in developing their social skills as well as promote accelerated learning. However, before we begin, keep in mind that each child is unique in their own way. Some are quick to pick things up while others are slow learners. This means that not every child will start to talk and walk right after they turn one. Some may be more expressive or active than others. If that is the case, there isn't a need to panic, as every child learns things at their own pace.

Socio-Emotional Developmental Milestones at Age One

Most of the social cues toddlers pick up are from their parents, especially mothers. It is the "the monkey see, monkey do" stage where they don't understand the reasoning behind a behavior but still do it.

You can expect them to point and express their intentions in whatever vocabulary they have learned in the past year. You can do the same. To promote accelerated learning, point towards things you want them to know about or remember. Keep in mind that it is less likely that they will remember it as their memory isn't equipped to do that just yet.

They are also able to recognize familiar faces like that of their parents, grandparents, siblings, babysitter, or doctor. They will start greeting them with a smile or a 'hi' and will willingly interact with them without supervision. By this age, they should be able to pay attention to the people around them and memorize their faces and voice. If they don't, this could be a red flag you need to talk about with your child's doctor.

They should also be able to engage with you on a one-on-one basis such as hand you things or take them from you. This again shows their eagerness to interact with you. They should also pick up the concept of taking turns, but this isn't a compulsion. Most kids have a tough time sharing their stuff with others.

They should also seek some independence whether they have started to walk or not. They will want to explore things and move towards them to give their curious mind some explanation.

Socio-Emotional Developmental Milestones at Age Two

By the time your child turns two, they should be able to better assess the things around them and become more engaged and inquisitive. They should be able to start parallel play by two. Parallel play refers to a child playing alongside another child but not together. They may occasionally exchange or share things together but don't expect too much too early. They still need to learn to wait for their turn and share their toys or food with others. If they are already doing so, go ahead and praise their effort. Otherwise, they are ready to defend their toys the minute someone tries to touch them. Their social behavior stems from egotism because they have egocentric thinking. Their behaviors are directed by their desires.

Moreover, this is the age when children start to engage with strangers with some confidence. They will wave at the cashier or smile at a passerby. Their reaction or response is a sign that they want to explore more and interact more. Not every child is this open and expressive about their desires which means if yours is, you need to encourage that. Inquisitiveness is a sign of intelligence. The more curious the child about the things around them, the more information they will take in about things.

Socio-Emotional Developmental Milestones at Age Three

By the time they turn three, you might be starting to think about putting them into preschool. They are more talkative than ever before. They are full of energy and the stability in their walking gives them more confidence to seek independence. Their social skills start to develop too as they interact with others more and more. They may even have a few friends they like to play with or share their toys with. It could be a sibling, a parent, or a child of their age.

This is the age when children start to engage in associative play. This means that they actively seek someone to play with them. Their attention span also increases and they are more motivated to pretend play. This is the right time when you, as their parent, have to provide them with ample opportunities to increase positive interactions so that they don't feel shy around strangers. This will give you and your child a less traumatizing time when they start preschool as they will feel comfortable around others.

They will develop a basic understanding regarding safety rules such as why they shouldn't play with the knife, why they shouldn't tease the pet, or why they must stay away from the stairs altogether.

They will also start to listen better which means you can start requesting and ordering things from them. These can come in the form of gentle reminders that don't seem like an order but rather a request.

They should also have a better grasp of emotions by age three. They may experience sadness or anger firsthand. This is the time when you need to encourage good social behaviors and how to deal with them without crying, whining, or throwing things. During such social complications, try to make them feel better by hugging or kissing them to show empathy.

Finally, their imagination will improve. They will start pretend-play. They will concoct scenarios in their head. If they are into cars, they may come up with a scenario like a traffic situation or a train that has gone over the rail, and an ambulance and fire-truck is headed to help them. When they reach this stage, start reading stories to them about the things in which they show interest. If they are into wildlife animals, read them stories about the animals helping each other out, obeying their parents, or portraying good basic manners. Stories are a great way to get your word across.

Now that we know of what to expect in terms of their social and emotional development, we can use strategies and parenting tips that seem appropriate for their certain age. In the following chapters, we shall discuss how parents can prepare themselves with the right tools and measures to develop excellent social skills that aid them when starting preschool.

Chapter 2: The Seven Proven Strategies for Toddlers to Develop Social Skills

E very child has a way of looking at the world. They have different styles approaching people and things. Some are shy and introverted while others just jump and leap for everything. Some have a hard time leaving their parent's side while others are running away from them. This is what we call a child's temperament. Your child's temperament may differ from their friend or your sister's child. Your toddler may take longer to warm up to others and prefer assessing situations from a distance rather than jumping into them. Temperament is an individualistic characteristic that makes parenting harder. There is no one-size-fits-all here or a GPS that voices in which direction you need to steer.

Many people are quick to judge other parenting styles. They think they have it all figured out and give their suggestions inconsiderably. They think that we aren't doing enough and therefore have children who behave poorly and are ill-mannered. This isn't always the case. Sometimes, despite trying, some kids just don't listen or obey commands. This is where knowing their temperament comes into play. You need to know what works for them and what doesn't. You need to find things that interest them enough to take action. You need to find their strengths and weaknesses to support their unique needs.

Connecting with them is the first step towards teaching any type of skill or habit. They need to look at you as an authority figure as well as a friend. They need to see you as their role model and idol, and this can only happen if they trust you and your judgment.

If you are responsive to their needs, they will stay attuned to yours. If they see you practicing good social skills and manners, they will learn the same. To teach good social skills and use them to improve accelerated learning will take time. Toddlers have poor attention spans and everything around them is more interesting than what you want them to focus on. Teaching effective social skills is an art and no parent has won the medal for it so far. There are, of course, millions of parents but everyone has a different reward in mind. Some want to teach their kids social skills because they want them to prosper in their careers, some want them to have deep and meaningful relationships, while some want them to build self-confidence and self-worth.

Whichever goal you are after, one thing is for certain: You want them to be the happiest child in the world. You want them to have the best of everything. You want to protect them from harm's way and ensure that they remain cared for and looked after.

We want to begin developing excellent social skills in them and improve their chances at accelerated learning. Below are seven effective strategies that will help teach them about manners, obedience, discipline, coping skills, communication, listening skills, and stress management as they grow older and enter into their teens.

Empathize

Empathy allows you to be closer to your toddler and understand them better. If you want them to obey you and be respectful, you ought to do the same. It is one of the most effective ways to get to know your child better. Sympathize with them and let them know that you understand what they are going through. Being empathetic offers parents a great opportunity to build strong relationships with their children. When the connection is strong, they will most likely do all that you want them to do out of love and mutual respect.

Teach Basic Manners

Basic manners and etiquette come well before social skills. Think of it as the first step of the ladder. With good manners, children have an easier time connecting with others, making new friends, and forming bonds. It makes them preferred playmates and it makes them disciplined.

Promote Parallel Play

Your child may not be into other kids and will prefer to play on their own, even when in a room full of kids. Firstly, there is no harm in that as it is the first step towards learning about collaboration and social play. Encouraging them will only make transitioning from parallel play to social play smoother and faster.

Encourage Expression

Expression or communication is one of the areas that they need to work on the most since they are only starting to build their vocabulary. The more responsive and talkative they are, the quicker they will learn things. Encouraging expression is also essential to build resilience and regulate negative emotions using healthy coping mechanisms.

Praise

Praise and appreciation is also essential to improve behavior and instill positive habits in children—especially in toddlers who have a mind of their own. Praise and appreciation can fuel them with the right motivation and support to fulfill their dreams and aspirations. It will also make it easier for you to communicate with them in a positive manner and help develop good social skills.

Fuel Passions

Being supportive of their passions and dreams allows parents to be an active participant in their lives. One of the most common complaints of parents is that their toddler doesn't listen to them. To eliminate misbehavior and to help them develop healthy social skills, one needs to spend time with them communicating. Showing support for their passions can be a great conversation starter and it can make you their go-to person to talk to. While they talk to you, you can continue to teach them about good social skills and their importance.

Role-Play Scenarios

Finally, role-playing scenarios with your toddler allows them to make sense of the feelings of others. It gives them a different perspective to look at life and helps them feel the impact of their actions and behaviors. It is a great way to teach empathy as well as build social skills, which ultimately helps parents raise confident, self-reliant, and resilient individuals.

Chapter 3: Empathize, Empathize, Empathize

E mpathy is the art of viewing the world from another's eyes. Empathetic people can understand what another person feels in a given moment and realize why someone else's actions in a particular situation make sense. Empathy allows us to understand the point of view of others when they wish to communicate their ideas and thoughts with us. It improves social interactions and it can be referred to as one of the most pivotal foundational blocks of social skills.

Since humans thrive on social connections, we all must learn about empathy and practice it in our daily lives. We are all born with seeds of concern and worry for others. Take the relationship between a mother and a child or a brother and a sister. We all hold compassion for one another and want to see each other succeed in life. As we grow older and we form more connections with others, we become less concerned about the immediate relationships we have. We forget about the love and attention our parents gave us when we were younger. We neglect their personal feelings and emotions and rarely have time to sit beside them and ask them how they feel. But, since we know that good social interactions rely on understanding one another, we need to take into account the fact that everyone wants to be heard. If we have a problem, do we not want to share it with someone and hope that they will understand? Similarly, others want the same care and attention that is genuine and is pure from all forms of judgment.

How do you nurture that? How do you become empathetic yourself and hopefully raise children who are empathetic too?

First of all, we are designed to empathize with others naturally. Our brains are wired in a way that we can feel the emotions that someone else is feeling. Have you ever seen a video where someone scares somebody during a prank? Do you not scream with them? Or perhaps you saw someone hit their hand with a hammer. Did you not wince? This is proof that humans are capable of empathizing with others.

For kids in their toddlerhood, their lack of communication skills often becomes a roadblock. They are unable to express themselves as they lack the right vocabulary for it. However, that doesn't mean that they don't experience any big feelings. If we think about it, it can all be rather confusing for them. This is where empathy comes in. They want to feel heard and validated and with empathy, you can do so. You can make them understand that you understand their state of despair and what they are going through.

How Toddlers Can Benefit From Empathy

Let's imagine for a minute a world without empathy. Everyone is mean and self-centered. No one cares about the opinions of others and everyone gets offended the second someone comes up with a conflicting viewpoint. Does it not seem like a toxic environment for a child to grow up in? Would you want your child to have the same self-centered and privileged beliefs?

As we get more innovative with technology and get artificial intelligence (AI) to replace most human jobs, employers start valuing only those who encompass a complex and varied set of skills. Today's world is a world of collaboration. Take conglomerates as an example. They have several products and services that fall into different niches. They need people who can collaborate, think effectively, and find solutions to unique problems with a unique and effective approach. The more minds working together, the greater the chance of a conflict. How well will your child do in such a competitive and collaborative environment if they are unable to hear what others have to say?

Numerous studies suggest a strong correlation between socio-emotional skills and a child's learning ability. We believe that if our child does well in studies, they must have good social and emotional skills too. Wrong. Research shows that achievements

465

and cognitive development only guarantee 50% success at school. The remaining 50% is guaranteed by how socially and emotionally developed the child is.

Other than that, empathy also nurtures the conditions essential for creativity. Creativity can strike at any minute. It can find us in the shower or during a traffic jam. It can't be summoned on command as it flourishes under openness, understanding, and acceptance. Being able to open oneself to the views of others takes courage as it accounts for trying something new. It also opens doors to being creative. When a toddler understands others and is accepting of their presence, it means that they are open to the possibility of taking risks and trying new things. An example of this would be going to new and unfamiliar places or meeting new people. If they don't cry, whine, or scream when someone touches them and they are inviting with big smiles on their faces, they are accepting of the newness and uncertainty.

Empathy also encourages logical thought processes and rational patterns. Many neuroscientists believe that when children come from a place of empathy, they are better equipped to cope with the daily stresses and challenges of life with reason, clarity, and purpose. They feel more competent to regulate their emotions and respond better.

Another benefit is less aggression in children. Toddlerhood is the age where children start to build vocabulary and of all the words they love the most, 'no' becomes their favorite. They respond to most things with 'no.' Additionally, when they can express themselves better and get their way, their demands increase too. When these demands remain unmet, children become angry and frustrated. However, if a child is empathetic, they might be able to see the reasoning and logic behind the rejection. Their reactions become less destructive and out of control. They will stop acting out and behave with calmness instead.

There is also evidence that children who lack empathy turn out to be selfish, boorish, and narcissistic. They are more likely to bully others and they have difficulty staying in a group. They are self-centered individuals who don't have compassion towards others. If this doesn't change, they may have a hard time making friends or finding the right partner for themselves. They can also have a troubled time being part of a community and they might remain alienated from everyone. They need to become tolerant of others. They need to learn compassion. Luckily, empathy teaches them to become compassionate and selfless.

Learning to Be Empathetic - Getting Started

We now know how critical empathy is for children and the role it plays in shaping their personality. It is best to start as early as possible. As parents, the first

467

thing you need to do is model empathy in your words and actions. Toddlers imitate the things they see. Even when they don't know the reasoning behind their actions, they mimic the actions of their parents. Teaching them about empathy will help them build good social skills and improve their interactions and bonds with potential friends and partners in the future. Here are some strategies for you to introduce the concept of empathy and model it yourself.

Use Play Cards

Use flashcards or books to depict various emotions and situations where the protagonist shows empathy towards the victim. Reading to your child about empathy using stories is a much better way to interact and get your word across. The more interactive and engaging the stories or cards, the bigger the possibility that they will pick the habit up.

Encourage Problem-Solving

Instead of coming up with a solution when your child is faced with a troubling situation or challenge, let them find one on their own. For instance, let's say their sibling has snatched a toy from their hand. What will they do? Do they cry right away and look for some help from you or do they let their sibling play with it for some time because they think the sibling needs it too? Their reaction will tell you two things. First, it will tell you how empathetic or non-empathetic they are in general, and second, it will let you know how much work needs to be done with them. When toddlers are allowed to do what seems fitting to them, it also builds their confidence and improves self-worth.

Reason Using Examples

Label the feelings or emotions that they are experiencing and try to normalize them. Secondly, show vulnerability in front of them so they know that others feel emotions too. Give them reasons compelling enough to understand and comply with. For instance, if you are afraid they will fall down the stairs, let them know your fears. Let them know how much it will hurt them and hurt you if they fall down the stairs and get injured. When toddlers think that the reasons make sense, they are more likely to abide by the rules set in place.

Show Moral and Ethical Support

If you ever find your child struggling with a difficult emotion such as sadness or pain, let them know that you understand their feelings and appreciate them for having the courage to go through it. Your support, even just verbal, will have a deep impact on them. They will feel a lot better if they know someone understands their situation. Use such instances to teach the importance of strong coping skills and show them how they can deal with big feelings in healthy ways. For example, if your child's trip to the zoo was canceled last minute, say something like, "I know you wanted to go to the zoo badly. I know you must be angry that we didn't get to go this weekend.

How about we go next week and later go for ice cream too?"

Chapter 4: Teach Basic Manners

T oddlers aren't old enough to distinguish between right and wrong. They will, however, do as directed. For example, they may not understand why they shouldn't hit others or maintain a safe distance from them but if they are directed to do so, they will. Why? It's because their parents told them to and also because they will be punished if they don't. They simply know that they must obey elders and respect others but without the literal reasoning.

This is where teaching them about basic manners comes in. They may not know why they need to say thank you but they will learn to say it if they are taught the right way. Teaching basic skills teaches them about courtesy, which is again important if they wish to have fruitful and happy interactions with others. Toddlers having difficulty controlling their impulses can be taught to use words like excuse me, sorry, and thank you to appear well-mannered. Being mannerly is a social skill that parents must develop in their children. It is important because it will allow them to get along with others in a kind and friendly way. Take an ill-mannered kid for example. Suppose you set up a playdate with an ill-mannered kid and your child. From the minute the two start to interact, the ill-mannered child pulls on your child's hair, hits him, snatches things from his hands, and makes your child feel miserable. Would you let that kid near your child again? Mannerly kids make preferred playmates. They get invited for playdates more than those who aren't mannerly. If your child is obedient and courteous, he already has a better chance to interact and make new friends.

Secondly, being courteous also demonstrates respect. Saying thank you upon receiving something or saying sorry for mistakenly hurting somebody shows that you come from a good and respectable family.

Toddlers who are taught manners early also build integrity. They become likable and desirable to be around. On the other hand, children who lack basic manners aren't the most pleasing to be around. They have a tough time at school and daycare because they can't get along with the rest of the kids and they feel alienated. No one wants to play with them and this only makes them act out more.

As a parent, it should be your goal to teach your child about basic manners as early as possible. Habits take time to set in. It is much easier to train a younger and eager mind than to train a developed and mature mind.

The Important Role Learning Good Manners Plays

Good manners allow young kids to convey respect. When one hears words like thank you from someone, they feel appreciated. When one hears sorry from someone, it removes the feeling of being wronged. When someone says excuse me, it shows respect for the person's right to not do something that has been asked. These are all signs of good character traits that teach one about respect for others and show appreciation for them.

If you teach your child these basic manners when they are young, you are doing them a big favor. From potential employers to partners, their ethics and morals will set the stage for them. Picture this: Your son goes for his first interview. He qualifies for the job in terms of his skills and qualification but lacks basic manners. Therefore, as he enters the room, he doesn't knock before entering, and when he moves towards the chair, he doesn't ask if he has the permission to sit. He interrupts the employer repeatedly, acts rude, and doesn't show respect towards an elderly manager. Do you think that company will see him as the right candidate? Do you think he will get the job? Let's not get ahead this far. Let's imagine a scenario where your child goes to the park. He doesn't let other kids have a turn on the swings, he pushes them around deliberately, and he complains back when confronted. What will the other parents think about you and your child? Do you think they will respect you or your child? Good manners go a long way when it comes to developing social skills in kids. It is the key to making interactions more conducive and pleasant.

How to Emphasize Teaching Manners

Toddlerhood itself has several stages. It expands over three years, each year with its unique features. Each stage promotes physical, emotional, and mental abilities. Behaviors differ in different stages of growth. As parents, we need to recognize which behaviors are expected at each age. For instance, if a child has just turned one, their communication skills will be different than when they turn three or four. But as always, starting early gives you an edge in shaping behavior and temperament. To build a solid foundation in social skills, you must approach them with the following strategies in mind.

Turn Dinner Times Into Conversation Times

Dinner time is a great opportunity to talk about the day's activities and highlights. If both parents work, you can ask the child about their day at the daycare. You can ask them if they made any new friends today, heard a new story, or learned a new poem. Dinner times offer an excellent chance to encourage communication and practice basic manners. You can teach them how they should eat, how to say thanks, and how to have normal conversations where one waits for their turn to speak and doesn't interrupt in between. You can also teach table manners, why they should respect the food they consume, and why they shouldn't waste things.

Reward Them When They Do Something Good

If you catch your toddler saying "thank you" or 'sorry,' never let it pass without appreciation or some form of reward. We are all motivated and driven by rewards. Be it a promotion at work or a sales coupon in a fashion magazine, we all love to be rewarded or appreciated. To emphasize and encourage the habit of good manners, never leave an opportunity to appreciate them when they depict good manners. Soon they will start to associate good manners with reward and be more motivated to use them.

Make It a Habit

Whenever your child receives something from someone, remind them to say thank you first and then hand it to them. The same goes for saying 'please' when they want something from someone. This promotes respect for others as well as increases the value of the things received. Teaching them to say thank you whenever someone gives them something will develop into a habit in no time.

Emphasize Graciousness

When competing, you don't always win. Sometimes you lose and it can be heartbreaking. You feel humiliated, mocked, and like the weaker person. No one likes to feel that and certainly not your little one. They may start to cry, scream, hit the other child, or act out by throwing things in aggression. This happens when they are unable to digest the loss.

Teach them healthy ways to accept defeat. Moreover, teach them not to gloat when they win or make the other person feel like the loser. Teach graciousness. Good sportsmanship is a must whether you win or lose. It must be taught to children early on as it prevents cases of jealousy, envy, and anger later in life.

Teach Good Playdate Manners

If you have been invited to a playdate with your toddler or have welcomed guests at your home, teach your child about how to make the other child feel welcome. Remind them of the rules like greeting, sharing, and waiting for their turn in a relaxed manner. Also, tell them to always clean up after they are done playing whether at their home or someone else's. If you are taking them to someone's house, sit them down and talk to them about not placing their feet on the furniture, running in the house, or touching things without permission. If you are the one hosting, tell them to let the guests eat first, be courteous, share their toys, and put the toys they don't want to share away before the friend comes over. This will prevent most of the snatching, hitting, or pulling.

Talk to Them About the Importance of Waiting

Kids this age can be restless. It can be hard to make them sit in one place. When they speak, they want to say as much as they can in a second. Teach them to calm down when expressing themselves so that they can be understood. Additionally, teach them about how important it is to hear others and to wait for their turn to speak. Model this by speaking calmly at all times and being genuinely interested in what they have to say. Also, don't encourage the habit of interrupting others and make it a point to let others complete their sentence first. Good listening and communicating skills are an essential part of developing good social skills. Be sure to make a note of it.

Chapter 5: Introduce Parallel Play

I magine this: You organized a playdate for your tot. You invited a few kids along with their parents. You laid out your child's many toys and told the parents to bring their child's favorite ones too. After an hour of play, you notice an odd thing. Your child is playing and so are the other kids. But they aren't playing together but rather alongside each other. What's up with them? Why aren't they socializing? At this age and stage, it should happen naturally, right?

Yes, but here's the thing. Unlike other skills, children don't learn social skills from their peers. Instead, they learn them from you. Your toddler is still young and prefers to play with familiar faces. Let's call that their inner circle. Even when positioned in a room full of toys and a few other kids, they would still prefer to play alone than with those kids. This happens because they haven't yet developed the social and emotional skills they need to interact with others.

Parallel play can be interpreted as a small phase in the life of a toddler where they choose to play alongside other children as opposed to with them. Interaction between the kids is nearly zero with an occasional smile, tug, or pulling incident between them. This is the first step to learning to play collaboratively and it sets the stage for shared play. As weird as it sounds, this is a normal phase. This should be encouraged, says Dr. Dana Cohen, a child psychologist at the Beaumont Children's in Royal Oak who specializes in children with autism and other special needs.

Why Parallel Play?

Ideally, parallel plays look exactly like it sounds. Two children play in close proximities, focused on their separate toys and games. Dr. Dana believes that children who don't engage in parallel play during their early years and prefer to remain isolated or are shy in the presence of another child may be showing signs of autism. There are many benefits to parallel play. For instance, it develops a child's motor skills. When a toddler engages in parallel play, they only focus on the resources they have in a controlled environment. They notice the behavior and actions of the other child and begin to imitate them. Their responses become coordinated. They learn to observe and modify. This is a great skill to foster in children as it shows that they can focus and follow. If they are to learn some sport or game, they will observe and learn to imitate actions by observing actual players. Suppose they are playing catch with you, they will soon learn to pick up the way you throw the ball at them and even pick up something entirely new.

Secondly, it helps in the development of communication skills. When children are left to play with themselves alongside other kids, they also pick up the words and language they use. They eventually start to talk to one another too. If they are at the park and someone yells to catch the ball, they will look at the child first and then at the ball and learn new words in the process.

Encouraging Parallel Play

How do you begin encouraging your child to parallel play? For starters, parallel play should occur in a safe and homely environment. This means that it has to take place in a place that isn't too crowded like the park or daycare, and second, it should occur in the presence of at least one parent of each child so that the children don't feel anxious around strangers. Keep in mind that the goal is to let them transition from this phase to the phase where they willingly start to interact with one another without being forced to. Keep the duration of the social play restricted but not too short. Give the child an ample amount of time to get accustomed to the surroundings and see if they seem interested in the other child or not. At first, the child will feel some stress and thus may not take part in any sort of play out of fear. Giving them some time to relieve their stress will prepare them to be more engaging next time.

Don't Force Them

When encouraging parallel play, let the toddler embrace momentary independence. If they don't seem interested in the play and would rather be roaming around the room, don't force them to sit down and play with the toys in front of them. Enforcement won't get you the desired results. Instead, it will only make the child act out and experience stress.

Have Enough Toys

Ensure that both the children have enough toys to play with. This means bringing out all the bricks, blocks, dolls, cars, stuffed animals, play dough, coloring books, and toy sets. A great tip is to have more toys that promote cognitive thinking and problem-solving so that you can kill two birds with one stone. No child should be made to feel left out with fewer toys. If you are determined to initiate social play early on, put all of the toys in the center of the room and let them choose their favorites themselves. However, keep an eye out for any fights, pulling, or pushing.

Keep Distractions to a Minimum

Limit the number of distractions in the room the kids are in. The more distractions there are, the less interested they will be in the actual play. If they aren't too clingy, you and the other parent can let them play on their own in a separate room and keep checking in on them every five to 10 minutes.

Remember, the goal is to build social skills and encourage social interactions. This is only possible when they are by themselves in the room. Also, if possible, reduce the number of toys after each playdate so that children feel more encouraged to interact with the limited availability of toys in front of them.

Know When to Upgrade

Finally, notice the behavior and actions of your child at every playdate. This will help you know when they are ready for the transition to collaborative play or play with another friend instead of alone. When you feel they are ready, subtly nurture direct interactions by making them sit together and share toy sets, puzzles, or coloring books. Encourage them to take turns playing and sharing their toys.

Chapter 6: Encourage Expression

With a limited vocabulary, toddlers aren't the greatest communicators. They need to learn to be able to express themselves better. Encouraging expression and seeking their opinion on little matters can help establish a trusted relationship and encourage toddlers to be more open about their problems and needs.

The more expressive they are about their wants and needs, the easier it will be to develop social skills since you will know exactly which areas they lack in. For instance, if you notice that your toddler loves to speak but is a poor listener, you can always encourage listening activities to teach them about the importance of listening and enhance that social skill.

All great ideas are born in the mind. However, they can die a terrible death if no one ever hears of them. The ability to express oneself effectively is an art. Children are natural storytellers. They are creative and imaginative. Nothing is impossible in their eyes. The better they are at expressing themselves, the better their quality of life and future prospects. The ability to communicate effectively is a key skill, and the better we are at it, the better our quality of life will be.

Humans have been communicating from the minute they were born. The first cry of a baby is a way to let the parents know they have arrived. As they grow from a baby to toddler, it becomes a parent's job to nurture good communication skills which will help them express themselves better and learn things at a quicker pace. When children feel confident in expressing themselves, their self-esteem also improves.

If we look at a child's developmental stages, we notice that they first start to communicate with their parents, then with their siblings, and then with their peers and educators. All that they learn, they learn from us–the parents. Thus, the more expressive, descriptive, and comfortable we are with our words and actions, the more comfortable they will be too.

Good Communication Skills and Social Skills Development

Communication is a fundamental developmental milestone in a toddler's life. We all want to be heard and be understood. Being able to express ourselves allows us to form relationships and improve social interactions. For a child, they need to express themselves in the same manner too. They use limited vocabulary and actions to express themselves. However, if we allow them to be more expressive by teaching them the right ways to say and do things, we can improve conversations and enhance the stability of parent-child relationships.

Communication also develops a special bond with the caregiver. The more time they spend together communicating, the stronger the bond gets. It leads to close connection with one or more of the immediate family members which becomes important as the child grows into a teenager and starts to keep things private and secret.

Having a vocabulary at an early age and knowing how to use it also helps the child learn things easily during school. It increases the likelihood that your child will pick things up faster than the other kids since they will already have an improved vocabulary by the time they start preschool. They will be quicker at taking instructions from their educators which will make learning easier and more interesting for them.

It must also be noted that children who aren't good at expressing themselves or have poor speech abilities have a difficult time with reading, spelling, and oral exercises. The parents have to work harder to improve the learning ability of the child. Besides, when they are unable to express themselves, frustration also sets in. You must know this if you have ever played charades with a partner that doesn't take the cues well. A minute into the game and you already feel frustrated for not being able to get your point across. The same is true with children. When they can't understand things clearly and they can't make others understand them, it becomes frustrating. The more they struggle, the more frustrated they get.

This is one reason why children with disabilities like autism or ADHD have a hard time with behavior modification. Children with diagnosed disorders can be hard to deal with for most parents and they will require assistance from schools that are designed particularly for their special-needs child.

Another aspect that often gets neglected is that when children don't know how to communicate, they have trouble making friends. Childhood friendships are especially important. When children suffer from poor self-esteem due to their poor communication skills, it can become a hindrance for them to get along with others. This can lead to increased anxiety and isolation which may become a mental health issue in the future.

Encouraging Openness

Your little one needs you and your support whether they can express themselves well or not. However, your job as a parent is to equip them with the right means to improve their communication skills as well as encourage expression. You need to get down on their level and make yourself approachable. You want them to see you as their supporter and mentor, not someone who will laugh at them for pronouncing something wrong or acting frustrated when they aren't able to convey their message. They should be able to see the willingness in you to understand them. Stay present and attentive to show your interest and concern for them. To improve any form of communication, both of the involved parties need to give their undivided attention. This is only possible when both are attentive to each other's needs and are active listeners. Some other great strategies to encourage the habit of expression so that children can learn great social skills include the following:

Read Stories

To improve vocabulary, foster the habit of reading in your children from an early age. Thanks to advancements in print media, you can always get your hands on interactive books. Some even come with sound effects to pique a child's interest. Make use of them and build the habit of reading with and to them. Stories are a great way to promote the expression of ideas, emotions, and thoughts. You can always ask questions about the characters or what they would do in a certain scenario.

Sing With Them

If they aren't into reading yet or are too young to understand, songs, rhymes, and poems can be your next best weapon. Poems and songs with simple and easy-to-recall lyrics can be a great way to build vocabulary and teach emotions. For example, if the poem is about a kid that has lost his bat, you can use it to teach sadness and happiness and how one experiences those emotions. If there are any difficult or unfamiliar words in the song or the poem, you can help your child understand them.

Listen to Your Child

Let them have some time to respond when you ask them a question or are talking to them. When you are speaking to them, ensure that you maintain good eye contact. Be mindful of the words you use around them, even when you're talking to someone else. Although these tips seem small and insignificant, they can have a huge impact on the way a child communicates with others. Essentially, you have to teach them good listening skills because they won't be able to contribute a response if they aren't listening. Asking them questions and noticing how they are responding to them will tell you if they listened or not.

Narrate Your Daily Routines

Narrating things as you do them is another great way to encourage dialogue and openness. This will allow your child to create connections between your words and actions. For instance, if you are watering the flowers, you can say, "You are flowering the plants in the garden." If we take a look, there are at least three news words that they can learn: gardening, watering, and flowering. They might ask you about it themselves, or maybe they won't need to as soon as they see what you are doing. Keeping them in the loop in such a manner will help them build vocabulary and become more curious about things around the house. Curious kids are often intelligent and fast learners.

Make Requests Clear

When teaching about openness and good communication skills, don't forget to set clear and realistic expectations. Every child has unique skills. They take their own good time to learn things. Just because a colleague's son is saying full sentences by age three doesn't mean your child should too. Sure, you can try a little harder with them but don't expect them to comply with the standards. They are too young to be thrown into a competition of "who does it better." They are kids, full of life and energy, let them be that! When making requests or giving instructions, be as clear as possible and ensure that they have understood what is expected of them.

Don't Correct Them

Sometimes, your child is going to pronounce words wrong. Instead of mocking or correcting them, simply repeat the right pronunciation of the word by using it in a sentence. This will prevent shattering their confidence and self-esteem. Keep in mind that the goal is to encourage openness rather than deter it. If you keep making fun of them, they might start to see you as a manipulator and stop coming to you with their ideas and problems altogether. Be subtle about the correction so that they don't feel judged.

Chapter 7: Praise Wholeheartedly

T o encourage good social behaviors, children need motivation. Praise and appreciation go a long way. Why else would they sit quietly and act well-behaved when there is nothing motivating them? Praising good behaviors increases the likelihood of repetition.

Praise and appreciation lets your little one know that you like something about their behavior. It is about you being vocal about something they did positively. Praise nurtures a child's skills, boosting their self-esteem and confidence. They will be competent in the face of challenges. When we praise our children, we demonstrate how they can think and talk positively about others and themselves. It is a way to tell children how much we like a certain behavior of theirs. It's like a pat on the back!

In earlier times, praising a child was considered bad. It was believed that it resulted in boosting their ego in a bad way and that it made them think of themselves as superior. It made them overconfident and full of themselves. But times are now changing and as we gain more and more information about mental health issues in children and their lack of self-confidence, it seems selfish not to praise them. Today, with the help of many scientific brain studies, researchers strongly believe that praise and appreciation is a great way to reinforce positive behavior in children and build their social skills.

According to one study, the human mind responds to social approval in the same manner that it does to monetary rewards. This means that verbal praise and recognition has become as important as monetary rewards to encourage good behaviors. Besides, who doesn't like to be praised? It makes us all feel gooey and accomplished inside, even if just for a minute. The best part is, praise doesn't even have to be lengthy or descriptive. A simple, 'yay,' 'wow,' or applause is a great gesture to show appreciation.

Importance of Praise and Appreciation for Toddlers

Praise and appreciation is an excellent and effective way to encourage children to try again after they have failed (Morris and Zentall, 2014). Toddlers seek praise and encouragement from their elders. They are already in that phase of development where they rely on communication. They look up to them and wait for their approval over everything. It all seems exciting as they are developing new vocabulary every day. They feel especially motivated when they are praised over day-to-day tasks like finishing their vegetables, walking, or putting aside all their toys after playtime. Many parents attach a reward for good behavior to further elevate the feelings of happiness and accomplishment.

When children feel supported, their natural curiosity is encouraged. They feel more in control of their actions and they have a strong will to do things with perfection. They even start doing things they previously hated doing, just for the sake of some praise and appreciation.

Furthermore, toddlers that feel motivated by their parents or teachers also report better mental health and wellbeing. You don't need science to prove that kids who grow up in supportive households find it easier to follow their dreams and passions than those who don't feel encouraged.

Finally, when tots feel appreciated, they are more likely to repeat that behavior. Thus, if they have been up to some mischief lately or are giving you a tough time with their temper tantrums and disobedience, try praising them for the things they do well and notice how their behaviors will change drastically.

Learning to Appreciate - A Guide for Parents

How do you get started? Are there any rules about which behaviors get praise and which don't? What words do you use so that your child will know when they are being appreciated? First things first, make it a rule to point out more of the good in them than criticizing them over negative behaviors. Ideally, you should say at least six good things about your child before you say one bad, or negative, thing to them.

They are at the age where good habits will find a home in their heart if they feel encouraged and motivated. Here is what you should appreciate.

Look for Small Successes

Praise shouldn't only be given over something major. Make it a habit to start praising your child for small and insignificant successes and accomplishments. Sometimes, we don't realize the amount of effort that has gone into something. Something that doesn't seem big to you might mean the world to them. Thus, don't hold back your praise and appreciation for big accomplishments only. Compliment them over little things too.

Reward Good Behavior

This isn't a requisite, but pairing your praise with something tangible (a reward) or intangible (a privilege) can also boost their confidence in their abilities and encourage the development of social skills and positive behaviors. Rewards add some oomph factor to a praise. They are the icing on the cake that can make all the difference.

Praise Efforts Too

Sometimes, your child will fail miserably. But that doesn't mean that they didn't make an effort. Praise shouldn't just follow an accomplishment. Effort should be praised too, equally. Doing so will motivate them to continue and not give up in themselves and their abilities. Let them know that you understand how hard they worked for something. They shouldn't have to feel like a failure.

Be Descriptive

Be clear and specific when praising them. If you want to encourage a particular behavior, they need to know that. Being descriptive allows you to hit the right mark. Being specific also makes the praise feel more wholesome and genuine. By doing so, you allow your child to know what behaviors and actions will earn them respect and appreciation from their parents, and they will hopefully try to be better at it too.

Chapter 8: Fuel Their Passions

L ike praises, being supportive and encouraging towards a child's passions and dreams is another essential and proven strategy to develop productive social skills in kids.

There are several perks to showing interest and motivating your toddler to seek their passions and dreams. They may seem silly and short-term currently, but by showing support and interest you make them see how excited you are. It also makes their small missions seem bigger, challenging, and important. In the process, they pick up some great habits like the importance of staying true and focused on a task, demonstrating resilience, and going after their goals and dreams.

What is a passion, and is it the same as a dream or goal? According to Merriam-Webster, passion is a strong feeling of excitement and enthusiasm for something or someone. It isn't necessarily a trajectory for success. It doesn't guarantee that your child will get into the best schools and colleges or get a high-paid job. It is more about intrinsic happiness. It is a source of excitement for the one experiencing it, and it may or may not reap promising success. If a child is passionate about something, it doesn't mean that they will forever remain stuck to it. For example, they may enjoy learning about dinosaurs right now but that doesn't mean that they want to grow up to be a paleontologist. They may want to pursue an entirely different career and goal in their adult life. The thing about passion is that it can change as the kid grows up. In most cases, it does.

The Benefits of Supporting Your Child's Passions

The real question is why you should be supporting their passions? Well, here are some excellent reasons why.

For starters, pursuing one's passions releases the feel-good hormone called dopamine. When we force our toddlers into doing something, we take away the joy from it. Suddenly, it becomes a chore and not an interesting passion. Conversely, when they do something purely out of joy and because they want to, it makes them feel happy and more driven to bring it to completion. When children do things out of interest, their brains kick into the auto drive mode. It releases substantial amounts of dopamine which makes children feel the accomplishment they have achieved.

Secondly, when they are driven by passion they also feel more focused and determined. If they don't feel motivated, they may still complete the task but not with 100% dedication. If the task doesn't spark joy and they just do it for the sake of doing it, it won't boost their self-esteem.

Thirdly, when children are motivated to pursue their passions and aspirations, they are more likely to talk about them with others every chance they get. This will improve their social interactions, both by number and quality. Their pure interest in the subject will compel them to discuss it proudly with others and may very well become the hub of their social circle. Who knows, maybe they will find someone like-minded as themselves and become friends with them!

Finally, we also know that when kids work passionately towards achieving something, they are open to taking in as much information as they can regarding it. This means that their learning and general knowledge will also improve. Passion-based learning is deep-rooted in science. The more interested the child is, the higher the chances of them learning new things about it. They will show more interest in studying and gaining knowledge about the subject and they will develop a greater understanding for it.

Showing Support - The ABCs

As parents, it is our job to support and nurture our child's interests and passions. By doing so, we show them that we care about their interests and understand how important it is to them. This helps to create a compassionate bond between us and allows for more strong and open communication. To get started, here's how you can support their passions and show them that you care.

Know Their Interests

It may seem ritualistic to do the same things other parents do with their children when it comes to finding their interests and passions. Perhaps you think that they have a thing for sports because they are always sitting beside their dad watching the sports channel. You assume that sports must be their passion, but we urge you to dig in deeper. Don't assume things when it comes to your children. Maybe the sole reason they are watching sports is because they want to spend more time with their dad. Sports may or may not have anything to do with their interests. Thus, take the time to really get to know your child and notice what sparks their interests and lights up their eyes with anticipation. Observe them during playtime, ask questions to know them better, and be an active listener to know what subjects they are passionate about.

Follow Your Own Passion

Toddlers do as they see. If they see you skimping on your own passions, they will do the same–sooner or later. As parents, be a great role model to encourage the habit of following their passions religiously. It is important for them to see that you follow the advice you have for them and spend time doing the things that you love. Cultivating your passions will allow them to do the same and invest their time and energy into what they love.

Avoid Judging

Just because your child is madly into stamp collecting and is not interested in some sport that has a definite and promised future doesn't give you the right to belittle them. You may have had other plans for them but forcing them to try the things you want is no different than mentally imprisoning them. Many expecting parents have aspirations to see their kids take after their interests. Maybe you were really into baseball and hoped that one day your son will be too, but it doesn't necessarily mean that they will. Maybe their interests are different in nature. Maybe they hate all things sports. When this happens, resist the urge to criticize and pull their leg. Avoid judging them for having interests that don't fit your ideals. Encourage them through thick and thin and show support. Let them fulfil their desired needs without being too judgmental about them.

Chapter 9: Role-Play to Convey the Message

Sometimes toddlers need a taste of things to build good social skills and promote accelerated learning abilities, and to fully understand them. Your lecture may not hold any value unless they experience the thing they weren't supposed to do. If they hurt someone, they won't be able to feel the pain unless it happens to them too. How else will they be more compassionate and careful the next time?

Role-play is interpreted in different ways. Essentially, it is learning via play. Role-play is an extremely strong technique in developing social skills. It fuels the young mind with imagination and creativity. Using role-play as a teaching method during toddlerhood proves effective and beneficial. It helps our little ones create scenarios in their head and experience various emotions and feelings during play. Everyone can learn how to read, write, or do the math. But it takes real skill to imagine worlds that exist only in the mind and interact with others around them. Since social skills can only be learned naturally through observation and training, role-play serves as a useful tool to get started.

The Power of Role-Play

If you have ever been to a therapist or counselor in troubled times, do you recall how they used visualization and role-play frequently to play out scenarios in real life? Did you ever notice how often they used it to make us see the things we have been unable to see or experience before?

The benefits of role-playing in kids are varied. For starters, they enhance social and emotional skills in children. During role-play, kids place themselves in settings where they are required to interact with others to find solutions and answers to their problems. This also allows them to experience what empathy feels like and it allows them to depict it. It also builds resilience in children as they feel more confident at regulating their emotions, gaining control over them, and controlling their reactions to them.

As discussed before, role-play allows kids to expand their vision by imagination. It promotes creativity and enhances their skills and talents by developing a strong problem-solving approach.

Role-playing also enriches language and communication skills. Kids can pick up new words and experience different emotions. When they are exposed to different scenarios, their cognitive development improves and their vocabulary increases too. The more words they know, the more expressive they can be. The more expressive they are, the more confident they feel. They are in a better state to convey their message. This also comes in handy when they start to read and write.

Finally, we also see role-play as an effective method to teach kids about conflict resolution. When we encourage them to view the world from a different perspective, we prevent conflict of opinions as well as physical fights and arguments. Sometimes, they are unable to see the logical side of things because they feel overwhelmed by their emotions. Their actions and behaviors aren't a product of rational thinking. If this continues or is allowed to continue, kids will never learn to cope in healthy and meaningful ways. They will always see the world as they want to see it and thus have a hard time accepting others' opinions. They won't be able to work as part of a team and they will always feel more privileged than the rest of their peers.

Using Role-Playing Strategies to Instill Good Habits

Learning social skills using role-play sounds like a solid strategy for toddlers. They are always curious about stories and imaginative scenarios. They must have already started to pretend to play. Role-play is more effective than just sitting in a corner and playing with themselves. It requires interaction which can help toddlers in many ways. For starters, they can seek attention from you. Second, they can experience what it means to be in someone else's shoes, and third, it encourages them to modify their behaviors and actions. It is also more effective than any school lesson written down in a notebook for a test. Its unique feature; interaction leaves a lasting impression. Thus, if you are convinced that this can be a great start to teach toddlers about social skills and accelerated learning, we have plenty of ideas to help you.

Reverse the Roles

Taking turns can help children see different sides of things. If they have been hitting or pulling another child's hair, sit them down and talk to them about how the other child feels. Ask questions like, "How would you feel if I pulled your hair?" and "How would you feel if I snatched that toy from your hand right now?" Let them see how their actions affect others and how they would feel if the same were happening to them.

Make Them Watch a Movie

The best thing about movies and cartoons is that they depict a vast majority of emotions that children go through but are unable to cope with in better ways. Let your child watch a movie and whenever a character experiences an emotion, positive or negative, pause the movie to ask them how they would have felt at that moment. Ask them what they would have done to observe how developed their emotional skills are. Once the child has provided you with an answer, see if it needs to be altered. If it does, then this is a teaching moment you need to take advantage of. The character would have done something sensible too. Once you are done explaining your point of view, play the movie and together see how the character overcomes the challenge too.

Identify Emotions

Using the same strategy used above, you can also ask them to identify which emotion the character is going through and why. "I think he is angry because the rain hasn't stopped and he wanted to go play outside with his friends." Let them label the emotion and ask them why the character feels a certain way.

Organize a Tea Party

Get a bunch of their toy figures and ask your toddler to arrange for a tea party for them. Tell them that they will be the host of it and help them prepare for the party. Once the table has been set and all the figurines have been seated, pretend to serve tea and biscuits. Pretend to have a conversation about emotions, feelings, and the importance of etiquette. Use language like "Could you please pass me the sugar pot?" and when your child does, say thank you in return. Similarly, you can celebrate the birthday of a toy figure and have your child prepare a gift for the character. You can tell them what to say upon meeting them at the birthday party such as "Happy birthday! I have brought a gift for you; I hope you like it."

Encourage Reading Stories

Stories that explore emotions, basic manners, and end with good morals to teach are a great way to encourage good behavior. You can read the book in different voices to pique interest, and stimulate their creativity by asking them open-ended questions during the reading to see what they would have done in that situation.

Conclusion

S ocial skills are a set of essential skills for children to learn. They comprise various habits and abilities that allow children to make social interactions more abundant and deep. They are what helps them find the right people, make friends, and have healthy relationships with their potential partners, colleagues, parents, and relatives in adulthood. The reason you need to start early in developing these skills is that their mind is still in the developmental stage. Whatever they hear, see, or learn today will find a permanent home in their mind. They pick up on the behaviors they see others exhibiting around them. They also take after the language they hear the most in the house, with or without assistance.

This means that everything starts with what kind of environment they are exposed to and the impact that it has on them. If both parents are naturally shy or spend little time with the child, the child has limited interaction and exposure to a healthy social environment. Thus, their vocabulary will be limited, and their habits will be non-concrete and undeveloped.

On the other hand, a child whose parents spend more time in the house with them and make every moment interactive and positive will have very developed habits and social skills. They will be more expressive, curious, and talkative. They will find approaching new people and making friends easier. They will also be more confident and poised in their nature.

This is the remarkable power of developing good social skills. As a parent, it isn't enough to teach them how to talk or walk, you need to build good habits right from the start. You need to enable them to express themselves and regulate their emotions better. You need to teach them healthy coping mechanisms to build resilience. They need to learn to listen to form better responses. Working with them using the strategies discussed in this book can help parents get started on the right track. Use these to boost their learning and encourage the formation of healthy habits.

Thank you for giving this book a read. I hope you loved reading it as much as I enjoyed writing it. It would make me the happiest person on earth if you would take a moment to leave an honest review. All you have to do is visit the site where you purchased this book: It's that simple! The review doesn't have to be a full-fledged paragraph; a few words will do. Your few words will help others decide if this is what they should be reading as well. Thank you in advance, and best of luck with your parenting adventures. Every moment is a joyous one with a child.

References

Abedon, E. P. (2005, October 3). *Toddler Empathy*.
Parents. https://www.parents.com/toddlers-
preschoolers/development/behavioral/toddle
r-empathy/

Bright Horizons Education Team. (2020). *Empathy:
A skill for future success.*
https://www.brighthorizons.com/family-
resources/empathy-a-skill-for-future-success

The Communication Trust. (2011). *Why
communication is important.*
https://www.thecommunicationtrust.org.uk/
media/2147/all_together_now_-
_section_2.pdf

Dedic, J. A. (2020, May 7). *14 ways to build your
child's social skills from home.* Parents.
https://www.parents.com/toddlers-
preschoolers/development/social/social-
skills-activities-for-kids-to-do-at-home/

Dewar, G. (2019). *The effects of praise: 7 evidence-
based tips for praising kids the right way.*
Parentingscience.Com.
https://www.parentingscience.com/effects-
of-praise.html

Diproperzio, L. (2013, July 4). *Social development milestones: Ages 1 to 4.* Parents. https://www.parents.com/toddlers-preschoolers/development/social/social-development-milestones-ages-1-to-4/

Jones, D. E., Greenberg, M., & Crowley, M. (2015). *Early social-emotional functioning and public health: The relationship between kindergarten social competence and future wellness.* American Journal of Public Health, 105(11), 2283–2290. https://doi.org/10.2105/ajph.2015.302630

Kumon. (2016, November). *The importance of children developing good communication skills.* https://www.kumon.co.uk/blog/the-importance-of-children-developing-good-communication-skills/

Lee, K. (2019). *How parents can teach their children good manners around others.* Verywell Family. https://www.verywellfamily.com/teaching-children-manners-620111

Lewis, M. (2015, September 29). *How to teach kids good manners - 6 benefits of proper etiquette.* Moneycrashers.Com. https://www.moneycrashers.com/teaching-kids-good-manners/

Myers, P. (2011, August 17). *The importance of teaching manners to kids.* Child Development Institute. https://childdevelopmentinfo.com/parenting/the-importance-of-teaching-manners-to-kids/#gs.agtnu2

Nair, A. (2018, June 29). *Parallel play: Why is it important for child development?* First Cry. https://parenting.firstcry.com/articles/parallel-play-how-does-it-benefit-your-child/

Newman, S. (2015, October 20). *How to support and nurture your child's passions.* Psychology Today. https://www.psychologytoday.com/us/blog/singletons/201510/how-support-and-nurture-your-childs-passions

Parentingni.org. (2016). *The importance of praise and encouragement.* http://www.parentingni.org/wp-content/uploads/2016/04/Importance-of-Praise-and-Encouragment-2.pdf

PBC Expo. (2020). *Reasons why role playing is important for your child.* https://www.pbcexpo.com.au/blog/reasons-why-role-playing-is-important-for-your-child

Playscheme. (n.d.). *Why is role play important for child development?* https://www.play-scheme.co.uk/why-is-role-play-important-for-child-development/#:~:text=It%20allows%20children%20to%20act

Raising Children Network (Australia). (2017, June 5). *Praise, encouragement and rewards.* https://raisingchildren.net.au/toddlers/connecting-communicating/connecting/praise#:~:text=Praise%20nurtures%20your%20child

Rector, J. (2019, May 9). *The importance of parallel play.* Tinybeans. https://tinybeans.com/articles/the-importance-of-parallel-play/

Resilient Educator. (2013, February 12). *Using empathy to teach social-emotional skills.* https://resilienteducator.com/classroom-resources/role-of-empathy-in-teaching-social-emotional-skills/

Roth, E. (2019, December 7). *Parallel play and toddlers: What it is and why it matters.* Metro Parent. https://www.metroparent.com/daily/parenting/toddlers/parallel-play-and-toddlers-what-it-is-and-why-it-matters/

Segrin, C., & Flora, J. (2000). *Poor social skills are a vulnerability factor in the development of psychosocial problems.* Human Communication Research, 26(3), 489–514. https://doi.org/10.1111/j.1468-2958.2000.tb00766.x

Stephens, K. (2007). *Everyday ways to teach children manners & social skills.* Child Care Exchange. https://www.easternflorida.edu/community-resources/child-development-centers/parent-resource-library/documents/manners-and-social-skills.pdf

Virtual Lab School. (2019). *Social-emotional development: Infants and toddlers.* https://www.virtuallabschool.org/infant-toddler/social-emotional/lesson-2

White, R. (2012, June 11). *Accelerated learning can benefit preschoolers.* Memorise. https://memorise.org/learning/accelerated-learning-benefit-preschoolers

Zero to Three. (2016, February 25). *How to support your child's communication skills.* https://www.zerotothree.org/resources/302-how-to-support-your-child-s-communication-skills

www.ingramcontent.com/pod-product-compliance
Lightning Source LLC
Chambersburg PA
CBHW070115100426
42744CB00010B/1843